Pensions

Drawing on the authors' extensive experience as actuaries, this work, originally published in 1987, provides a thorough examination of the problems which had arisen, and those that seemed likely to arise, with regard to both public and private pension funds at the time. It ranges in scope from the realities of individual plans and schemes devised by employers and employees to the management of pension funds and investment portfolios. The concept of socially responsible investment is discussed.

Reliable statistical information on the health, age and occupation of the population is an important tool in planning pension schemes for both the public and private sectors, and this book includes a careful analysis of the available data, leading to many useful projections for the thirty to forty years which followed. Although the statistical information is derived from UK sources, the problems it relates to, and its analysis was applicable to pension planning in all developed countries.

The breadth of the authors' approach, fully embracing the apprehension at the time about the demands of an increasingly ageing population and a partially unemployed workforce, would give this book added interest to a wide range of academics and professionals in financial institutions, government and the social services. Today it can be read in its historical context.

Pensions

The Problems of Today and Tomorrow

Bernard Benjamin, Steven Haberman, George Helowicz, Geraldine Kaye and David Wilkie

Routledge
Taylor & Francis Group

First published in 1987
by Allen & Unwin

This edition first published in 2024 by Routledge
4 Park Square, Milton Park, Abingdon, Oxon, OX14 4RN

and by Routledge
605 Third Avenue, New York, NY 10017

Routledge is an imprint of the Taylor & Francis Group, an informa business

Publisher's Note
The publisher has gone to great lengths to ensure the quality of this reprint but points out that some imperfections in the original copies may be apparent.

Disclaimer
The publisher has made every effort to trace copyright holders and welcomes correspondence from those they have been unable to contact.

A Library of Congress record exists under ISBN: 0043321275

ISBN: 978-1-032-74296-0 (hbk)
ISBN: 978-1-003-46862-2 (ebk)
ISBN: 978-1-032-74303-5 (pbk)

Book DOI 10.4324/9781003468622

Pensions

The Problems of Today
and Tomorrow

**Bernard Benjamin, Steven Haberman,
George Helowicz, Geraldine Kaye
and David Wilkie**

The City University

London
ALLEN & UNWIN
Boston   Sydney   Wellington

Allen & Unwin, the academic imprint of
UNWIN HYMAN LTD
PO Box 18, Park Lane, Hemel Hempstead, Herts HP2 4TE, UK
40 Museum Street, London WC1A 1LU, UK
37/39 Queen Elizabeth Street, London SE1 2QB

Allen & Unwin Inc.,
8 Winchester Place, Winchester, Mass. 01890, USA

Allen & Unwin (Australia) Ltd,
8 Napier Street, North Sydney, NSW 2060, Australia

Allen & Unwin (New Zealand) Ltd in association with the Port Nicholson Press Ltd,
60 Cambridge Terrace, Wellington, New Zealand

First published in 1987

British Library Cataloguing in Publication Data

Pensions, the problems of today and tomorrow.
— (Studies in financial institutions and markets; 4)
1. Old age pensions — Great Britain
2. Pension trusts — Great Britain
I. Benjamin, Bernard II. Series
331.25'2'0941   HD7105.35.G7

ISBN 0-04-332127-5

Library of Congress Cataloging-in-Publication Data

Pensions, the problems of today and tomorrow.
(Studies in financial institutions and markets; 4)
Includes index.
1. Old age pensions — Great Britain. 2.Pensions —
Great Britain. 3. Pension trusts — Great Britain —
Investments. I. Benjamin, Bernard, 1910—
II. Series.
HD7165.P46   1987   331.25'2'0941   86-32086
ISBN 0-04-332127-5 (alk. paper)

Phototypeset in Plantin by Grove Graphics
Printed by Billing & Sons Ltd., London and Worcester

Contents

Preface

In 1954 a report on 'The Growth of Pension Rights and Their Impact on the National Economy' was presented to the Institute and the Faculty of Actuaries (Bacon, Benjamin and Elphinstone, 1954). Some thirty years later a similar second report was presented to the Institute of Actuaries (Benjamin *et al.*, 1985). This was produced by the Centre for Research in Insurance and Investment at the City University under the guidance of its director, Bernard Benjamin, who had been one of the 1954 authors. The team for the second report was:

Bernard Benjamin PhD, DSc, FIA, Foundation Professor of Actuarial Science at the City University and first director of the Centre for Research in Insurance and Investment.

Steven Haberman MA, PhD, FIA, Professor of Actuarial Science and director of the Actuarial Science Unit at the City University.

George Helowicz BSc, MA, FIA, lecturer in actuarial science at the City University.

Geraldine Kaye BSc, FIA, research fellow at the City University.

David Wilkie MA, FIA, FFA, consultant actuary and formerly a professor of actuarial science at Heriot Watt University.

It is this report that forms the basis of this book. The views put forward do not necessarily represent those of either the Institute or Faculty of Actuaries nor is any individual author responsible for or necessarily in agreement with views expressed in chapters written by any of the other authors.

In Chapter 1 George Helowicz traces the development of state and occupational pensions and concludes that, as in the past, the arguments will continue over the relative roles of state and occupational pensions in the national pensions framework.

In Chapter 2 Geraldine Kaye discusses the 1985 White Paper *Reform of Social Security – Programme for Action.*

In Chapter 3, she outlines the types of retirement benefit provided by state and occupational pension schemes. She also describes sources of information on pension funds and related matters.

Geraldine Kaye discusses in Chapter 4 the relative roles of public and private enterprise in pension provision and in the latter case whether the responsibility should be the employer's or employee's. The function of a pension scheme is examined and how this has changed over time. The history of the move to a final salary structure is described and the demise of money purchase schemes is discussed. Further topics discussed include early leavers, the indexing of benefits to pensioners, cross-subsidies between members, the degree to which a pension fund should be run by and for the employer and the extent to which it should explicitly represent the individual savings of the employee, and whether the provision of pensions should be related to need.

In Chapter 5 David Wilkie writes about the macroeconomic aspects of funded pension schemes and how they represent an addition to savings that may then be used for additional capital formation to create the capacity for higher production in future years. He also contrasts funded schemes with the pay-as-you-go type such as the current state scheme. The conclusion of the chapter is that the way in which pension funds (both state and occupational) operate tends to conceal the reality that present prosperity comes from present work, assisted by the accumulated capital that has been inherited from past work, and that there is no one to pay for our own pensions but ourselves.

In Chapter 6 George Helowicz discusses the large investment potential of pension funds and the desirability of directing this to the financing of the development and reconstruction of domestic industry and the creation of jobs. This leads him to explore socially responsible investment strategies and the constraints imposed by the Megarry judgment. He points out that large financial institutions such as the pension funds undoubtedly have considerable influence in deciding where new investment is placed, which new property developments are carried out, which companies are able to raise money satisfactorily by rights issues, which new companies will be successful on the unlisted securities market, and so on, and wonders whether this power is being used to national advantage. As a supplementary question he asks whether the presence of very large funds under unified investment management facilitates or hampers the flow of savings into the right sort of new capital formation.

Taxation is discussed in Chapter 7. Geraldine Kaye presents a condensed discussion of the advantages and disadvantages of taxing pensions on the present approximate expenditure tax basis or on a possible income tax basis or on an intermediate basis in which only the investment income would be taxed, the treatment of contributions and benefits remaining as at present. The point is made that it is difficult to see why personal savings for retirement through occupational pension schemes should receive a favoured form of tax treatment when individual provision before retirement through personal savings does not, and until recently has been penalized. A plea is also made that it would be a great simplification in the administration of occupational pension schemes if the Inland Revenue limits were removed entirely. An important concomitant of this abolition would in her view be the taxation of lump sums at least in excess of some limit.

In Chapter 8 Bernard Benjamin looks briefly at the demographic history of the United Kingdom over the period 1871–1981. A set of variant population projections is then described up to the year 2031. The demographic trends from 1901 to 2021 are then reviewed by the use of an index of dependency to answer the question: what are the overall effects of past changes and anticipated future changes in population structure on the proportion of the population who represent the dependent groups? In discussing the numerical results, his main concern is to dispel the hysteria evident in the government and in other bodies about the relative growth in the elderly population. There will be strains, but not much greater than have already been faced and borne before. The major dependency strains arising from the lower birth rate will not arise until thirty or forty years from now, giving ample time for a resolute and farsighted government to plan ahead.

Steven Haberman is the author of Chapters 9, 10 and 11. In the first of these he takes the argument of Chapter 8 further by considering employment as well as demographic trends. Whereas for men there has been little change between birth cohorts in economic activity rates, for women there has been an increasing trend in labour force participation since 1951. This means that successive cohorts of women have an increasing probability and duration of economic activity over their lifetimes. The results of Chapters 8 and 9 are combined in Chapter 10 and lead to refined projections of the dependency ratio over the period 1981–2031 with explicit allowance being made for employment trends, in particular for women.

In Chapter 11 Steven Haberman looks at future pension expenditure (state and occupational schemes) in relation to the size of the national economy, using a range of economic, demographic and actuarial assumptions. The total pensions expenditure for 2031 (in terms of 1981 earnings levels) is estimated to lie between £32b and £38b (on a medium mortality assumption) and between £38b and £45b (on a low mortality assumption). He then expresses these amounts as a proportion of the aggregate of wages, salaries and pensions expenditure (TWSP). These proportions are 19–22 per cent and 22–25 per cent respectively. For 1981 the total equivalent is estimated to be £20b or 12 per cent of TWSP. However, the financial strains created by this growth in pensions expenditure due to an ageing population, the maturing of SERPS and the possible increased coverage of occupational schemes can, he argues, be met if there is moderate economic growth in the future.

References

Bacon, F. W., Benjamin, B. and Elphinstone, M. D. W. (1954), 'The growth of pension rights and their impact on the national economy', *Journal of the Institute of Actuaries*, vol. 80, pp. 141–202

Benjamin, B., Haberman, S., Helowicz, G., Kaye, G. and Wilkie, D. (1985), 'Pensions: The Problems of Today and Tomorrow', report presented to the Institute of Actuaries, June

List of Abbreviations

APPP	appropriate personal pension scheme
CBI	Confederation of British Industry
CPIC	Company Pensions Information Centre
CPS	Centre for Policy Studies
CSO	Central Statistical Office
DHSS	Department of Health and Social Security
ECI	Equity Capital for Industry
EIRIS	Ethical Investment Research and Information Service
FCI	Finance Corporation for Industry
FIG	Financial Institutions Group
FSSU	Federated Superannuation Scheme for Universities
GAD	Government Actuary's Department
GHS	General Household Survey
GLEB	Greater London Enterprise Board
GMP	guaranteed minimum pension
ICE	Inner City Enterprises
ICFC	Industrial and Commercial Finance Corporation
IPM	Institute of Personnel Management
LAPR	life assurance premium relief
LEL	lower earnings limit
NAPF	National Association of Pension Funds
NCB	National Coal Board
NHS	National Health Service
NIB	National Investment Bank
NUM	National Union of Mineworkers
OPAS	Occupational Pensions Advisory Service
OPB	Occupational Pensions Board
OPCS	Office of Population Censuses and Surveys
PEP	Personal Equity Plan
PP	personal pension
SERPS	State Earnings Related Pension Scheme
SFO	Superannuation Funds Office
SRI	socially responsible investment
TPFR	total period fertility rate
TRS	Teachers' Retirement System
TUC	Trades Union Congress
TWSP	total wages, salaries and pensions

UEL	upper earnings limit
USS	Universities' Superannuation Scheme
VAT	value added tax
WMEB	West Midlands Enterprise Board
YOP	Youth Opportunities Programme
YTS	Youth Training Scheme

Pensions

1 A Look at the Past

GEORGE HELOWICZ

The social progress of society this century has been such that most individuals expect to receive a pension in their old age from the state. In addition, many people will receive a further pension from the occupational pension schemes of their previous employers. Today, retirement from work is a normal practice. However, the idea that people are entitled to give up work at a certain age and receive a pension is a relatively new concept that provided a solution for employers faced with the problem of old workers who were no longer economically useful to them. At the turn of the century there was no state pension scheme and private employers offering formal pension arrangements were a rarity. It was only within the public sector, particularly in the Civil Service, that some progress had been made in formalizing pensions.

This brief look at the past begins with state pensions and then goes on to explore the development of occupational pension schemes in the public and private sectors.[1]

The struggle for state pensions

The first half of the nineteenth century was dominated by the 'Puritan Ethic' – a belief that poverty was the result of idleness and moral inadequacies. Provided a person was careful with their money whilst in work and set aside amounts to cover periods of sickness, unemployment and old age, then they should have no fear of poverty. Unfortunately, those who could not work or count on financial support from their families often found themselves with no choice other than to join other paupers in the semi-penal conditions of the workhouse.

The main medium of saving for these contingencies of life was through friendly societies. These 'were a typical manifestation of the Victorian ethic of providence and self-help' (Gilbert, 1966, p. 165). In return for a financial contribution they granted sick pay, medical care and a death benefit. Through the holding of regular meetings they also provided social companionship for their members. Membership of a friendly society showed independence and respectability, and to be elected an officer of a local society was a measure of status within a local community. Friendly societies were mainly the prerogative of the skilled worker. 'They made no appeal whatever to the grey, faceless, lower third of the working class

. . . membership was not for the crossing sweeper, the dock labourer, the railway navvy, any more than it was for the landowner, the Member of Parliament, or the company director' (Gilbert, 1966, p. 167).

A number of surveys on the extent of poverty in London seriously challenged the notion that poverty was an individual failing. One of the earliest surveys was carried out by Charles Booth and published as 'Life and Labour of the People of London'. Booth frequently discovered that the most important contributory factor to poverty was old age. These surveys demonstrated the need for a more positive role from the state and questioned the effectiveness of voluntary saving with institutions such as friendly societies. Evidence was such that many people were unable during periods of employment to earn enough to be able to save.

The discovery of a separate class of the 'aged poor' led to calls for state pensions. In a paper presented to the Royal Statistical Society in 1891, Booth proposed a non-contributory tax-supported weekly pension of 5 shillings from age 65. Opposition on the grounds of cost came from the government, which if a state scheme were to be introduced would have preferred a contributory one. On the other hand, the friendly societies felt threatened by a contributory scheme as this would compete for working-class savings. In the tradition of Victorian laissez-faire, they were suspicious of the state's role in an area that had been their sole prerogative. Yet, ironically, a non-contributory scheme would have helped some schemes with the financial difficulties they faced.

Decreasing mortality due to medical and sanitary improvements meant that members were living longer and that more was being paid out in sickness benefit than anticipated by the actuaries. The fall in the birth rate only helped to compound these difficulties in that it resulted in a smaller number of young lives from which the societies could recruit. Inevitably the sickness experience worsened as the average age rose. In addition, many societies, because they felt a commitment to look after older members through their lives, paid out sickness benefit as if it were a pension, producing further actuarial deficiencies. A non-contributory scheme offered them financial relief because the burden of sickness payments in old age would be taken away from them.

The reluctance of successive governments to commit themselves to what was perceived as a horrendous cost ensured that progress towards a state pension scheme was slow and tortuous. Delay would be created by the setting up of Royal Commissions. On other occasions, events would occur that either placed pensions low on the government's list of priorities or else thrust them prominently into the political limelight. The following timetable of selected events clearly illustrates this process:

July 1892   A Liberal government is elected. In response to the growing interest in pensions it sets up the Aberdare

Commission on the Aged Poor. The Commission reported back in 1895, recommending that pensions should be left in the hands of the friendly societies.

July 1896   The Rothschild Committee is set up to examine possible plans for old age pensions. Its terms of reference prohibited the examination of any but contributory schemes. The Committee reports back two years later that it cannot agree on any scheme.

November 1898   The adoption by New Zealand of a non-contributory old age pensions plan acts as the catalyst for a national campaign on pensions organized by Herbert Stead.

March 1899   The success of the Stead campaign results in the appointment of a Select Committee on the Aged Deserving Poor (the Chaplin Committee).

May 1899   The National Committee of Organized Labour on Old Age Pensions is formed, based on the principle that every old person should be entitled to a free pension from the state. Activists were encouraged to approach influential newspaper editors and 'lay on their consciences the sad plight of more than a million aged poor' (Gilbert, 1966, p. 194).

July 1899   The Chaplin Committee proposes a weekly pension of 5 shillings financed partly by the poor rates and partly by the state. Payment would only be made after a thorough investigation of an applicant's need and character.

October 1899   The Boer War breaks out, and in an orgy of patriotism the attention of the working class and government is diverted away from pensions.

January 1906   The general election sees a large increase in the number of working-class men in Parliament. This forces the Liberal government to recognize that the working-class vote will have to be bought and that the price may have to be pensions.

May 1907   A Private Member's Bill is introduced in Parliament proposing a weekly pension of 5 shillings from age 65. The Bill achieves a second reading.

July 1907   Unexpected parliamentary by-election defeats for the government concentrate its attention on pensions.

May 1908   The government announces its intention to introduce the Old Age Pensions Bill. After amendment the Bill was enacted later in the year. The Act provided for a weekly pension of 5 shillings for a single person or 10 shillings for a married couple to those who had reached

age 70. There was a sliding scale of reductions to offset
income from other sources. In the House of Lords, the
Act 'was roundly criticized both on the grounds of
expense and as a vast extension of charity that would
lead to the demoralization of the working classes'
(Gilbert, 1966, p. 225).

In 1925 a contributory scheme was added to the non-contributory one.
It took under its umbrella those who were insured under the National
Insurance schemes for sickness and unemployment and gave them an
entitlement to a weekly pension of 10 shillings from age 65. Entitlement
was determined by the contribution record rather than by a means test.
This pension on its own was never meant to be sufficient to meet fully
a person's needs. This was made clear by Neville Chamberlain during the
second reading of the 1925 Bill when he stated the intention was that it
should be supplemented by additional resources through, for example, an
employer's own pension scheme.

In contrast, 1942 saw the publication of the Beveridge Report
(Beveridge, 1942) which laid much of the foundations of the post-war
welfare state. The report was not only concerned with old age pensions
but dealt with all aspects of social security. The flat-rate benefits proposed
were intended 'to be sufficient without further resources to provide the
minimum income needed for subsistence in all normal cases' (1942, p.
122). With regard to pensions it considered that:

any Plan of Social Security worthy of its name must ensure that every
citizen, fulfilling during his working life the obligation of service
according to his powers can claim as of right when he is past work an
income adequate to maintain him. This means providing, as an
essential part of the plan, a pension on retirement from work which is
enough for subsistence, even though the pensioner has no other
resources whatever (Beveridge, 1942, p. 92).

However, Beveridge's levels of subsistence did not include allowances for
such things as newspapers, cigarettes, beer, entertainment, etc., and
therefore bore no relationship to pre-retirement levels of income.
Recognizing this, the Report states that 'direct encouragement of
voluntary insurance or saving to meet abnormal needs or to maintain
standards of comfort above subsistence level is an essential part of the
Plan' (Beveridge, 1942, p. 93). The main provisions of the Beveridge
Report were later incorporated in the 1946 National Insurance Act.

The general belief that the standard of living in retirement should bear
some close relationship to that enjoyed before retirement prompted the

Phillips Committee (1954) in 1954 to view occupational pension schemes as both the remedy for inadequate state pensions and a possible method for easing the financial pressures on the Exchequer from pensions. This approach contrasted sharply with that put forward in a 1955 Fabian Society pamphlet 'New Pensions for the Old' where the prominent role in providing wage-related pensions would be taken by the state.

State pensions since Beveridge

Until the 1959 National Insurance Act both contributions to and pensions from the state were flat amounts independent of income. The 1959 Act was a departure from this and introduced the graduated scheme. The pension consisted of two components – a flat-rate one and a graduated one. The flat-rate pension, which was paid for by a flat contribution, was paid to everyone. The graduated one was paid for by a graduated joint employer/employee contribution of 9.5 per cent of earnings between £9 and £18. In return, an additional weekly pension of 2.5p was paid for each £7.05 and £9 paid in graduated contributions by men and women respectively.

The Conservative government's White Paper, *Provision for Old Age* (Ministry of Pensions and National Insurance, 1958), declared that one of the aims of the scheme was 'to make provision for employed persons who cannot be covered by an appropriate occupational scheme to obtain some pension benefits related to their earnings' whilst at the same time seeking 'to preserve and encourage the best development of occupational pension schemes'. The graduated scheme provided a pension that was clearly inferior to that offered by the better private schemes and, because it resulted in an increase in contributions without an immediate corresponding increase in pension outgo, helped to achieve another aim which was 'to place the National Insurance scheme on a sound financial basis'.

The 1959 Act also introduced the concept of 'contracting out', which was copied by later governments and which today 'remains almost unique in the world' (McKelvey, Round and Fairclough, 1985, p. 5). Employers were able to contract their employees out of the graduated part of the state scheme. If this was done, no graduated contributions were paid and the right to a graduated pension was forfeited. Contracting out was allowed only if an employer undertook to provide an occupational scheme that gave benefits as good as those given up. Given the low level of graduated benefit offered this was not a particularly onerous condition.

In 1969 the Labour government produced its proposals for state pensions (the Crossman scheme). Pensions, like contributions, would be wholly earnings related. The pension was to be calculated in two parts.

The first part would be equal to 60 per cent of lifetime average earnings up to a half of national average earnings, which at the time was £11. The second part was one-quarter of the remainder of earnings up to a ceiling of £33. In both cases earnings were revalued up to the retirement date to compensate for the loss in value due to inflation. Contracting out was also permitted. However, the government lost the general election of June 1970 and the proposals were never implemented.

With a new government came fresh proposals on pensions. The Conservative government's 1973 legislation gave a predominant role to occupational pension schemes. It was proposed that the state scheme should consist of a flat benefit financed by earnings-related contributions together with an additional benefit earned through the State Reserve Scheme. The latter was to be a funded money purchase scheme administered by the Reserve Pensions Board. A joint contribution of 4 per cent (2.5 per cent from the employer and 1.5 per cent from the employee) was payable to the State Reserve Scheme, which offered a guaranteed rate of return and the prospects of a profit-sharing bonus. Contracting out from the State Reserve Scheme was permitted and the Occupational Pensions Board was created to supervise the appropriate arrangements. The 1973 legislation, under certain conditions, gave early leavers the right to receive a deferred pension as an alternative to a return of contributions. Once again, before all these proposals could be introduced, the government lost the February 1974 general election to the Labour Party.

Given that state pension plans changed every time a new government was elected, it was clearly necessary for there to be a degree of consensus amongst the political parties if further uncertainty was to be avoided. 'Finally, in 1974–1975 a truce was called. Subject to endless discussion, negotiation and bargaining, it proved possible to find support within both major political parties for the Social Security Pensions Act 1975' (McKelvey, Round and Fairclough, 1985, p. 5). This Act, which is often referred to as the 'Castle scheme', brought into operation on 6 April 1978 the State Earnings Related Pension Scheme (SERPS), which at the time of writing is still in existence.

Earnings-related contributions are payable on earnings up to a ceiling known as the upper earnings limit (UEL). As with previous schemes, the Act provides a two-tier structure of pension payments. The first level of pension is a flat amount approximately equal to what is known as the lower earnings limit (LEL), whilst the second level is related to earnings between the LEL and the UEL. Both earnings limits are changed at the beginning of each tax year. The second pension is 1.25 per cent of pay earned between the two limits in the best twenty years prior to retirement. Earnings are revalued to the date of retirement to maintain their purchasing power.

Contracting out of the earnings-related pension is permitted provided the employer offers a pension scheme that meets certain minimum standards. These include the provision of a pension at least as good as that given up, the so-called 'guaranteed minimum pension' (GMP). Additionally, the pension has to be related somehow to final earnings and based on a minimum pensions fraction of 1/80 for each year of service. Those contracted out pay a reduced contribution on earnings between the LEL and the UEL. A vigorous campaign by the National Association of Pension Funds and the Insurance and Pension Industry in favour of contracting out resulted in a very large percentage of occupational schemes doing so.

Then in the early 1980s a number of researchers (for example, John Kay at the Institute for Fiscal Studies) began to look at the ultimate costs under SERPS, suggesting that these were beyond the state's financial resources. In addition, proposals emerged from the Centre for Policy Studies on personal pensions as part of an ideology of individual responsibility and freedom. These proposals have found considerable sympathy with the present Conservative government's preoccupation with Victorian values and its desire to limit public expenditure.

With regard to personal pensions a consultative document appeared in July 1984 from the Department of Health and Social Security, proposing that:

- personal pensions (PPs) should be available as of right to all employees, and would normally be of the money purchase type – that is, based on contributions rather than on earnings, as with final salary schemes;
- PPs should qualify for contracting out of SERPS and the test should be based on the level of contribution calculated to produce an adequate level of pension;
- the employee would bear the risk of their PP failing to provide the same level of benefits as would have been available from their employer's scheme or from SERPS.

Concern was expressed in some quarters over the proposals; the following comment is illustrative:

It is reasonable to assume that the intentions of the Government lying behind its proposals for personal pensions is the philosophy that as many people as possible should be able to control their own financial destiny and not be beholden to the Government in particular or to any gigantic financial institution. Whilst this concept cannot, we feel, be challenged in the case of a small number of directors and senior executives for whom, in effect, personal pensions are already set up, we are concerned as to the serious implications of such practice spreading to the general level of employees. The danger here, as we see it, is that whilst informed comment will be available from professionals, this could easily be swamped by the massive selling efforts of commercial organizations, principally assurance companies which in the efforts to obtain ever-increasing amounts of business, will gloss over the practical difficulties to the employees involved and perhaps exaggerate the likely returns available from the premiums paid. (McKelvey, Round and Fairclough, 1985, pp. 225–6)

At the same time the government took the opportunity to review the whole social security system and produced a Green Paper (DHSS, 1985a), which suggested the abolition of SERPS. Following almost universal condemnation of the proposal, the subsequent White Paper (DHSS, 1985b) sought only to modify the scheme, whilst giving encouragement to personal and occupational schemes – with, for example, an extra 2 per cent reduction in the national insurance contribution for those newly contracting out of SERPS. It was proposed that the earnings-related pension should be based on lifetime earnings rather than the best twenty years' earnings, and that the maximum pension available should be 20 per cent of earnings rather than the previous figure of 25 per cent. The contracting out facility would also be available to those opting for a personal pension plan provided a minimum contribution of 4 per cent (shared equally between employer and employee) was paid to the plan.

These alterations are planned to take effect in 1988, but it remains to be seen whether they will ever be implemented.

The growth in occupational pension schemes

Pension schemes set up by employers are an integral part of the pensions framework in the United Kingdom, but the growth in the numbers of employees covered by such arrangements has been far from even. By 1936 the United Kingdom membership of occupational pension schemes had reached only 2.6 million and, of these, 1.0 million were public sector employees. Since the end of the Second World War, however, membership has grown considerably, as Table 1.1 indicates. The increase in numbers has been influenced by factors such as the greater awareness of employees of the value of an adequate pension and recognition by employers that a pension scheme is something that ought to be provided by a good employer. Government policy on pensions, including tax reliefs and the ability to contact out of any state pension arrangements, has also been a factor that has encouraged growth.

Table 1.1   *Employees in ocupational pension schemes,*
UK, 1936–1979 (millions)

Year	Private sector	Public sector	Total
1936	1.6	1.0	2.6
1953	3.1	3.1	6.2
1963	7.2	3.9	11.1
1979	6.2	5.6	11.8

Source: Government Actuary (1981).

Occupational pension schemes and tax relief

Until the 1921 Finance Act an employee's contributions to a pension scheme received no tax relief and the interest income of the fund suffered tax in the normal way. Neither was it always the case that an employer's contribution would attract tax relief as an expense of management. After the First World War, income tax rates rose to levels much higher than pre-war ones. The effect was seriously to reduce the net return from investment and as a consequence to deter employers from setting up and maintaining funds. The solution provided by the 1921 Act was to grant tax relief on the contributions paid by both employers and employees to funds approved by the Inland Revenue. In addition, the investment income of such funds was exempt from tax, and the pension once it became payable was taxed as earned income.

These reliefs are still in existence today but are granted only to 'exempt approved' schemes defined under the Finance Act 1970. Any cash sums payable on death or at retirement are also tax free. An 'exempt approved' scheme is one that has been set up under an irrevocable trust and that also meets certain criteria laid down by the Inland Revenue. The approval of pension schemes is looked after by a separate branch of the Inland Revenue known as the Superannuation Funds Office.

Occupational pension schemes in the public sector

The earliest pension arrangements for public sector employees were those relating to civil servants. Early in the eighteenth century, for example, a contributory scheme had been set up for those working in the Customs and Excise department. Schemes such as these enabled an employer to deal in a humanitarian way with workers who were either too old or too infirm to be of economic use to them.

By the nineteenth century the system of remuneration within the Civil Service had become very complex. Gerald Rhodes describes the situation as follows.

Some civil servants were remunerated by fees as well as or instead of salaries; some held sinecures providing an income with no duties; others again held office for life but paid a deputy part of the remuneration to perform the actual duties of the office. The confusion of arrangements for appointing and paying public servants was reflected in the confusion of arrangements for providing for both old age and retirement. Those who held sinecures, for example, were not necessarily retiring in the modern sense, although the acquisition of a sinecure might well serve as a means of providing an income in retirement. (Rhodes, 1965, p. 16)

Such practices were of course open to abuse and corruption, and in 1785 a Commission was set up to examine the whole payments system. Because many of the payments were in effect pensions it is not surprising that the Commissioners also had to deal with the existing pension arrangements. It is therefore important to appreciate that 'the first move towards a system of civil service superannuation was incidental and subordinate to a much wider concern and movement to check corruption and reduce cost in the public service' (Rhodes, 1965, p. 17).

By 1810 a comprehensive review had been carried out on the conditions of service in the Customs and Excise department. As a result, parliamentary legislation was passed in 1810 giving these employees a non-contributory pension paid for out of public funds. Some twenty-three years later, the 1834 Superannuation Act granted pensions to the whole of the Civil Service. Those who had entered before 1829 could, after fifty years' service, expect a pension equal to their full salary, whilst those entering after this date would qualify for a pension of two-thirds of salary after forty-five years.

In 1856 a Royal Commission was appointed to consider whether any changes were necessary to the 1834 Act. Restating why it believed the provision of pensions to civil servants was in the public interest, the Commission commented: 'the evil consequences of retaining a single Civil Servant in an important post for which he had become incompetent, cannot be estimated in money and may be much more than an equivalent for the expense of the superannuation of a whole department' (Rhodes, 1965, p. 18). Thirty years later, the Ridley Commission suggested further reasons why Civil Service pensions were a good thing. Recognizing that 'the growing practice, too, of railway companies, banks, and other large commercial undertakings, is to establish systems of superannuation', it commented that 'pensions help to retain in the service men who might otherwise be tempted elsewhere' (Rhodes, 1965, p. 19). The 1903 Courtney Commission also noted that a pension dependent on years of service was a convenient way of keeping staff long term, 'as there is thus secured an inducement to maintain continuous service on the part of the servant' (Rhodes, 1965, p. 20).

The early years of the Civil Service scheme saw an emphasis on the advantages accruing to the state. Gradually this view was moderated and subsequently relaxed by the Courtney Commission, which saw the role of the state as one of offering 'a moderate provision for the commonest contingencies of life' (Rhodes, 1965, p. 21). This role envisaged not only the payment of a pension to a civil servant but also the payment of benefits to his dependants on his death. In 1909, a death benefit equal to one year's salary and the payment of a cash sum at retirement were introduced. Subsequently in 1935 and 1949 widows' and dependants' pensions were also added.

In contrast, there was a marked reluctance to introduce pensions for teachers. 'It seems to have been felt that unless some restriction was placed on the giving of pensions, the virtues of providence and thrift would not receive their due honour. But this could only be done if pensions were discretionary and not embodied in a general scheme' (Rhodes, 1965, p. 24). Those pensions that were available were strictly limited; for example, in 1851 the number of pensions in payment at any one time was restricted to 270. Gradually arguments for a pension scheme based on efficiency and to a lesser extent on humanitarian grounds began to be accepted. A pension scheme, it was argued, would attract better-quality teachers, improve teacher morale, reduce the wastage of certificated teachers, and ease the government's embarrassment over the lack of pension for thousands of teachers. Not until 1898 was a scheme introduced and then only for elementary school teachers. Other teachers had to wait until 1918 before a more general scheme was introduced.

Prior to 1922, the only way a local authority could set up a pension scheme was by means of a private act of Parliament, and a small number had in fact pursued this course of action. Under the 1922 Local Government and Other Officers Superannuation Act, local authorities were enabled to introduce schemes without recourse to Parliament. The Act, which did not compel the employers to set up schemes, set standards of benefits and provided a basis for those transferring from one local authority to another to transfer their pension rights. It was not until 1937 that pension provision was made compulsory.

The early years after the Second World War saw the creation of the National Health Service and the nationalization of the coal, gas, electricity and transport industries. At the same time, the opportunity was taken to introduce a comprehensive pension scheme for all employees, some of whom had previously been members of their former employer's occupational scheme.

Today, public sector pension schemes are broadly similar in the benefits offered. Pensions are based on final salary, years of service and a pensions fraction of 1/80, and once in payment receive a degree of inflation proofing. A cash sum is also provided at retirement. Lump-sum death payments and widows' pensions are also provided. It would be true to say that these schemes provide a yardstick by which private sector schemes can be judged.

Occupational pension schemes in the private sector

The initial growth of occupational schemes in the private sector was to a large extent motivated by considerations of business efficiency, although the driving force for some employers was benevolent paternalism. Amongst the larger employers, the East India Company and the Bank of England had formal pension schemes at a very early date; the Gas Light and Coke Co. established a contributory scheme for staff in 1842 and for manual workers in 1870; the Prudential had a widows' scheme in 1866 and a retirement pension in 1872; in 1904 Lever Bros set up a fund providing benefits on injury, illness and retirement; in 1906 Rowntrees of York set up their contributory pension scheme. By 1900 nearly thirty pension schemes were run by the railway companies for both staff and manual workers.

That efficiency was a motivating force for the railway companies is clearly illustrated by the following comments of the manager of the North Eastern Railway:

> Surely a pension is an act of grace. . . . I do not quite see where the obligation to pension comes in. My view of the pension is that it is an act of business common sense . . . not as philanthrophy. . . . Unless you have something like an efficient pension fund, the directors would be under a constant compulsion to keep on the men. It is a choice between keeping them on and sending them to the workhouse, and they could not resist keeping them on. (Rhodes, 1965, p. 41)

Conclusions

The arguments over the relative roles of the state and occupational pension schemes in a national pensions structure have been an important feature of the past, particularly in the last forty years. What emerged from time to time reflected the government's ideology and the influence that groups such as the National Association of Pension Funds and the Centre for Policy Studies could exert. Writing in 1965, Gerald Rhodes suggested that the 'future debate is likely . . . to centre round the questions "how much pension?" and "who should provide pensions?" ' (1965, p. 45). Time has shown this to be a correct prediction and there is no doubt that these questions will continue to be debated. But the debate has widened beyond simply a state versus occupational pension argument to one where pension rights are seen as akin to property rights such as home ownership and share ownership. From this viewpoint personal pensions follow naturally, as individuals then become responsible for their own savings and therefore their own pensions. The philosophy of personal pensions is thus an individualistic one that can serve only to undermine collective provision for retirement whether from the state or occupational schemes.

The future debate will also be concerned with the investment practices of pension funds. They represent an important source of investment funds for the United Kingdom economy and the questions being asked are whether the economic ills of the country can be attributed to the failure of their investment programmes and whether the investment actually undertaken is beneficial to the national interest. These questions, as Chapters 5 and 6 show, are already receiving close scrutiny from the Labour Party and the Trades Union Congress. It remains to be seen whether pension fund investment will come under some form of state control.

Note

1 I would like to acknowledge the work of Bentley Gilbert (1966) and Gerald Rhodes (1965). The parts of the chapter dealing with the origins of state pensions and the development of occupational pension schemes have drawn from their work.

References

Beveridge, Sir W. (1942), *Social Insurance and Allied Services*, Cmnd 6404, London: HMSO

DHSS (1984), *Personal Pensions – A Consultative Document*, London: HMSO

DHSS (1985a), *Reform of Social Security – Programme for Change*, vol. 2, Cmnd 9518, London: HMSO

DHSS (1985b), *Reform of Social Security – Programme for Action*, Cmnd 9691, London: HMSO

Gilbert, B. B. (1966), *The Evolution of National Insurance in Great Britain*, London: Michael Joseph

Government Actuary (1981) *Occupational Pension Schemes 1979*, Sixth Survey by the Government Actuary, London: HMSO

McKelvey, K. M., Round, T. and Fairclough, M. (1985), *Hosking's Pension Schemes and Retirement Benefits*, London: Sweet and Maxwell

Ministry of Pensions and National Insurance (1958), *Provision for Old Age*, Cmnd 538, London: HMSO

Phillips Committee, *Report of the Committee on the Economic and Financial Provisions for Old Age*, Cmnd 9333, London: HMSO

Rhodes, G. (1965), *Public Sector Pensions*, London: Allen & Unwin

2 Current Regulation

GERALDINE KAYE

The growth of occupational pension schemes during the twentieth century has occurred in an environment affected substantially by legislation. The influence of the government can conveniently be described under the four headings of competition, cooperation, concessions and control. Competition has come in the form of the provision by the state of a compulsory pension scheme, first a flat-rate one, and later an earnings-related one. Cooperation has come in the form of permitting occupational schemes to act as an alternative to parts of the state scheme through the arrangements called 'contracting out'. Concessions have come in the form of tax relief for pension funds subject to certain conditions. Controls have come through legislation restricting how pension schemes may behave, particularly in respect of early leavers.

At the time of writing in 1986, the world of pensions is again in legislative turmoil. The Social Security Act 1985 introduced a significant number of new controls on pension schemes, which are slowly coming into effect. The Social Security Act 1986 makes substantial changes in the State Earnings Related Pension Scheme (SERPS), and also changes the way in which contracting out may be done, introducing the possibility of contracting out through the provision of an individual personal pension. The Finance Act 1986 introduces new provisions for the tax treatment of pension schemes that are deemed to be in surplus.

Both these 1986 Acts will depend for their effect mainly on Regulations, which, at the time of writing, had not even been circulated in draft form for consideration by the various interested bodies, never mind published. Since a very large amount of the detail of the new provisions is left to Regulations, it is only possible at this time to give an outline of the various new proposals. How they will work out in practice is still to be determined.

A further factor is the existence of the Financial Services Bill, which at the time of writing had not yet completed its progress through Parliament. It will substantially reform the way in which the investment world is regulated, and will impinge upon the activities of the investment managers of pension funds, and set the framework within which personal pensions may be marketed and investment advice of all sorts, including advice about pensions, may be given.

Yet another piece of new legislation is the Building Societies Act 1986, which, amongst a great many other things, will allow building societies to administer and market personal pension schemes. It remains to be seen how much the building societies will take advantage of this possibility.

Finally, the Finance Act 1986 introduced the concept of Personal Equity Plans (PEPs). These will give individuals tax concessions for personal investment in individual ordinary shares. Although expressed in a different form, the tax concessions for PEPs are of similar effect to the tax concessions for pensions, at least in some circumstances, and therefore they will be potential competitors to voluntary personal pension schemes and additional voluntary contributions made by individuals to their occupational pension scheme. Again, the details of how these will work are yet to be prescribed by Regulations and those who might administer PEPs have not yet publicized their plans.

With all this mass of legislation in the pipeline it cannot be clear to anyone how the pensions scene will develop in the next few years. No one can know the extent to which individuals may choose to contract out of SERPS in order to effect an 'appropriate personal pension', or the extent to which those who do will add to their minimum required contribution by additional voluntary contributions. No one knows the extent to which individuals will choose to withdraw from their employer's occupational scheme in favour of a personal pension or the extent to which employers will encourage or discourage such moves, or indeed which institutions will actively promote appropriate personal pension schemes (APPSs). The opportunity will exist for occupational schemes to contract out of SERPS on a 'money purchase' basis; no one knows how many employers will take up this option. The extent to which PEPs will successfully compete with pension fund money and the extent to which potential managers will promote PEP schemes is also unknown. Anything written here is therefore extremely speculative, and may well be proved wrong by events. It is convenient to consider the various changes under way under the four headings – competition, cooperation, concessions and controls. Before discussing the possible impact of the changes, it is desirable to review briefly the *status quo ante* and how that position was reached.

Competition

Old age pensions on a means-tested basis were introduced by the Old Age Pensions Act 1908. Contributory old age pensions for all employees were introduced in 1925. Following the Beveridge Report (Beveridge, 1942) these two schemes, along with various other social security benefits, were consolidated into one system in the National Insurance Act 1946. This provided a flat-rate pension for all employees and for the self-employed, subject to sufficient contributions having been paid, for men at 65 and women at 60 who had then retired. The basic pension for a single person was £1 6s. 0d. per week when the scheme came into force in 1948, and from July 1986 is £38.70p per week. A married man receiving pension gets 160 per cent of the single person's pension, and his widow, provided she is above pension age, gets a single person's pension. The husbands of married women and widowers do not get these benefits.

The amount of the basic pension has been increased fairly regularly. Currently the system is that it is increased strictly in line with any increase in the Retail Price Index; but in fact over the nearly forty years since 1948 it has been increased more or less in line with average earnings. It is reasonable to assume that in the long run the amount of the basic pension will continue to increase in line with earnings, since if it falls too far out of line political pressures will ensure an appropriate increase.

The system of flat-rate pension is the one unchanging element of the present situation. Contributions for the flat-rate pension were originally also on a flat-rate basis, with both employer and employee contributing; and the Treasury chipping in a certain proportion from general taxation. From 1961 the contributions have been earnings-related, up to 1978 in a limited way, and after that on a level percentage basis between a lower and an upper limit; in 1985 a sliding scale basis was introduced, so that the contributions paid by the lowest paid and by employers on their behalf are at a lower percentage rate than the standard rate. These contributions pay not only for the retirement pension but for all the various other benefits obtainable under the social security scheme.

Earnings-related benefits were introduced into the state scheme in 1961 at a modest level. After several false starts and abandoned proposals the Social Security Pensions Act 1975 introduced the present earnings-related scheme. It is this scheme that the present government has felt may become too expensive, and has legislated to modify.

In November 1983, the Secretary of State for Social Services, Mr Norman Fowler, announced the setting up of an enquiry, 'to study the future development, adequacy and costs of State, occupational and private provision for retirement in the United Kingdom including the portability of pension rights, and to consider possible changes in those arrangements taking account of the recommendations of the Select Committee on Social Services in their report on retirement age'. The enquiry was chaired by Mr Fowler himself, and included both civil servants and outside members who were familiar with pensions. It took evidence from the general public – including the institutional bodies concerned with pensions – but it did not publish a report. The government having considered the evidence and the views of the members of the enquiry published a Green Paper entitled *Reform of Social Security – Programme for Change* in June 1985 (DHSS 1985a). This appeared to pay rather little attention to the majority evidence presented, but picked up ideas that had been vigorously argued by a minority. This may have been because the government saw the same few firms of consultants representing various interested bodies and therefore felt that it was not receiving a satsifactory spread of views. The main proposals for pensions in the Green Paper were the phasing out of SERPS and the introduction of a system of compulsory contracting out, either through occupational schemes or through personal pension schemes. The proposals in the Green Paper were almost universally opposed, both by the main pension institutions who favoured the existing system, and by some of the proponents of change who felt that the practical difficulties of the government's proposals were overwhelming.

In December 1985 the government published a White Paper *Reform of Social Security – Programme for Action* (DHSS, 1985b), shortly followed by the Social Security Bill, which completed its stages through Parliament and received the Royal Assent in July 1986. The government retreated considerably from its radical proposals in the Green Paper, and seemed to accept that its strategic objectives could adequately be achieved by reforms that were, if not like, at least accepted as practicable by those responsible for administering occupational pension schemes.

The changes to SERPS will come into effect in April 1988. This is ten years after the introduction of SERPS in 1978, and the pension accrued during these ten years will remain almost unchanged. The new system will apply in respect of employment after April 1988. The pension of an employee under the old SERPS rules built up to 25 per cent of the average of the best twenty years revalued relevant earning, where revaluation is in line with increases in national average earnings and relevant earnings are earnings between the lower and upper earnings limits, which for 1986/87 are £1,976 and £14,820 per annum respectively. For those whose whole working lifetime is after April 1988, the ultimate SERPS pension will build up to 20 per cent of lifetime revalued relevant earnings, where the working lifetime is taken for men as the forty-nine years from age 16 to 65, and for women the forty-four years from age 16 to 60. Adjustment is to be made for potential years work lost through incapacity or time away from work to bring up children, but not for years spent in full-time education.

An extended period of transitional arrangements will smooth the progress from the old to the new system. Those who retire before April 2000 will accrue SERPS pension on the old basis throughout, so that their pensions will be 25 per cent of the average of the best twenty years. The accrual rate for contributions after April 1988, and those retiring after that retiring between April 2000 and April 2010, and those retiring after that date will receive pension based on 20 per cent of relevant earnings under the new scheme. However, it will not be until 2032 (for women) or 2037 (for men) that benefits under the old scheme will cease to be relevant (such is the time scale of pension arrangements; but one must have considerable doubts whether the new SERPS scheme will last unchanged for anything like this period).

Benefits for surviving spouses under SERPS are also to be changed. Under the old scheme the surviving spouse, whether a widow or a widower, can inherit the whole of the late spouse's SERPS entitlement subject to a certain maximum. For deaths occurring after April 2000 the surviving spouse will inherit only one-half of the previous pension, whether this accrued during the old or the new regime.

The overall effect of the changes in SERPS will be to reduce considerably the ultimate level of pensions under the scheme compared with what they would have been had the changes not taken place. The halving of spouses' pensions means that the ultimate level of these will be reduced even more than the basic pension. This reduction in the prospective SERPS outgo during the next century should achieve one of the government's objectives, which was to cut back on the prospective cost of SERPS as it reached maturity, and in particular as the bulge of births from 1947 to the mid-1960s reached retirement in the early decades of the next century, presumably having to be 'supported' by the contributions of a working population that, unless the present trend in births alters considerably, will be rather smaller than at present.

If participation in SERPS were compulsory, the proposed changes to the scheme need not significantly affect occupational pension schemes. Those schemes that participate in SERPS but arrange the total prospective pension for members on an integrated basis, that is taking account of the entitlement to pension under the flat-rate state scheme and SERPS, would have to consider whether to revise their occupational pension benefits to take account of the prospective reduction in the SERPS pension; but those schemes that are not so integrated could ignore the changes. The complications occur because of the existence of the option to contract out of SERPS. We therefore turn to our theme of cooperation between the state and occupational pension schemes.

Cooperation

Since the introduction of the graduated earnings-related scheme by the National Insurance Act 1959, the government has allowed occupational pension schemes that provided a satisfactory alternative benefit to contract out of the State Earnings-Related System. Since 1978, the alternative to SERPS has been the provision by the occupational scheme of a guaranteed minimum pension (GMP). GMP accrues over the working lifetime of the employee, but otherwise is designed to produce the same pension at retirement as the SERPS scheme. The actual mechanism is that an employee's pension is calculated on the basis of his earnings records, and the amount of GMP is deducted from this. At retirement the two are supposed to match in general. However, the SERPS pension will have been based on the best twenty years' revalued relevant earnings, whereas the GMP will have been based on lifetime earnings (or at least post-1978 earnings), so that the two will not match exactly for any one individual. If GMP is less than the SERPS pension, the state scheme makes up the difference, so the individual is no worse off than if he had not been contracted out. During retirement the total SERPS pension including GMP is increased in line with the Retail Price Index, whereas the GMP paid by the employer and deducted from the pension paid by the state (under the 'old', pre-1988 system) remains fixed in money terms. This does not affect the employee, but it means that the government in effect pays for the index linking of GMP.

The same principle will apply after 1988, except that GMP will accrue so that it will reach 20 per cent of average earnings for a full working lifetime, just like the new SERPS pension. Indeed, since the new SERPS pension will be based eventually also on lifetime earnings, the two should match more closely, at least after 2032 or 2037!

Instead of GMPs after retirement remaining fixed in money terms, for post-1988 accruals they will have to be increased each year in line with the increase in retail prices, with a maximum of 3 per cent (and a minimum increase of zero; i.e. they will not be reduced, even if the Retail Price Index falls).

Under the old rules, a widow's GMP of one-half of the member's GMP has to be provided. For GMPs that accrue after 1988 it will be necessary also to provide widowers' pensions on the same basis.

Under the old system, schemes that wished to contract out had to satisfy various other conditions in respect of the total pension provided, as well as providing the guaranteed minimum pension. The so-called 'quality' tests have been abandoned, and it will only be necessary for contracted out schemes to provide GMPs for members and their surviving spouses.

The various changes to take effect from 1988 in fact bring the systems for SERPS and GMPs rather closer together. The accrual basis will eventually be the same, and benefits for surviving spouses will be on the same basis. The only remaining major difference will be in the rate of post-retirement increase. However, this eventual convergence is at the expense of continuing complications in emerging benefits being calculated on two different bases for decades to come.

Since the introduction of SERPS in 1978, contributions by employee and employer to the National Insurance Scheme, which provides state retirement pensions, including SERPS, and other benefits, have been a percentage of earnings below the upper earnings limit (and since 1985 employers have paid contributions on the total earnings of the employee). Members of conracted-out schemes and their employers have paid lower contributions, attracting a rebate on contributions in respect of earnings between the lower and upper earnings limits. The amount of the contribution approximately compensated for the cost to a scheme as a whole of providing GMPs for all members. It did not attempt, nor was it intended, to provide exactly for the cost of the GMP for each individual member.

Under the new system, the contracting-out rebate will continue, though it is not yet clear at what level this will be after 1988. The present rebate is 6.5 per cent of relevant earnings, and it was in any case expected that this would reduce slowly as the cost of providing GMPs on a slowly reducing accrual basis also reduced.

The major innovation in the field of cooperation is in the possibility after 1988 for occupational pension schemes to contract out of SERPS by providing a pension only on a 'money purchase' basis, and also for individuals to contract out either from SERPS or from their occupational scheme to effect an appropriate personal pension.

Although the principles for an occupational money purchase scheme are clear, the detailed implementation of such schemes still has to be worked out. In principle, a contracted-out money purchase occupational scheme will need to have a minimum contribution equal to the contracting out rebate. Benefits will need to be based on the amount of contribution for each individual member, increased (or perhaps increased or decreased) in accordance with the investment performance of the funds in which the contributions have been invested or deemed to be invested. At retirement, the proceeds resulting from the investment of the minimum contribution will have to be taken wholly in the form of pension, which will need to be incremented in the same way as GMPs in future, and spouses' pensions on a similar basis will also need to be provided. Presumably additional benefits on the death of the member before retirement, or on earlier retirement due to ill health, will need to be provided through additional contributions, of either the employee or employer. It will be possible for a contracted-out money purchase scheme to provide certain additional benefits on a defined benefit basis.

Appropriate personal pension schemes will be somewhat similar. A variety of institutions will be permitted to set up such schemes, apparently either through a separate fund, something like a unit trust, or through a life insurance policy. It is to be expected that most such schemes will be on a unit-linked basis, analogous to investment in a unit trust or a unit-linked life policy, rather than being on a fixed money basis like a non-profit deferred annuity contract, which was the style of older money purchase schemes, mostly now superseded. The individual employee will be able to choose a particular institution as the recipient of his contributions for a particular tax year. Unfortunately, it appears that the employee and his employer will pay the full national insurance contributions to the DHSS, which will remit them to the chosen institution only some months after the relevant tax year, which may therefore be up to eighteen months after the date when the first contribution was made. How this will work out in practice, and whether any interest will be allowed for the delay, is yet to be seen, but it is clear that there will be considerable complications because of contributions in the pipeline when an employee dies or reaches retirement. The Act gives the Secretary of State power to regulate the expense charges made by institutions offering APPSs, and to control the classes of asset in which the funds can be invested, but it remains to be seen what these regulations will be.

On retirement, the proceeds of the minimum personal pension contributions must be taken in the form of a pension, incremented in the same way as GMPs (that is, in line with the RPI with maximum of 3 per cent each year but no decreases), and the surviving spouse's pension at one-half of the previous level. If the employee dies before reaching retirement there are provisions for requiring that the proceeds are converted into a pension for a surviving spouse, but if the employee is not married or the amount is small the proceeds may be taken as a lump sum.

It is assumed that many life insurance companies will offer APPSs. It is not yet clear how many of the other institutions that the government have in mind as possible providers – banks, building societies, friendly societies, unit trust managers – will actually be able to, or will wish to. Many commentators fear that the necessarily high cost of selling these contracts to individuals will mean that they get poor value for money for their contributions compared with the same contribution applied within an employer-sponsored scheme. If expense charges are controlled at too low a level, it will not be attractive to institutions to offer APPSs, and if they are allowed to be sufficiently high to attract institutions they may be uncomfortably high for the contributors. Others feel that competition in this field, combined with explicit expense charges, will be sufficient to restrain overcharging, and that in any case the potentially good investment performance may be sufficient to outweigh any likely charges. It remains to be seen how the market settles down, and what controls prove necessary for the protection of individuals.

An inevitable consequence of the freedom of individuals to choose, even within limits, the investment medium for their retirement savings is that the investment performance of different APPSs will be different, and even for one scheme will differ from time to time. It remains to be seen whether individuals will be enthusiastic about personal pensions if they find that the proceeds of an investment have been particularly poor. Individuals will not be discouraged if the investment performance turns out to be particularly good, though invidious comparisons may be made by the less fortunate. However, unless the Inland Revenue changes its rules, those who benefit from exceptionally good investment performance will find themselves disappointed. The present system of Inland Revenue restrictions, discussed in Chapter 7, restrains the amount of pension that can be received to a maximum of two-thirds of 'final salary', suitably defined. It might be only rarely that the proceeds of the minimum contributions would breach this limit, but certainly if an individual invested considerable additional contributions in personal pension schemes, as he will presumably be allowed to, it would not require exceptional investment performance to reach the upper limits.

It is clear that the system of controls for tax relief on pension schemes will need to be changed, so that the amount of contribution for defined contribution schemes is limited, rather than the amount of benefit. A statement of the Inland Revenue's policy in this respect might be expected in good time before the introduction of the new scheme in 1988, but so far this has not yet appeared.

One aspect of the new proposals that has received almost universal opprobrium is that individuals who effect a personal pension and employers who introduce a new contracted-out scheme will receive an extra 2 per cent rebate on the national insurance contributions for the years 1988–1993. While it is clear that the government's intention is to encourage those who at present participate in SERPS to establish a new personal pension, or their employers a new contracted-out scheme, it is felt to be particularly unfair on those schemes that are already contracted out, and will not receive the rebate. The issue is complicated by the fact that a mere rearrangement of an existing contracted-out scheme will not qualify for the rebate, but nor, apparently, will the extension of an existing scheme to cover a class of employee at present not contracted out. Instead, a new scheme would need to be set up to cover such people – who in fact form a very significant number of those who participate in SERPS.

A few figures may help here. According to the seventh Government Actuary's survey of occupational pension schemes (relating to the year 1983; Government Actuary, 1986), some 22 million employees are included in the state pension scheme. About half of these are currently in occupational schemes, and the vast majority of these are contracted out. About 11 million people currently participate in SERPS. Of these 11 million, some 5 million are employed by employers who do have occupational schemes, and about 6 million by employers who have no occupational scheme at all. About 3 million of the 5 million are not in their employer's scheme because they are part-time employees. A further 1 million were excluded because their service was too short or they were too young. If these employers were to include such employees in new schemes – perhaps money purchase schemes based on the minimum contribution required – nearly half of those who at present participate in

SERPS would become contracted out, and they and their employers would get the advantage of the 2 per cent additional rebate.

The new market for personal pensions probably lies among the 6 million who are employed by firms with no schemes at all. Quite a large number of these are employed in industries where pension provision is not the first thought for either employer or employee or where the employees are taken on on a fairly casual basis – agricultural workers perhaps come into the first category, construction workers and shop workers into the second. There will indeed be some smaller firms, perhaps newly founded ones, where the provision of pensions through personal pensions is attractive to both employer and employees, who may in such firms work very closely together.

The other possible field for new personal pensions is in attracting individuals away from existing occupational schemes. Whether this is attractive to the individual will depend very much on the attitude of the employer. At one extreme, it is possible that some employers will cooperate wholly with the concept of personal pensions, for example by attributing the entire employer's contribution to the pension scheme to individual members, and allowing these contributions to be transferred to a personal pension scheme, along with the minimum contribution required. But such employers perhaps already arrange pensions on an individual insured money purchase basis, and they are likely to be few in number. At the other extreme, an employer who provides a non-contributory final salary scheme that he does not wish to see disturbed may be required by an employee to pay the minimum contribution to an appropriate personal pension scheme along with the required contribution by the employee; but he need do no more. An existing member of such a scheme might get no more than the deferred pension he would receive as an early leaver. It will not be obligatory for him to be able to take a transfer value out of the scheme unless he actually leaves the employer's service. For a long-standing member of such a scheme, a deferred pension and a future minimum contribution personal pension will appear distinctly unattractive. New entrants, and those who have been in such a scheme for only a short time, will have to take two things into consideration: will their immediate rate of contribution be higher or lower if they effect a minimum personal pension, and will their ultimate benefits be higher or lower?

If the scheme is non-contributory, then the contribution rate to a personal pension must be higher, but if the scheme requires a contribution of, say, 5 per cent of salary then the minimum personal contribution required may well be lower. This may influence some people, regardless of which scheme gives better value for money. Value for money will be difficult to judge, particularly for young people, since it will depend on a comparison between two sets of unknowns: on the one hand, the investment performance over perhaps forty years or more of a personal pension; on the other hand, either the proceeds of a final salary scheme if they should remain with that employer until retirement, or the proceeds of a deferred pension, if they should leave that employer at some unknown future date. Faced with such uncertainties, there is no way that an individual can make an informed decision, or even receive informed advice, and his (or her) decision will have to be made on the basis of possibly irrelevant factors, prejudice, hunch, or persuasion from the employer or the personal pension salesman. It is quite unclear how many people will be persuaded thereby out of occupational pension schemes into personal pensions.

Concessions

We now turn to the taxation concessions granted to occupational pension schemes. The Finance Act 1918 first allowed tax relief for an employee's contributions to a suitable retirement benefit scheme, which at that time included schemes providing wholly lump sums on retirement, similar to endowment assurance policies. In the Finance Act 1921 the present style of relief was first permitted, with the contributions of the employer to the scheme not being attributed to the income of the employee (but nevertheless allowed as an expense of the employer), investment income being exempt from income tax, and the final pension benefits becoming taxable as earned income. These two systems continued in parallel until 1970, when the system currently in force commenced, combining features of both the previous regimes. The system that provided wholly lump sum (but did not get tax relief on investment income) ceased to be approved, but the system providing pensions was allowed to yield a larger lump sum than it previously could, based on final salary near retirement.

A rather similar tax regime for the self-employed was set up by the Finance Act 1956, which allowed the self-employed to effect retirement annuity policies with life assurance companies, with broadly the same tax privileges. However, whereas for employer-sponsored schemes there were limits on the amount of benefit that could be taken, for self-employed retirement annuities the amount of contribution was limited.

The details and the financial effects of these tax concessions to pension schemes are discussed more fully in Chapter 7. The one obvious inconsistency of the system is the tax-free lump sum permitted at retirement. Indeed, were it not for this, it is arguable (and, indeed, it is argued in the chapter on taxation) that no limits need be put on the contributions or benefits at all, since all the outgo would then be in the form of pension benefits that would be taxable. Although in the early part of 1985 rumours were circulating that the Chancellor of the Exchequer intended to restrict the amount of tax-free lump sum, no changes in the system were in fact made.

We have already commented that the introduction of significant numbers of defined contribution schemes would appear to require a new regime in which the amount of contribution will be limited but not the amount of pension benefit – though the proportion of benefit that could be taken in the form of lump sum could be restricted as it is for the self-employed. It is not yet clear whether the Inland Revenue will grasp this nettle before 1988, or will wait until the inconsistencies that will undoubtedly arise if the present system remains in force become intolerable.

The pensions industry received a quite different surprise in the Chancellor's Budget speech in 1986, which proposed the introduction of restrictions on the amount of 'surplus' that could be maintained in an approved pension fund. A number of developments had in fact led up to this. Because of redundancies in which large numbers of pension scheme members received only the benefits of early leavers, a small number of pension schemes had found themselves with considerable surpluses, and had been permitted by the Inland Revenue to return these surpluses to the employing companies – which, indeed, were not necessarily in the best of financial health as evidenced by their need for redundancies. These refunds were taxable as income of the company, though if the company were making losses such a refund would only serve to reduce the carried forward losses, and for the time being would appear to be tax free. Secondly, several years of good investment performance, at least in market value terms, had given the impression that pension funds should have large surpluses in hand. In fact, an increase in market values of shares or property that is not matched by an increase in dividends or rental just means that pension funds have to invest future contributions on less favourable terms, and is a disadvantage to them. Nevertheless there was an appearance of surplus because of the rise in share prices. Thirdly, it was suggested that the effect of redundancies, which had certainly been advantageous to some schemes, was actually very widespread. In fact, however, many firms operated early retirement schemes rather than redundancy schemes, and these were generally costly either to the pension fund or to the company itself.

Probably the main impetus to the Chancellor's proposals was the desire of the Inland Revenue to clarify the circumstances in which refunds of pension fund money could legitimately be taken. The effect will be that after some date, presumably in 1987, it will have to be determined whether or not a pension fund is 'in surplus', according to a prescribed basis. Details of the proposed basis will be published in Regulations, and are not yet known. Proposals put forward by the Government Actuary suggest that assets will require to be valued, not on the basis of market values, but by discounting the expected future income on the assets on a constant basis, equivalent perhaps to valuing ordinary shares at twenty times the annual dividend. The liabilities will be valued on a rather conservative basis, taking into account prospective salary increases up to retirement and prospective pension increases thereafter. If the value of the assets on this basis exceeds 105 per cent of the value of the liabilities, then the trustees of the pension fund will have to indicate to the Inland Revenue how they propose to reduce the surplus over the following five years. The options available to them are to increase benefits, to reduce contributions from the employer or the employee, possibly to nil, or to take a refund into the employer's accounts. If this last option is chosen, the refund will be subject to tax at a special rate of 40 per cent, with no allowance against losses elsewhere.

The effect of these provisions is yet to be seen. They will certainly discourage funds that may have intended to grossly overfund, hoping that a surplus could be taken back at a later date; but many of the existing Inland Revenue restrictions prevented gross overfunding anyway. Because it is very difficult to forecast the amounts that may be required to meet future pension liabilities to a high degree of accuracy, unless the required basis were to be a very conservative one (as it appears likely to be) then a system that allowed only a 5 per cent margin would lead to considerable instability, with employers perhaps being forced to take refunds and to alternate with uncomfortably large extra contributions. The proposals, however, do not require compulsory refunds at all. Indeed, some trust deeds would not permit this. Instead, a fund that fails to reduce a surplus over the required period will simply become only partially approved for income tax purposes.

It seems likely that the new proposals will encourage some employers to increase pensions in course of payment more than they otherwise would have done, and possibly to fund for a higher level of benefit. Indeed, some employers may find that their funding is so far below the permitted maximum that they may be inclined to increase their funding target towards it. In the immediate future it seems likely that contribution rates would have been reduced somewhat anyway. It seems unlikely that many employers will willingly pay the 40 per cent penalty in order to receive a refund if other alternatives are open to them.

It therefore seems unlikely that these measures will have any significant effect in total on the tax relief obtained by pension funds or on the tax that may be paid by them. However, a period of low inflation and high interest rates and significant real increases in share dividends and property rentals could disprove this forecast.

Controls

Pension funds were subject to no direct controls on their activities for many years, other than operating within the normal constraints of trust law and complying with the requirements of the Inland Revenue if they wished to qualify for tax relief. The Superannuation and Other Trust Funds (Validation) Act 1927 ensured that in England and Wales pension funds that wished to take advantage of its provisions could remain in force in perpetuity, unlike an ordinary private trust. In Scotland, perpetual trusts were in any case possible. The conditions of validation were, however, easily met, relating mainly to procedure, accounting and actuarial valuations.

The position began to change after the Social Security Act 1973, which first required pension schemes to provide benefits for those who left the service of the employer before normal retirement age – early leavers – or at least for those who had at least five years service to their credit. The preserved deferred pensions that were required did not, however, have to be increased in any way to allow for inflation between the date of leaving service and the date of retirement. The high inflation of the 1970s showed the limitations of such provisions and stricter provisions were introduced in the Social Security Act 1985. For service after 5 April 1985, the amount of the deferred pension will have to be increased between the date of leaving service and the date when the member reaches normal retirement age by the proportionate increase in the Retail Price Index, but not by more than 5 per cent compound over the whole period. These compulsory provisions will be slow to take effect, though many schemes do allow increases in deferred pension on the prescribed basis for all service, and some may choose to allow full indexation rather than restricting the indexation to 5 per cent.

Provisions requiring schemes to have the same conditions for entry to a pension scheme for male and female employees were introduced by the Social Security Pensions Act 1975. A very recent EEC directive (Council of the European Communities, 1986) will require schemes in due course to provide equal benefits for males and females. But no steps at all have been taken to equalize permitted retirement ages, which are different in the state scheme (65 for men, 60 for women) and may remain different in occupational schemes.

The Social Security Act 1985 inroduced further controls on what pension schemes could do. Schemes were required to provide transfer values on an equitable basis – equitable, that is, in relation to the deferred pensions and other preserved benefits provided under the scheme. Schemes are also required to provide considerably more information for members than most had done previously. This information includes an explanation to members at the time they join the scheme, statements of benefits each year while they are members of the scheme, and statements of the benefits to which they would be entitled if they left the scheme, on request. Regulations under the 1985 Act also prescribe various items that must appear in the annual report to members. Most of these provisions have yet to be seen operating in practice. Whether members will see them as being usefully informative, so that they take a more active interest than previously in the pension scheme, or whether the provisions will simply remain a tiresome necessity for the pension scheme administrators, with little appreciable benfit to members, remains to be seen.

Conclusion

A great many of the above conclusions have been of the 'wait and see' variety. This seems to be an inevitable consequence of a period in which there has been so much reform of the pensions structure, and so much change in the investment scene beyond pensions is also under way. On the one hand are those who wish to see individuals having both much greater knowledge about and much greater involvement in the investment of their personal savings and in the pensions savings made on their behalf. On the other side are those who have developed an efficient and economical, if somewhat paternalistic (and not necessarily equitable) way of providing reasonable incomes in retirement for large numbers of people. There are those who wish to provide a service to individuals or to firms in furtherance of either of these ends, and there are no doubt those who see the opportunity of financial gain to themselves through providing such services. The stage is set for an interesting interplay between these various forces. One thing, however, seems certain: pension schemes will have to operate within a substantial legislative framework, and changes to that framework will come about, not only for administrative, but also for political reasons.

References

Beveridge (1942), *Social Insurance and Allied Services*, Cmd 6404 London: HMSO
Council of the European Communities (1986), *Directive of 24 July 1986 on the implementation of the principle of equal treatment for men and women in occupational social security schemes (86/378/EEC)*, *Official Journal*, No. L225, 12 August, p. 40
DHSS (1985a), *Reform of Social Security – Programme for Change*, 3 vols, Cmnd 9517, 9518, 9519, London: HMSO
DHSS (1985b), *Reform of Social Security – Programme for Action*, Cmnd 9691, London: HMSO

Government Actuary (1986), *Occupational Pension Schemes 1983*, Seventh Survey by the Government Actuary, London: HMSO

Social Services Committee (1982), *Age of Retirement*, Third Report from the House of Commons Social Services Committee, Session 1981–82, HC26–1

3 Retirement Benefits

GERALDINE KAYE

Description

The British system for providing income for people during their retirement years has four main elements:

- supplementary benefit
- private saving
- state pension
- occupational pension.

Supplementary benefit
When people discuss pensions in a formal setting, social security is not usually considered as an item of pension provision. However, at least 1½ million pensioners (DHSS, 1985) are entitled to supplementary benefits of one kind or another, because either their occupational pension is too low or they are not even entitled to one.

State benefits are now so extensive that almost everyone in the UK has been or will be in receipt of some form of state benefit. As well as the many non-cash benefits, at least seventy cash benefits are available. Most of the benefits must be claimed separately; most have different qualifying conditions and levels of income, and complicated claims forms; most are administered from different offices by overworked and under-qualified staff. Most importantly, for those really in need, the levels of benefit do not provide enough to support anything approaching a normal lifestyle, whereas for others they may provide the jam for the gingerbread which, although always nice to have, cannot be considered necessary for the state to provide.

Each November the DHSS publishes a leaflet entitled *Which Benefit*. Its code number is FB2 and is obtainable from HMSO. It is prepared by the Central Office of Information and lists the range of benefits available together with the code numbers of further relevant leaflets. That such a publication is necessary and requires the caveat 'This leaflet gives general guidance only and should not be treated as a complete and authoritative statement of the law' shows just how complicated the system has become.

As a result of piecemeal changes, our social security system has become unwieldy and difficult to communicate. After retiring from his post, A.

H. Robertson, who served as Chief Actuary of the Social Security Administration in America until 1978, wrote:

> Any social insurance system if not properly designed and communicated can
>
> (a) Effectively dictate retirement age patterns followed by a nation at an age which may not be in the best interest.
> (b) Discourage individual initiative and private saving for retirement, yet fail to provide adequate retirement benefits.
> (c) Create unrealistic expectations for retirement which when unfulfilled will result in frustration and disatisfaction.
>
> (Robertson, 1981, p. 136)

Our system is exhibiting all the characteristics of which he warned. The present government therefore set up an investigation into the whole pensions and social security system and has presented its results. The details are contained in Chapter 2.

It must be acknowledged that the future distribution of resources between 'pensioners' and others can never be guaranteed. For all practical purposes there will always be 'dependency' by the non-productive members of society, whether those too old or too ill to work or simply those who, for varying reasons, voluntarily or otherwise, simply choose not to work. This 'dependency' will arise because, whether these individuals collect their 'pensions' by drawing on their savings or by making a claim on future PAYE taxes, they will need to convert them into goods and services. Money must be exchanged into consumables. Thus there will always be dependency on somebody else's production, on future food, drink, goods, services and supply of amenities. Just as somebody has to provide the cash, so somebody must generate the goods for purchase. It can be seen in the above context that 'pensioners' refers to anyone in receipt of income from the state in the form of social security payments or in income from occupational pension schemes, as it matters little when considering consumption from which source of income it is derived. In any discussion about pensions, therefore, it is important that all types of monetary social security benefits, as well as occupational benefits, are considered and some attempt is made to quantify them. It must be noted that not all benefits are easily quantifiable – for example, the geriatric drain on the health service or pensioners' free transportation, although some estimates could be made by introducing suitable questions into the General Household Survey or by *ad hoc* national sample surveys.

Private saving
This requires no comment.

State pension scheme
Employers, employees and self-employed make compulsory contributions to the state scheme, which provides three types of retirement benefit:

- a basic rate state pension, payment in full depending on past contributions – for a single person this is £38.70 per week and for a married couple £61.95 per week (1986/7)
- a 'graduated pension', based on contributions under a scheme introduced in 1961 and superseded in 1975 – the maximum payments are £3 per week
- a state earnings-related pension (SERPS), for which the self-employed cannot qualify. The important fact is that, before retirement, potential benefits are revalued each year in line with national earnings and, after retirement, pensions are indexed to the cost of living.

Employers have a choice whether or not their employees participate in the earnings-related part of the state scheme. If an employer has an occupational scheme for his employees that is good enough to pass certain stringent tests as to the scope and adequacy of its benefits, the employer can 'contract out' his employees from the earnings-related part of the state scheme.

If the employer has chosen to contract out, then the employees are no longer eligible for the earnings-related state benefit, but as a condition of contracting out the employer has to provide a benefit at retirement that is referred to as a guaranteed minimum pension. The GMP must approximately equal the forgone state benefit. Where an employer has contracted out his company from the state earnings-related scheme, both the employer's and the employee's contributions to the state scheme are reduced. The employees are, of course, still entitled to the basic flat-rate state benefit.

In general, it is the larger schemes that contract out. Only 10 per cent of private sector schemes are contracted out, but they cover 80 per cent of the members of private sector schemes. In the public sector, 77 per cent of schemes are contracted out, covering 99 per cent of the membership.

Occupational pension schemes
It is difficult to make any general statement about the benefits provided by the average occupational pension scheme because of the great variety that exists. The difficulty is further compounded by the secrecy and

mystique engendered by the many vested interests involved. Additionally there is no comprehensive register of all 'approved' occupational pension schemes.

A register for inquiries to private sector funds was originally held by the Inland Revenue, but this has not been kept up to date. The manual records were never weeded and to do so now would probably be more time-consuming and costly than to start from scratch again. There are, of course, commercial registers, but one can never be certain if they are comprehensive for the large schemes, and one can be certain that they are not for the small schemes.

A register is required for two main purposes:

- to assist with the drawing of statistically reliable samples and in particular to allow total assets to be estimated,
- to provide a tracing service for early leavers.

When someone leaves a scheme they have no more contact with it until they retire. If, in the meantime, the company has changed its name, been taken over or merged, they will find it very difficult to trace the original scheme. If, in addition, they have changed their address, so that when the scheme tries to contact them it cannot, the coming together of the two parties is likely to be a lost cause.

The government has recently passed enabling legislation for such a register, but its actual implementation has been delayed for at least three years (Mackay, 1985) after meeting opposition from the trade and professional associations, mainly on administrative grounds.

Statistics

Without an accurate register, there is no data base from which one can draw samples to conduct surveys and hence provide meaningful answers to the questions regarding typical retirement benefits posed later in this chapter. Most organizations 'duck' the problem and produce statistics based on those schemes to which they have access. For example, the National Association of Pension Funds (NAPF), which is the principal trade association of the pensions movement, produces an annual survey based on its own membership. The survey makes no attempt (or pretence) of representing the whole pensions movement. While the NAPF is recognized by government departments, etc., as representative of the pensions industry, in practice it is likely to be representative only of the 'better' schemes, since to join the NAPF one presumes that the fund management must have been concerned and interested in its pension scheme. Another feature of the NAPF is that its members are generally the larger pension schemes. It is estimated by the Government Actuary's Department that well under 5 per cent of employers with pension funds are members of the NAPF and yet almost 50 per cent of employees who are members of pension schemes are represented by it. The survey results make no attempt to allow for those schemes that do not respond to the survey – usually about 50 per cent of the membership. Schemes that do not respond are likely to be the small ones and do not have the staff available to fill-in voluntary questionnaires. This makes the survey even more representative of large schemes.

It may seem from this that the NAPF survey is without value, when quite the reverse is true. The survey is produced annually and is comprehensive (the questionnaire covers eleven closely typed pages) in the topics covered, thus proving a valuable guide to trends. The survey results are published in booklet form. The booklet contains a copy of the questionnaire and all tables are cross-referenced to the appropriate question. The results are analysed and discussed. The commentary gives an explanation of changes in statistics from year to year where the reason is not immediately obvious. The NAPF survey is the one most widely quoted in the popular press. One must always remember, though, that it does not present a true picture of smaller schemes or the 'less good' ones.

For many purposes the fact that the survey represents only the larger schemes does not matter too much. Theoretically it is absurd to give equal weight to, say, the ICI scheme and a one-person scheme. In practice, 1,000 schemes with average membership of 1,000 members each may be more likely to influence the thinking of members than a single scheme with say 1 million employees. Employers are interested in the policies of firms of comparable size and tend to take no more than a passing interest in those of industrial giants.

Statistics produced by commercial consultants tend to follow the same line taken by the NAPF and are based only on their own clients. As consultants have 'control' over their own clients, they can, of course, achieve a 100 per cent response. Such results reflect the recommended practice of that consultant. Many consultants are very large, and others group together in an attempt to make their statistics more representative. The problem with the statistics produced by consultants is that very often they are not made available to the general public.

Where then can we go next in our attempt to find information about the average pension scheme? The government recognizes the gap in available statistics and every four years produces a survey of its own under the auspices of the Government Actuary's Department (GAD). They have used various methods to obtain a sample reliably representative of all schemes. The survey relating to 1983 was based on a sample achieved by asking people in the General Household Survey if they were members of an occupational pension scheme. Positive respondents were given a further questionnaire asking, among other questions, the name and address of their employer. These employers were then sent detailed questionnaires about their pension schemes. The purpose of the GAD's survey is to examine the extent to which employers in the UK are covered by occupational pension schemes and to describe the nature and amount of benefits that become payable on retirement and on death and the contributions they pay. In addition, it covers such matters as the income and outgoings of pension funds, and the number and amounts of pension being paid.

The survey is the most significant in the pension field, not only because of its coverage of all types of employers and sizes of business throughout the UK, together with members of HM Armed Forces, but also because of the comprehensiveness of the subjects covered, such as membership, size of funds and benefits on change in employment. Employers are requested to return a copy of their printed rules and/or explanatory booklet together with the completed questionnaires. This enables the Government Actuary's Department to analyse topics not directly covered by the questionnaire. The commentary accompanying each table in the survey results identifies such information. The subject on which questions are asked as well as their precise content can change from survey to survey to reflect matters of topical interest and points raised in critical reviews in the press as well as to incorporate requests from interested parties such as the Trades Union Congress, the Confederation of British Industry and the Occupational Pensions Board.

The survey is conducted on a voluntary basis and suffers from all the usual problems of non-response that afflict voluntary surveys. The survey organizers are diligent in their follow-up procedures, but there are limits to how many times someone who has been chosen as part of the sample can be questioned before one must accept that they are refusing to participate.

The published survey results extend to over seventy tables. Most tables distinguish between schemes that relate to the public sector and private sector, and some differentiate in the public sector between public corporations, central government, local authorities and HM Armed Forces. Each table is preceded by a paragraph giving background information and analysing the results.

The results of the government's survey on pensions are hopelessly out of date by the time they appear. Only preliminary results of the 1983 survey were available in May 1986 (Government Actuary, 1984). The value of the survey is that it is the only one considered to be representative of the whole population. Many of its results are split by size of fund and it therefore provides the only source of statistics about small funds. Statistics quoted in this chapter are derived from the 1979 Government

Actuary's survey (Government Actuary, 1981) unless relating to 1983, in which case they represent preliminary results from the later survey. Other sources will be specifically referenced.

Having briefly reviewed the main sources of information about typical benefits, what are these benefits? There are vast differences between private and public sector occupational pension schemes and because of that they will be detailed separately in most cases.

In outlining the benefits let us consider a potential member of a pension scheme and consider what points would be important to him. (The potential member is referred to as 'him' not because of any inherent bias, but merely for convenience.)

The first question this potential member might ask is 'Am I eligible to join?' Not all employees are eligible for pension scheme membership – either their employer does not have a pension scheme, or there is a minimum period of service before they can join, or in some cases part-time and temporary workers are ineligible. Despite this, in 1983, 11.1 million people – just over half the people in employment – were members of occupational pension schemes. Pause here for a few moments to reflect on this statistic.

Half the working population may be in pensionable employment, but half are not. As it is mainly the large employers who have pension schemes, it seems unlikely that this coverage will increase greatly without government intervention. One of the aims of the current Conservative government is to promote industry-based (as opposed to an individual employer-based) occupational schemes in the hope that this will increase coverage.

For eligible employees, membership of a scheme has generally been a condition of employment, although from 1986 this is no longer permitted. Public sector schemes generally cover all full-time permanent employees. The same is increasingly true for larger firms in the private sector, but many firms still operate schemes for staff only or have separate staff and works schemes.

Data from the Women and Employment survey (Martin & Roberts, 1984) show that, whereas 58 per cent of employed women worked for an employer who had an occupational pension scheme, only 34 per cent belonged to such a scheme. The survey indicates that the principal reasons for not being a member are the ineligibility of part-timers and failure to satisfy the minimum qualifying age and/or the minimum qualifying period. There is a difference between the minimum age at which employees are admitted to public as against private schemes: 87 per cent of public sector members become eligible by age 18, but for the private sector this figure is not reached until age 21. The Social Security Pensions Act 1975 required no sex differential in the minimum entry age.

The potential member's next question might well be 'How much is it

Table 3.1   *Employees in pension schemes, UK, 1953–1983 (millions)*

Year	Private sector		Public sector		Total members	Total employed	Percentage of members
	Men	Women	Men	Women			%
1953	2.5	0.6	2.4	0.7	6.2	21.9	28
1956	3.5	0.8	2.9	0.8	8.0	22.7	35
1963	6.4	0.8	3.0	0.9	11.1	22.9	48
1967	6.8	1.3	3.1	1.0	12.2	23.2	53
1971	5.5	1.3	3.2	1.1	11.1	22.5	49
1975	4.9	1.1	3.7	1.7	11.4	23.1	49
1979	4.6	1.5	3.7	1.8	11.6	23.2	50
1983	4.4	1.4	3.4	1.9	11.1	21.1	52

Note: The table excludes employees who have some pension rights from their current job, but are not currently accruing benefits.
Source: *Department of Employment Gazette*, 5 December 1985.

going to cost me?' Nearly 80 per cent of all members of occupational pension schemes are in schemes where employees as well as employers contribute. Such schemes are usually referred to as contributory schemes. In almost 80 per cent of these schemes, the members were required to pay 5–7 per cent of their salary as their contribution. Now that membership is no longer compulsory, there is likely to be a further movement towards non-contributory schemes. What member is going to 'opt out' of a scheme that he feels costs him nothing?

The next question is likely to be 'How soon can I retire?' In the private sector, 90 per cent of members were in schemes where the normal male retirement age is 65. Although females must have equal access to pension schemes, once they are in there are no further regulations and 90 per cent of women in private sector schemes retire at 60, five years earlier than their male counterparts. The public sector is somewhat more favourable with regard to retirement age and even 35 per cent of male employees retire at 60. This situation is likely to change as the result of a successful test case brought by a women who had objected to being retired earlier than her male colleagues. The resulting EEC ruling of 25 February 1986 that women should have the right to retire at the same age as men is however only a directive and not compulsory. Changes may therefore be slow.

Finally, he might ask 'What will I be paid when I retire?' This is likely to be an income for life plus a one-off capital sum. Almost all public sector scheme members and 92 per cent of private sector scheme members are covered by a final salary pension formula, i.e. the pension is calculated by reference to the member's pensionable earnings for their entire working life – a period ending at or not long before retirement or leaving service. In the public sector, pensions are normally based on 1/80 of pensionable earnings for each year of service plus a lump-sum payment equal to three years' pension. In the private sector, there is far more variation, the most common practice being to pay 1/60 of pensionable earnings for each year of service, but where a lump sum is paid this is usually an equivalent exchange of part of the pension rather than an addition to it. For a person with forty years' service, a pension based on 80ths with a lump sum of three years' pension can be approximately equal in value to one based on 60ths but with no lump sum.

In the public sector and in the majority of private sector schemes an employee with forty years of service could expect a pension of about two-thirds final salary. The pension actually received can depend crucially on how many times a person changes jobs and the consequent arrangements for transfer values. For men actually retiring in 1983 the average retirement pension paid was £45 per week in the public sector and £30 in the private sector. These figures compare with average adult male earnings of £170 a week. The higher figures for the public sector could be due in a large measure to the existence of the 'transfer club' – a group of employers and pension schemes that have agreed a common basis of transfer payments. Unfortunately, the club is at present mainly confined to public sector pension schemes. Apart from job changes, a possible reason for the low figures could be that benefits have not had time to build up fully as many of the private sector schemes were formed in the 1950s and 1960s. The setting up of nationalized industry and public sector schemes occurred at the same time (e.g. the NHS and the National Coal Board) therefore few employees have had time to maximize their benefits.

Virtually all public sector pensions enjoy complete protection from inflation, though there are differences in the way this is guaranteed. Pensions of civil servants, HM Armed Forces, employees of the National Health Service and local authorities (including teachers and police) are inflation-proofed by statute. (It must, however, be noted that the cost of this inflation-proofing is taken into account in all public sector salary negotiations. Contrary to popular belief, indexing for public servants is *not* completely free.) Pensioners of most of the nationalized industries enjoy inflation-proofing according to the rules of the scheme, though in some cases there is an element of discretion. Elsewhere pensions have, in fact, been increased in line with prices, even though there may be no rule or statutory obligation. Rules and practice in the private sector differ widely from one scheme to another. Hardly any scheme guarantees full inflation-proofing; however, at least 75 per cent gave some increase between 31 December 1981 and 31 December 1983. Most preserved pensions in the public sector are also inflation-proofed up to normal retiring age.

A very valuable benefit provided by most pension schemes – and one that our potential member is unlikely even to enquire about is the benefit should he die. The death benefit is particularly valuable to a member because it is usually available even if he is so unhealthy that he would be uninsurable if he went to an insurance company in his own right.

The general pattern of benefits on death in service is for a lump sum to be paid, with, in most cases, a dependant's pension. In 1979, 90 per cent of schemes provided a lump sum (other than a refund of contributions) on the death in service of a married man. In the private sector, lump sums payable on death in service are usually defined as a multiple of salary. The average level of benefit is about 2 times the annual salary at the date of death. In the public sector, the lump sum depends on both salary and length of service (possibly augumented) – this calculation results in a lump sum usually between 1 and 1½ times the annual salary at death. These averages include an allowance for the refund of contributions. In most schemes the lump sum benefit on death in service is calculated in the same way for all members, irrespective of marital status, sex, and the presence of dependants.

By 1979, 94 per cent of all (male) scheme members had an entitlement to a widow's pension should they die in service. For most members, the widow's pension is based on the member's salary and service. The method of calculation varies widely, but there is a strong tendency to use a pension formula based on either 120ths or 160ths of member's salary per year of service. Should the widow remarry it is normal in the public sector for her pension to be stopped (or suspended), except for the GMP. But in the private sector, about 60 per cent of members are in schemes where the pension is unaffected by remarriage.

About 52% of members are in schemes where no provision is made for widowers' pensions or pensions to other dependants. For the rest, in most private sector schemes a pension is provided to the legal spouse on the death of any member, although a few schemes only allow a spouse's pension if he/she was financially dependent on the member.

Most schemes provide for payments to be made not only on the death of the member while in service but also on death as a pensioner. The benefit takes various forms. In the private sector, a guaranteed period of pension is common. Public sector schemes often provide a minimum total benefit equal to the lump-sum benefit that would have been paid on death immediately before retirement. About 95 per cent of male members are in schemes with some provision for a widow's pension on death after retirement. It is usual for the mode of calculation to involve the member's salary and service, and the pension is often calculated as one half of the retired employee's pension. In 1979, about two-thirds of male members in schemes granting unconditional widow's pensions on death after retirement are covered in respect of marriages contracted after retirement (although a sizeable fraction would not be covered if marriage had taken place within six months of death).

Addresses for further information

Few, if any, people conform exactly to the average. How then does one find out more about one's own pension scheme? First, each member of a scheme is meant to have at least a booklet that sets out details of his benefits and the names of the scheme's trustees and how to contact them if he wants further information. Many scheme members, not realizing the importance of this booklet, will not have kept it. Others, because possibly it has been poorly written, will not understand it. Some of these people will not ask their personnel manager or the trustees for more information because they are frightened they will look silly – not realizing that their lack of understanding is not their fault but the fault of the booklet. (The NAPF organizes competitions under the heading of 'Golden Pen Awards' designed to improve the clarity of pension scheme literature.) Still others are frightened to enquire because they do not wish management to know that they are thinking of changing jobs, or may be retiring early on ill-health grounds. They suspect that if management is aware of these thoughts, it will force the issue for them. Where then can such people go for advice?

The Company Pensions Information Centre (CPIC) has been set up as a non-profit-making educational organization that gives general information about company pension schemes but not individual advice. Although it can give only factual information and not specific advice, it finds that it can satisfy a large proportion of callers.

It publishes the following books and will provide one free copy of each to members of the general public. Subsequent copies must be paid for:

How to understand your pension scheme
How a pension fund works
Pensions for women
What is a pension fund trustee?
How changing jobs affects your pension
What pension terms mean

It can also provide speakers on a wide range of pension topics.

The address of CPIC is:

7 Old Park Lane
London W1Y 3LJ

01 493 4757

If, after speaking to CPIC, readers find that it is not factual information that is wanted but advice, they must find a consulting actuary, pensions consultant or one of the many other professionals specializing in this area. The organizations to which such professionals are likely to be affiliated are as follows:

Association of Consulting Actuaries, Rolls House, 7 Rolls Building, London EC4A 1NH
Association of Pension Lawyers, Richard Butler, 5 Clifton Street, London EC2A 4DQ
Association of Pensioner Trustees, 417 Midsummer Boulevard, Saxon Gate West, Central Milton Keynes, Bucks, MK9 3BN
Faculty of Actuaries, St Andrews Square, Edinburgh EH12 2AQ
Institute of Actuaries, Staple Inn Hall, High Holborn, London WC1V 7QJ
National Association of Pension Funds, 12–18 Grosvenor Gardens, London SW1 0DA
Pensions Management Institute, 124 Middlesex Street, London E1 7HY
Pensions Research Accountants Group, Metropolitan House, Northgate, Chichester, West Sussex, PO19 1BE
Society of Pension Consultants, Ludgate House, Ludgate Circus, London EC4A 2AB

All of these organizations will be willing to provide details of their members who are available for consultation in the relevant area. Of course, professional consultants charge. Although fees are not always as high as may at first be feared, good advice is always worth having.

A member of a pension scheme or a pensioner who cannot afford to go to consultants and has first put his query, or complaint, in writing to the authorities of his scheme can seek help from a charity – the Occupational Pensions Advisory Service (OPAS) – which has recently been set up with the objective of 'proferring advice and assistance on all matters relating to occupational pension schemes to individual elderly members of the public requesting such advice and assistance (including in particular beneficiaries under occupational pension schemes and their dependants), or, to relieve such other members of the public as are considered deserving of such advice and assistance by reason of their necessitous financial circumstances'. The normal way to contact them is through the Citizens' Advice Bureau, but more information can be obtained from:

The Honorary Secretary
Occupational Pensions Advisory Service
Room 327
Aviation House
129 Kingsway
London WC2B 6NN

01 405 6922 ext. 205

References

DHSS (1985), *Social Statistics Facts and Figures*, London: HMSO

Government Actuary (1981), *Occupational Pension Schemes 1979*, Sixth Survey by the Government Actuary, London: HMSO

Government Actuary (1984), *Occupational Pension Schemes Survey 1983*, Press Release

Mackay, Andrew (1985), Parliamentary Question, *Hansard*, vol. 88, col. 684, 11 December

Martin J. and Roberts C. (1984), *Women and Employment: A Lifetime Perspective*, Department of Employment/Office of Population Censuses and Surveys, London: HMSO

National Association of Pension Funds (1983), *Ninth Annual Survey of Occupational Pension Schemes*, Croydon: NAPF

Robertson, A. H. (1981), *The Coming Revolution in Social Security*, Security Press, Mclean, Virginia

4 Current Problems in Pension Provision

GERALDINE KAYE

Introduction

Later chapters will deal with problems that might be described as macro-economic – the strains on the national economy exacted by population structure changes, the emerging growth in social needs and expectations, the complementing of state and private sector pension provision, as well as the consequences for income redistribution in claims upon the gross national product and in national and international investment. First, there is the need to comment upon a number of topical issues at what might be referred to as the micro level of pension provision. These issues are partly economic, partly political since they are concerned not only with the relative roles of public and private enterprise in pension provision but also with, in the latter case, whether the responsibility should be the employer's or the employee's. The question of the protection of the pension entitlement of the individual, especially in the event of a change of employment, is also touched on.

The government announced an all-embracing enquiry on 16 December 1983 and required evidence for the first of the parts into which this enquiry was subdivided (very much concerned with these issues) to be submitted by 31 January 1984. Despite the very tight deadline, written evidence was obtained from over 1,500 different sources. This serves to show just how much interest was currently being aroused. The unprecedented speed with which the government has proceeded demonstrates the importance that it attaches to the issues raised. As a result of that enquiry, the government has produced a White Paper that will lead to changes in the way employees provide for their pensions. (Chapter 2 has dealt with the implications of this White Paper.)

Many research papers as well as new journalistic articles still seem to be being published almost daily. At one end of the spectrum are papers presented by those who fear that a rapidly growing elderly retired population will place such severe financial strain on the working population that they will be unable or unwilling to permit continued transfer of resources (by taxation or pension contributions) to the pensioner population at the implied future rate. This school of thought separates into two: (a) those who feel that the answer lies in privatizing the state pension scheme (Adam Smith Institute, 1983) and, (b) those who advise that privatizing state pensions is not even part of the answer. The latter school of thought argues that the source of the pensioner's income (taxation or pension contribution) is irrelevant if the workers perceive that the pensioner is enjoying a level of living that is too high relative to their own level (Lyon, 1983).

At the other end of the spectrum are the charitable organizations, such as Age Concern, associated with the care and welfare of the elderly. The main fear of such bodies is that the total needs of the elderly (many of them only partly financial) are not properly understood or provided for. Such organizations are not particularly concerned about the source of the finance to provide for the elderly, as long as the needs are met – though, to be fair, they are concerned with cost-effectiveness. (In Chapter 8, Bernard Benjamin reviews some of the problems of social welfare that concern these organizations.)

Groups at each end of the spectrum have generally been objective in setting out the problems, as they have seen them, and their solutions – again as they have seen them; however, it must be said that although there has also been special pleading (and some marketing distortion) there are also groups and individuals who take a middle-of-the-road view. Individuals from all parts of the spectrum regroup when dealing with the specific problems associated with early leavers – that is, employees who change jobs, are made redundant or retire early from a pension scheme of which they are members, for whatever reasons. Here there is a division between those who, when designing occupational pension schemes structures, believe that in the main it is the contribution level that should be specified – *the defined contribution school* – and those who believe that in the main it is the benefit level that should be specified – *the defined benefit school.*

The *defined contribution* school is, at its extreme, represented by the Centre for Policy Studies (CPS, 1983), which could be said to support a sophisticated form of money purchase arrangement. CPS have coined the phrases 'portable pensions' as well as 'personal pension provision'. Both expressions have now become accepted journalistic (and advertising) terminology and are unfortunately apt to be regarded as requiring no further explanation when used in articles published in the financial pages of magazines or newspapers even though in practice they have tended to acquire meanings that differ from journalist to journalist. The *defined benefit* school is, at its extreme, represented by the National Association of Pension Funds (NAPF), which could be said generally to support final salary arrangements.

The function of a pension fund – past

The NAPF has described the purpose of pension funds as enabling people to enjoy retirement rather than to endure old age. This, though true, is an oversimplification (NAPF, 1983).

Over the years the function of pension schemes in the United Kingdom has changed. In the late nineteenth century, private pensions were granted on an *ex gratia* and personal basis to favoured employees of a company as a reward for long service. Often there was no formal scheme, only statements of intent or merely expectations based on custom. Informal arrangements of this character, without legal protection, offered opportunities for abuse and preferential treatment of individuals, and often soured employer/employee relations since the arbitrary nature of the pension award could tempt an employer to use the threat of withholding a pension as a means of placing pressure on an employee. More formal and legally protected arrangements were clearly advisable and there was soon pressure to introduce them generally. Section 32 of the Finance Act 1921 set the pattern for occupational pension funds as they are known. (Similarly, the Beveridge Report, 1942, is often considered as the founding document of the modern welfare state.)

The state retirement pension is usually paid to men at the age of 65 and to women at the age of 60 and not before. For people who draw the pension and go on working there is a system of reductions in the state benefit corresponding to the amount earned. This is commonly referred to as the earnings rule. For those who defer their drawing of a pension there is a system of corresponding increases. This, combined with the Superannuation Funds Office's (SFO) insistence on a normal retirement age, has forced firms to introduce a fixed retirement age into their occupational pension schemes. Any younger retirement age would lead to a sharp increase in the level of retirement income at age 65 (60 women) and to the operation of the earnings rule for several years. Despite this, some occupational schemes do have retirement ages other than 65 (60 women), but even in these schemes the retirement ages tend to be fixed rather than flexible. In 1979, 90 per cent of members of occupational pension schemes were in schemes with a normal retirement age that coincided with that of the state scheme (Government Actuary, 1981).

In the past, pension schemes have been seen as a way of providing an orderly pattern of retirement and career progression. A contracted pension from a fixed age reduced the pressure on the employer to retain old staff and was also a means of encouraging continuous service. Trends are developing away from this practice of a fixed retirement age, and the existence of a pension scheme may no longer be the means by which a company can retain staff that it feels are useful and by which it can divest itself without conscience of staff at the end of a useful working life.

The following are extracts from the Trades Union Congress (TUC) evidence submitted at the end of 1981 to the Social Services Committee of the House of Commons looking into the age of retirement:

> We do not consider that there should be a blanket requirement to give up work at any age, but it is accepted that through collective bargaining it can be agreed that employees should give up particular occupations at a specific age.

> the most acceptable change would be to allow flexibility for both sexes to retire within a specified period before and after a notional common pension age. (Social Services Committee, 1981)

After considering evidence from the TUC as well as from many other organizations and individuals, the committee reported (Social Services Committee, 1982). The report recommended a scheme of pensions based on a new notional common pension age of 63 with flexibility of actual retirement age. The report emphasized that 63 was not to be regarded as replacing either age 60 or 65 in the present system, but merely to be used as a reference age on which the new concept of a flexible retirement might be based. In addition to this, the Council recommendation in 1982 from the EEC on the subject of community policy towards retirement age contains the following two commitments (Council of the European Communities, 1982):

- after a certain minimum retirement age – identical for men and women – workers should be free to choose the date of their retirement;
- financial incentives to promote the early departure of elderly workers should be used only in exceptional economic circumstances and are not to be considered as an integral part of flexible retirement system.

The function of a pension scheme – present

It is not easy to determine a consensus view of the main function of a pension scheme at the present time. People have differing ideas, if not about what scheme functions are, at least about what the schemes should or should not achieve. This is illustrated by a government survey into public attitudes to various aspects of pension provision in February 1984 (Gallup, 1984). One of the questions asked of people employed by employers who had sponsored occupational pension schemes was: 'How do you personally view your employer's pension?' (see Table 4.1); a far more detailed breakdown may be obtained from the actual survey results.

Table 4.1   *Public attitudes to pension provision*

How do you personally view your employer's pension? I mean do you see your eventual pension as:

	Replies (% of total)*
means for your employer to retain staff	13
method of compulsory saving	38
reward for loyalty	19
gift from employer	2
deferred pay	25
means for employer to recruit staff	10
stability/security/investment for future	5
employer's obligation	4
other	4
don't know	7

* Affirmative replies were permitted in more than one category.

This question was posed only to employees. It would be very interesting to have a similar question inserted in the next Government Actuary's survey addressed to employers. Meanwhile, it will be necessary to use the following examples to illustrate that employers' views are also divergent.

In the initial evidence given by the Institute of Personnel Management (IPM) to the Occupational Pensions Board (OPB) for its report on early leavers (Occupational Pensions Board, 1981), the IPM wrote: 'In order to ensure the best use of manpower, employee mobility should not be discouraged. It considers that the different treatment in relation to pension rights of people changing jobs can often act as an impediment to mobility.' By implication, the IPM feels that one of the functions of a pension scheme should be to provide 'no impediment to the mobility of labour'. In fact, one of its conclusions in this original evidence was that 'full transferability of pension rights should be the ultimate aim'. Others, such as the National Union of Miners president Arthur Scargill, in his widely reported conflicts with the investment managers of the mineworkers' pension scheme, feel that pension funds have a role to play in the wider community and that the funds have a function in relation to their investment obligations to the whole economy. Many others would agree with the NAPF's simplistic view that pensions are provided to enable people to enjoy retirement rather than to endure old age.

It is always unfair to take quotations out of context, so it is only right and proper to preface the following quotation from a recent Institute of Actuaries Students' Society paper (Wilson, 1984) with the observation that it comes at the end of a far more conventional list of functions of pension funds. None the less, it is stated as one function that 'pension funds present a challenge to actuaries and other professionals to ensure that a flow of contributions now is transformed into a retirement income for each individual with his particular history and characteristics'.

It is clear from current discussion that the functions of a pension fund are neither mutually exclusive nor very restricted. The following are some other functions that are currently quoted: morale booster, aid to recruitment, tax protection, deferred salary, good industrial relations, compulsory employee saving. If any three functions stand out from the rest they are probably the concepts of compulsory saving, deferred pay and the means to enjoy retirement. It would appear that it is not only the absolute function of a pension scheme that we should consider but also the public concept of what a pension represents.

The pension concept

The concept of a pension as deferred pay has been around for a long time, at least since a paper published in the *Journal of the Institute of Actuaries* in 1901 (Manly, 1901). More recently this concept, widely promoted by the TUC, has gained official recognition in the evidence supplied by the Government Actuary to the Wilson Committee (1980). The first paragraph of this evidence reads as follows:

> For the 11.5 million employees who are members of occupational pension schemes, the pensions and other benefits provided by these schemes are normally part of their terms of service. The employer promises that, through the media of his pension scheme, future payments will, in specified circumstances, be made to his employee or his dependants. Although the pension scheme benefits will normally be paid after the employee has retired or left service for some reason they effectively form part of his remuneration. Indeed, pensions scheme rights are often referred to as 'deferred pay' and this concept underlies the preservation provisions of the Social Security Act 1973.

The concept of the pension as deferred pay has become universally accepted partly because it is an apparently simple concept to understand. It is generally accepted that, if pension contributions were not made by the employer and/or employees, it is likely that the employees would receive more pay. Furthermore, pensions do resemble pay in that they are paid by the former employer or his nominated insurance company, are related to the former employee's salary at retirement date (according to the sixth Government Actuary's survey, 1981, at least 90 per cent of schemes are final salary related), and are taxed under the pay-as-you-earn system.

There is a danger, however, in using the term deferred pay synonymously with pension since this may lead to unrealistically raised expectations in the minds of the members of pension schemes. Viewing pensions as deferred pay and the employer's contribution as effectively part of remuneration has led the layman to think that a regular contribution, which in some ways bears a fair and reasonable relationship to the salary from which it is notionally deducted, is put aside each year and invested to pay each individual's deferred salary when the time comes. This may be how the popular image of pensions as compulsory saving arose.

Pension costs are frequently quoted in terms of x per cent of payroll to employer and y per cent of salary to employee (where y can be as low as 0). This method of expressing costs as a rate rather than a definite sum makes allowance for changing membership and salaries. If in practice any attempt were made to allocate costs back to specific individuals they would not necessarily be of regular application or smoothly progressive. When the layman hears that a figure of $(x+y)$ per cent of payroll is being allocated to the pension fund to provide deferred pay, he may assume – incorrectly of course – that this precise percentage is applicable to each individual specifically rather than (as is really the case) to the fund globally. If Mr A aged 45 joins a company his pension will probably cost the company more than the average $(x+y)$ per cent of his salary, but this piece of information does not make headlines. If Mr B aged 25 leaves the same company early with little or no transfer value he may feel harshly treated. This is the type of situation that can provoke adverse public comment. The fact that such comment is based on a lack of understanding does not make it less damaging to the pensions movement. Pensions are deferred pay but people must be made to understand that the same absolute pension may require a different incidence of contributions for different people of the same entry age but with different durations of employment and different salary histories and different expectations of life after retirement (for example, men and women).

It may be that pension scheme members would like the structure of their schemes amended to make provisions for early leavers and the maintenance of real values and other difficulties. It is quite natural, in the absence of attributable costs, that members should want the best of all possible worlds. It is mainly for this reason that, whilst the present low level of understanding of the working of a pension scheme persists, rational changes cannot be made. Even where payments form only a notional deduction from salary it is important for members to understand that each benefit has its cost and to how much that cost amounts. Pension contributions now form such a high proportion of payroll (an overall figure of 15 per cent is not unusual) that cross-subsidies between members become very important. The concept of equal pay for equal work becomes untenable if the pension contributions (notionally) allocated on a member's behalf (and of course any other fringe benefits, although these fall beyond the scope of this chapter) are not quantified.

It must be stressed at this juncture that an employer is free (in the UK) to adopt entirely different pension arrangements for different employees or classes of employee (for example, senior executives), and this of course permits a more specific allocation of costs. Moreover, there are other benefits to be considered, such as those paid to widows or children on the death of an employee (an important consideration at younger ages) or early retirement.

The concept of pensions as deferred pay has led people to question the fairness of the complex cross-subsidies between one individual and another that are implicit in the structure of a pension scheme based on defined benefits. Before considering the problems caused by cross-subsidies, it will be useful to summarize and comment on some of the reasons for the trend in favour of collective arrangements based on final salary as opposed to individual policies or schemes based on other types of benefit formulae.

Reasons for the move to final salary structure

With so much attention devoted to the concept of pensions as deferred pay, the function of pensions as a means of preserving a reasonable level of living in old age is sometimes forgotten. The public interest in this function is evident from the strong lobby for the maintenance of real values of pensions. It was this that gave impetus to the introduction of the final salary type design of pension scheme, which, it was claimed, avoided the danger of newly awarded pensions lagging behind current wage levels.

Final salary schemes introduced a new problem – how to deal with the early leaver – and did not really solve the original problem of pensioners' incomes lagging behind those of the workforce. The principle of safe-guarding the real value of pensions can be stated more generally as maintaining the relationship between the level of living of pensioners and that of the economically active population so that pensioners shall have a share in national economic growth. Final salary schemes in themselves achieve this only at the exact instant of retirement and methods have to be found to complement them – currently by various forms of contractual or voluntary indexing.

Another important factor in the move from individual to group arrangements was administrative cost. Group arrangements do not usually require any individual records to be kept of yearly contributions or benefits. This is true for final salary funding where the contribution is defined as a percentage of company payroll and the benefits of any individual can be easily calculated, when required, by a simple formula. The reduction in overheads involved was considerable. But it is questionable whether this differential in overheads will still apply in future. The advent of computers has made it physically possible to hold more records pertaining to an individual. If it is necessary to hold a record that contains name, sex, age and address, it does not require much more space and effort also to restore the notional contribution. Whereas it may previously have taken many man-hours to calculate individual pension contributions and only minutes to calculate percentage of payroll, it is now possible for the computer to calculate and store individual contributions almost instantly. Moreover, although individual information may not previously have had to be supplied to pension scheme members on a regular basis, its provision will shortly be compulsory. The difference in cost between supplying a benefit statement that contains a box with an individually calculated contribution and one that does not is considerably less than the cost comparison between supplying any statement and not having to supply one at all. It could be a simple automatic print-out in a uniform format just as monthly salary statements or electricity or telephone bills are produced. Indeed, it would be a simple extension of existing computerized wage or salary statements.

The ability of collective arrangements to cope with a much wider spread of circumstances than individual policies has, no doubt, also contributed to their popularity. When a new group scheme is set up, an employer is able to fund back service pensions over a fairly long period. With individual arrangements, funding would normally be required immediately. Yet another advantage, if it can be called an advantage, of group schemes is the opportunity they offer employers to mask the cost of ill-health retirements and other forms of *ex gratia* payments.

At a recent pensions meeting, a participant (professionally engaged in the field) remarked that he did not like the idea of moving from the final salary structure for occupational pension schemes to an individually costed system because the employer would no longer be able to afford to take elderly recruits into his scheme. There are many arguments for retaining the final salary structure for pensions, but this is not one of them, although it is heard surprisingly frequently. The fact that the costing of a final salary pension scheme takes into account as one of its many assumptions just who the employer is likely to recruit lulls him and many of his non-technical advisers into thinking that their recruiting policy has no effect on costs. (This is discussed further in the section on cross-subsidies.) In practice, management rarely considers pension costs when framing recruitment, or in fact any other policy, because it is probably not impressed upon management that it is essential to do so.

The Inland Revenue benefit limitations for approved schemes are largely based on the model of the Civil Service pension provisions and these are final salary based. This may be the most important factor encouraging the introduction of final salary-based pension schemes. Further encouragement has been given by the conditions imposed for contracting out of the earnings-related state scheme (SERPS). (At the date of writing this book it has been proposed by the government to permit contracting out of money purchase schemes.)

The term 'money purchase costing' for allocating the overall company pension contributions to individuals has acquired a bad image in the industry. In the past, the benefits provided by money purchase schemes have proved inadequate, and this too is one of the reasons why the design of occupational pension schemes was generally changed to a final salary basis. However, if as much money had been paid in contributions to the original money purchase schemes as currently to final salary schemes, the benefits might now be adequate. It is also important to remember that a money purchase funding method does not have to imply an equal allocation of contribution levels (as a percentage of salary) as between individual members. An age-related scale of contributions would not necessarily be inequitable since each member would be aware of his own entitlement. If he stayed, he too would in turn receive the higher contributions. More important, if he left early he would be in no doubt about the benefits that he was forgoing.

The most well known of the old money purchase schemes was the Federated Superannuation Scheme for Universities (FSSU), which existed without major revision from 1913 to 1975. Despite the title of the scheme, the majority of its members are not employed by UK universities. In 1975 the Universities' Superannuation Scheme (USS), a modern final salary scheme for academic staff in the UK, was introduced. There was a transitional period, between 1975 and 1980, during which the vast majority of the UK university membership of FSSU opted to form USS. (The non-UK university members were mostly unable to transfer because of essentially Inland Revenue reasons.) FSSU still exists and has over 4,000 members, but they tend to be employed by agricultural and other research associations such as wool, rubber and brewing and by the commonwealth universities, particularly in third world countries. All these employments involve considerable short-term interchange of staff. It is necessary to study a little of the history of the FSSU to understand the reasons for its demise.

Modern pension schemes are based on the 1921 Finance Act. Any scheme that predated it, such as the FSSU, escaped its provisions. However, any scheme that escaped the immediate provisions of the 1946 Act following the Beveridge Report – as did the FSSU – was immune only until such time as a material change was made to the scheme rules. If such a change was made, then the scheme would have to conform to the

1921 basis, as later revised and consolidated. Any modernization therefore would have resulted in the loss of the member's ability to take all his retirement benefits in cash. A feature requiring modernization was the fact that tax relief on FSSU policy contributions was normally based on the relief given to life assurance policies. A further reason for the demise of FSSU, and usually the only reason quoted, was the effect of inflation. Many FSSU members had their contributions invested in non-profit policies which patently did not keep up with inflation.

The universities set about trying to cope with inflation. In 1950 a supplementary scheme was invented, based on the grade upon which the retired member had been paid. In 1960 a new supplementary scheme was created based on 9/75 of final salary. Finally, in 1975 the USS was launched and by April 1980 most of FSSU members had joined. Many changes would have been needed to make FSSU work in the modern conditions. It is not fair, however, to use it as an example of the failure of the money purchase concept without first detailing its historic background.

For those interested, far more detail is contained in a paper by Peter Stirrup (1984) to the 22nd International Congress of Actuaries.

The early leaver problem

What exactly is the early leaver problem? In the majority of occupational pension schemes membership for eligible employees is compulsory (although the government has now produced a consultative document with proposals to change this) and members will normally be required to contribute some 5–7 per cent of their salary. Many schemes provide the employee with a pension of 1/60 of final salary for each year of working life with the employee. (Actual benefit formulae are far more complicated and are subject to various caveats for tax and other reasons, but this simple formula will serve for illustrative purposes.) This means that an employee who remains with an employer throughout his working life – or at least the last forty years of it – can aspire to a pension of two-thirds of final salary.

If an employee leaves to take up an appointment with another employer, then there is, at present, a price to be paid. Let us consider a very simple example of two individuals, A and B, who live in an ideal world in which inflation does not exist. They have both contracted with the pension scheme to receive, in return for maintained contributions, a pension when they retire of 1/60 of final salary for each year of service. For the first twenty years they earn identical salaries of £x per annum. A is then offered a once-for-all promotion, which involves trebling his salary, and he thus earns £$3x$ per annum each year until he retires twenty years later. B is not offered promotion, but moves to an appointment exactly similar to A's with an enhanced salary of £3x per annum in a new firm. He too retires twenty years later without having any further salary increase. We assume that the new employer has an exactly similar pension scheme to that of the former employer.

A's pension is $\frac{40}{60}$ (3x) = 2x per annum

B's pension is $\frac{20}{60}$ (x) + $\frac{20}{60}$ (3x) = $\frac{4}{3}$ x per annum, which is less than

2x per annum

B who has changed jobs will no longer receive the two-thirds of final salary pension that he still aspires to and he cannot understand why.

The word 'aspired' has been deliberately chosen because the problem of the early leaver is partly a problem of false expectation and only partly a problem of the way in which pension schemes currently work. All that B's former pension scheme has actually promised him is that, for each year that he was working for the former employer, he would receive a pension of 1/60 of final salary, that is, the final salary received from the former employer, not the final salary he would be receiving immediately prior to retirement from some new employer. The ex-employer can justify this situation by asking why should he have to contribute to an increased pension that has been caused by subsequent pay rises over which he has no control and may well have decided not to give had he been in control. There will often be two different concepts of final salary: (a) for the ex-employer, final salary means the salary paid to the employee at the time of leaving; (b) for the employee, final salary will usually mean the salary paid at the point of ultimate retirement.

This problem has been recognized for many years. In 1970 Stewart Lyon, in opening a discussion at the Institute of Actuaries on the then proposed National Superannuation and Social Insurance Bill (Lyon, 1970), predicted that 'occupational schemes would never fulfil their proper role in the pensioning of employment so long as an employee's accrued pension rights, if they were significant, could be lost on a change of job'. The problem has now become a serious issue occupying much attention of the government. This is because, for various economic reasons outside the purview of this chapter, there has been a growing pressure for job mobility.

The government too has proposed a solution to the problem that only solves the problem from its viewpoint. It has recognized that there is a problem with early leavers, but it has been convinced that the problem is that inflation is eating away the value of the pension promise of the first employer. It has therefore legislated that the ex-employer inflates his ex-employee's pension entitlement by 5 per cent per annum up to the ultimate retirement. This is tantamount to asking the first pension scheme to provide for national salary increases of 5 per cent a year subsequent to the employee's departure to a second and/or subsequent employer.

It is true that inflation causes many problems and hardships, but the problem of the early leaver in relation to final salary pension schemes cannot justifiably be attributed to it. Inflation could only be regarded as wholly or even mainly to blame if it were demonstrable that employees received only inflation-linked salary increases. This is patently not so. There are still age, length of service, merit and productivity increases.

Adequacy problem

When presented with the question 'Why are final salary schemes considered less primitive than money purchase schemes?' at a DHSS conference, the chairman of the Occupational Pensions Board (OPB) commenced his reply – reflecting a majority view – with the assertion that 'employees need a pension related to their pre-retirement earnings and money purchase schemes cannot guarantee this'. As he developed his reply it was clear that he assumed that an income-related final salary was necessary to maintain a reasonable level of living in retirement. But this leaves in question the meaning of reasonable level of living, and its relationship to pre-retirement income would depend upon the value of that income. For the low paid a mere subsistence pension would be a very high proportion of pre-retirement income. For the chief executive of a large enterprise a small proportion of income would still, to most people, represent comparative affluence. But it might not be regarded by him as reasonable if this level of comparative affluence was significantly lower than that to which he had become accustomed in the last few years of employment.

It is clear that for most people an adequate pension has little to do with subsistence and more to do with the expectations of the social group to which they have progressed before retirement. This is a fact of life in both a private enterprise society and a planned economy (though perhaps in the latter case the range of affluence levels is not so wide). It is not appropriate here to make judgments about matters of political economy. It is a fact that adequacy is a matter of relativity to income. In this respect the assertion by the chairman of the OPB is justifiable. But one should substitute 'expects' for 'needs'. Need only comes into the picture at the lower end of the scale where the concept of social welfare has to be considered. As will be demonstrated in Chapter 8, there are still many people who have not been members of occupational pension schemes long enough to secure a pension that is more than a very small fraction of pay prior to retirement, or who have not even been members of schemes at all. They have real subsistence needs that have to be met by the state pension scheme and other forms of welfare.

The 1946 legislation that introduced compulsory social insurance for all was concerned with this concept of welfare. Since then, however, this has been overtaken by the concept of an income-related pension. There is a fundamental issue between, on the one hand, those who think that the state should confine its role to the provision of a welfare pension and that further provision should be by personal saving through either contribution to an occupational pension scheme or payment of a premium to an insurance company or other financial institution or simply personal investment (or combinations of these three), and, on the other hand, those who think the state should deal comprehensively with pension provision. The debate, which is political rather than technical, continues.

The level of living

Employers realize that employee satisfaction and good staff relations will not be maintained if the pension scheme members feel that they are part of a bad scheme. It has always been difficult to measure in any quantitative manner the staff relations return of the investment of an employer in a pension plan, but it is obviously very small if the members do not value the scheme. The public is becoming more knowledgeable about pensions and about the difference between the value of money now and in the future, and this must inevitably lead to a situation where any plan that does not automatically provide for inflation will not be classed as a good plan. A company can afford only a limited sum of money; it must decide how to allocate this sum so as to satisfy as far as possible the aspirations of all employees. This is not easy. Each member of staff is an individual with individual needs. What is considered essential by one individual can just as easily be considered superfluous by another, especially if they have differing family responsibilities. This makes the provision of fringe benefits, including company pensions, a difficult task for any employer. A compromise has to be reached between the desirable and the possible (within the limits of cost that the enterprise can afford to bear).

It is important that each individual should understand the extent to which he, as an individual, is responsible both for himself and for his dependants in the event of retirement, disability, death or sickness, and the extent to which the employer and/or the government (via the resources of the working population) are responsible. It is not easy for an individual member of a typical final salary scheme to determine what level of additional savings he may require. As will be shown in the final section of this chapter, the amount of money funded in a final salary scheme on behalf of any individual progressively increases throughout service. He is therefore unable at a young age to make a rational decision whether or not to make separate provision for his retirement. If he decides to make separate provision on the assumption that he will change jobs and then does not do so, he may have caused unnecessary hardship in his younger years to himself and to his family (if any) by his (in the event) unnecessary saving campaign. Conversely, if he does not make provision and does change jobs, he (and his family) may be caused unnecessary hardship after his retirement.

If a specified percentage of his income were funded on a true money purchase scheme the problem would not arise. But introducing a money purchase scheme raises another important question. If an individual gets only what he pays for, why should he not arrange it himself without the patronage of the employer (who would, however, have to pay higher salaries or wages to compensate). It cannot be argued that lower-paid employees are less able to save, since the money that would have gone to pension contributions could be paid out as higher salaries. If it is then argued that this money, if paid as a salary increase, will be used for necessary living expenses, then it would appear that the original salaries were not high enough and the pensioners, assuming that they receive pensions less than the salary that they are intended to replace, almost certainly would not be receiving enough income to provide for necessary living expenses in retirement.

In modern conditions, it is not necessarily true that a pensioner requires less than the working person to maintain himself. He no longer has travel expenses or possibly as great expenses for clothing or meals out, but to offset that saving there are also increased costs such as heating and lighting during the longer hours that a pensioner is at home. These pensions would therefore require supplementing by the state (even if indirectly in the form of rent rebates, etc). But it is important, as has been stressed earlier, not to confuse the welfare and insurance objectives of providing pensions. The welfare aspect should be dealt with by government and can be by way of a flat-rate pension; the insurance aspect should be covered by the individual or company as appropriate. Additionally, on the insurance side it would be important to make provision for permanent health insurance to allow for benefits that cannot be self-financing (such as those on early retirement from ill-health). The provision of such benefits must depend on the true principles of insurance, viz. the pooling of risks.

If general agreement could be reached that it is desirable for the state to cover, as of right, the basic welfare needs of the retired population – the 'endure old age' part of the retirement – and for companies and/or individuals to provide pensions beyond that minimum – the 'enjoy' part of retirement – we will have recovered the Beveridge concept. At the date of writing this book, it appears that such a consensus view is unlikely to be reached in the short term.

It could be possible for there to be general agreement that individuals and/or companies should cover the basic welfare needs of the retired as well as the additional benefits. But it is difficult to imagine, in a caring society such as ours is meant to be, that agreement will not be reached that it is desirable for the state to look after the basic welfare needs of the elderly − if only because each of us will be old in our turn. If, nevertheless, the opposite is decided upon, there would have to be a complex social security system to look after those who, through no fault of their own, were unable to work and to provide sufficient for their old age. This is just the sort of situation that those who believe in self-help usually wish to avoid.

The cost of extending state pensions to cover the basic welfare needs of individuals must be calculated, but it is likely to be lower than at first imagined. If the benefits are taxable under the normal PAYE system, any payments to those not in need will be recouped to the extent of basic rate tax at least. Payment to those in need, by far the larger grouping, will be offset to the extent that other supplementary benefits, which were previously paid, will no longer be required. It must not be forgotten to include in this offset the vast costs of administering the present supplementary benefits scheme.

It must be remembered that when a person becomes infirm (a state almost entirely independent of age once the age of, say, 65 has been passed) and thus dependent on the help of others it is the provision of care not money that is needed. No matter how generous a pension scheme may be under current circumstances it cannot afford to pay benefits that will enable each retired member to employ a day nurse and a night nurse, and domestic assistance. Most present-day schemes would not even pay enough benefit for a member to enter a charitable old age home, let alone one run by private enterprise.

It is to be hoped that the schemes of the future will see their function as the provision of care as well as money, that is, they will consider themselves insurers of old age in much the same way as PPP and BUPA now consider themselves insurers of health in that they are indemnity insurers, meeting bills payments when incurred. What might in practice happen is that the pension funds, instead of investing in traditional investments, such as ordinary shares, may decide to build sheltered housing, old age homes and hospitals, thereby investing directly in the economy and providing jobs now as well as ensuring the welfare of their pensioners when their time comes.

Cross-subsidies

We can now look in more detail at the problem of cross-subsidies, although still within a simplified framework. As has been stated in the section on the pension concept, it is usual for pension costs to be expressed as x per cent of payroll of employer and y per cent of salary to employee, which makes allowance for changing membership and salaries over future decades. Such assumptions can be made only because fairly large numbers of employees are involved and therefore actuarial techniques can be employed to calculate rates of contribution. If we want to look at the actual cost of a pension to a specific individual, we can be certain about its nature only when the person has died and payment of the pension has finished. In the real world of pension fund management, this technique of calculating the cost of the pension retrospectively serves no useful purpose, but theoretically it can be used to shed much light on what occurs in practice. We shall return to this later.

Perhaps the simplest way to look at the present cost of an individual's eventual pension is to look at each year's cost separately. If a given calendar year of contribution is considered in isolation it is obvious that for a given salary a younger employee should have a much smaller percentage of his salary going into the pension fund than an older member because the younger man's contribution will be invested for a longer period before retirement. It can be argued that this does not matter. The younger employee who pays too much in relation to his pension promise in the earlier years will pay too little later and on the average justice will be done. However, if there is to be employee mobility, it is not to be presumed that he will stay with the one company until retirement. Nevertheless, let us assume that both employees stay with the same employer until retirement. For the same pension promise, the older employee will still cost the employer more than the younger employee because it will be funded over a shorter period. This extra cost can be met only by a subsidy from the employer or, if the average contribution is raised to meet it, by a subsidy from the younger employee.

It can be argued that cross-subsidies of the kind described above are part of the normal insurance principle that equal premiums are paid for equal risks but unequal outcomes. But here we are dealing with unequal risks (promises). It is important for the employer (and employee) to bear in mind that, when costs for the whole company are calculated, the assumptions take into account certain proportions of employees at each age. If company policy is changed so that those assumptions are no longer valid, then the costing would need to be recalculated. If, for example, the company were to have a massive recruitment of older, more experienced employees than had been allowed for in the original assumptions, the cost would increase. If, on the contrary, it were decided to have a massive recruitment of apprentices at a younger age than had been allowed for in the original assumptions, the cost would decrease. This seems obvious, but when an employer takes on only one new recruit the effect is masked and overlooked because that new recruit is so insignificant in relation to the total numbers.

Consideration must also be given to the effect of salary increases that are out of line with the salary progression that has been taken into account in costing the pension arrangements and in subsequently fixing contributions. If contributions are a percentage of salary it might be thought that a rise in salary will automatically increase the contribution proportionately. But the reserve held in the scheme to cover the liability for past service will now be inadequate unless also proportionately increased. A shortfall in reserves will thus be created and will add to any deficiency revealed at the next valuation of the scheme. This deficiency will have to be met either, as is often the case, by a payment from the employer or by some general upward adjustment in contributions. Here then is another element of cross-subsidy. This is not a criticism of pension schemes or of the practice of awarding exceptional salary increases to exceptionally valuable employees, but it is a reminder to the employer that there are hidden costs in the practice. In effect, the reward to the favoured employee is greater than the actual increase in salary.

Some model calculations have been conducted by Professor David Wilkie in order to quantify the extra cost (Wilkie, 1985). The model contained the following simplifications and assumptions, amongst others:

1. There is a staff of eight individuals all starting at age 25 with a salary of £5,000.
2. There is a specific salary scale within the firm that happens to coincide with that given in Formulae and Tables for Actuarial Examinations, which is purely a specimen table.
3. The staff all have a personal rate of salary progression that is lower or higher than the given scale by a specified percentage ranging from −2 per cent to +5 per cent.
4. There is in addition a general level of salary increase in excess of inflation by 1 per cent per annum.
5. The rate of inflation is 7 per cent.

It can be seen from Table 4.2 (p. 62) that the cost of the pension to the 'high flyer', C, is nearly 35 per cent, whilst for the plodder, A, it is only 10 per cent.

The insurance principle

Let us return for a moment to consideration of the insurance element. It is generally accepted that some people will receive more benefits from a scheme than they put in, and some less, since this is the principle of

Table 4.2   *Cost of pension*

Individual	% increase in salary relative to salary scale*	Final salary	Level contribution (% of salary)
		£	
A	− 2.0	6,500	10
B	0.0	14,000	15
C	5.0	100,000	35

* This is in addition to the general level of salary increases in the company overall.

insurance. But the principle of insurance in the context of pension schemes would normally be regarded as applying (as it does in life insurance) to the individual differences in longevity amongst homogeneous groups so that the prolonged enjoyment of a pension by the member who lives to an older age is paid for partly by contributions attributable to the member who dies at an earlier age. In pension schemes we not only see the averaging between individuals with similar life expectancy but with different actual longevity; we also see cross-subsidies from the lower to the higher paid, from young to old, from men to women, as was discussed in the previous section. If one considers a scheme in an industry in which the workforce is known to have a high occupational mortality risk not experienced by the office staff and the mortality experiences of these two groups are merged (as may be quite likely), then one even has cross-subsidies from the poor to the rich. It is to be noted that these cross-subsidies can therefore operate in a non-egalitarian manner, which is the reverse of what is usually considered to be the object of pooling of risks. Moreover the cross-subsidies are hidden, the benefactor receiving no credit and the recipient remaining unaware that he is receiving any benefit.

If the cross-subsidies were to be more open and the members of a pension scheme were to realize that the level *x* per cent contribution that the company is paying on their behalf actually means differing amounts on behalf of Mr A and on behalf of Mr B, a more rational decision could be taken about the use of the cross-subsidy not as an insurance element but as a deliberate benefit to the well-promoted (that is, valuable) stayer as part of management policy, justified on the grounds that the employer is underwriting the solvency of the pension scheme and providing a large proportion of the cross-subsidy. It is not intended here to suggest any redistribution of the contribution level merely to make members aware of those to whom the relevant costs are attributable. Provided the members of a pension scheme realize that the level *x* per cent contribution they are told that the company is paying on their behalf comprises differing actual amounts on behalf of different sub-groups, this will be sufficient to enable them properly to judge the value of the scheme to them.

Pension scheme members may well decide it is worthwhile their subsidizing older workers, since they too will become old in their turn. Equally the employer may decide that the older worker is worth a higher salary by virtue of his experience and may decide to pay this increase partly by means of a pension contribution. In such circumstances the final salary scheme structure as we know it would remain unchanged, but it would be based on rational acceptance. It is, of course, possible that when greater knowledge enables members and employers alike to make more rational choices, there will be a redistribution of contributions that would fall somewhere between the distribution necessary for (a) the current final salary structure, where members are told *x* per cent of salary is paid into the pension fund on their behalf, but it is on average *x* per cent comprising varying amounts for individuals depending on their circumstances and final benefit entitlement, and (b) assigning an actual level uniform contribution rate for different benefit entitlement, which would be very popular with younger members but very unpopular with their older colleagues. Changes would be gradual because of the time scale required to alter scheme rules and also because sudden change would leave those near to retirement with small benefits through no fault of their own.

The design and function of pension schemes are continuously evolving. What is acceptable today may not be so tomorrow, although changes are gradual and not abrupt. As a result of political or marketing pressure or employee preference, occupational pension schemes may give way to individual money purchase plans, or to some way of providing benefits not rigidly linked to pre-retirement salary. At present there seems to be no general desire on the part of workers to contract individual money purchase pensions that may be more costly than equivalent benefits in a group scheme and certainly more trouble to them, individually, to arrange and maintain. The proposed legislation may, however, change this.

To sum up so far, there are two distinguishable approaches to pension provision. These are based on either the defined benefit or the defined contribution principles. Either approach is tenable, as indeed is some combination of the two. It must, however, be noted that where the defined contribution system is chosen the payment into a scheme of like amounts for individuals in like circumstances is easily arranged. It will appeal to those people who argue that cost is the logical and only criterion for assessing equal treatment in pension schemes. In defined benefit schemes it is very difficult to determine the cost for each individual. The defined benefit method would therefore appeal to those who argue that equality of benefit is the only valid yardstick. The division between the two approaches is highlighted in the context of the debate about equality of the sexes: this is thoroughly discussed in a recent paper presented to the Institute of Actuaries (Wilkie, 1985).

For a company paying a level percentage of payroll to the pension fund and making advance funding provisions for salary increases, attributing costs on the money purchase scheme is neither elegant nor easy to explain, especially because of the allowance for future salary increases. None the less, the money purchase method of explanation does have the overriding advantage of exposing the cross-subsidies in a scheme. Its general acceptance might influence the design of schemes. One insurance company has been marketing an occupational pension plan that combines the principles of money purchase and final salary benefits within one group scheme. This provides the early leaver with the money purchase guarantee and the member that stays with the advantage of final salary benefits. It achieves this objective by splitting the pension contribution into two separately identifiable elements. One element, which the insurance company recommends should not exceed 75 per cent of the total contribution level, is used to provide a money purchase benefit. When an employee retires, the second element is to be administered in a deposit administration way to top up benefits to final salary level if the member's money purchase pension falls short of the amount that would be attributed on the final salary formula. The plan does not go far enough. It is still not possible to see to whom and at whose expense the deposit administration part of the final pension is allocated. Cross-subsidies in any form should be open.

References

Adam Smith Institute (1983), *Privatizing Pensions*. A report to the Secretary of State for Health and Social Security. Restricted publication

Beveridge, Sir W. (1942), *Report on Social Insurance and Allied Services*, Cmnd 6405, London: HMSO

Council of the European Communities (1982), *Council Recommendations on the Principles of a Community Policy with Regard to Retirement Age*, 10 December

CPS (1983), 'Personal and Portable Pensions for All'. A memorandum prepared by the Personal Capital Formation Study Group of the Centre for Policy Studies

Gallup (1984), *Gallup Report*. A DHSS enquiry into attitudes of members of occupational pension schemes to portable pensions published in March 1984 by Gallup

Government Actuary (1981), *Occupational Pension Schemes 1979*, Sixth Survey by the Government Actuary, London: HMSO

Lyon, C. S. S. (1970), 'National superannuation and social insurance bill', *Journal of the Institute of Actuaries*, Vol. 96, p. 163

Lyon, C. S. S. (1983), 'Presidential address: The Outlook for Pensioning', *Journal of the Institute of Actuaries*, Vol. 110, pp. 1–16

Manly, H. W. (1901), 'On the valuation of staff pension funds', *Journal of the Institute of Actuaries*, Vol. 36, p. 209

NAPF (1983), Verbal comment by the NAPF representative at a special conference on 14 September 1983 on 'Early Leavers' convened by the Rt Hon. Norman Fowler, MP, Secretary of State for Social Services

Occupational Pensions Board (1981), *Improved Protection for the Occupational Pension Rights and Expectations of Early Leavers*, Cmnd 8271, London: HMSO

Social Services Committee (1981), *Minutes of Evidence on Age of Retirement to Social Services Committee, given on 21 December 1981*, Session 81/82, London: HMSO

Social Services Committee (1982), *Age of Retirement*, Third Report from the House of Commons Social Services Committee, Session 1981–82, HC26–1, 24 November, London: HMSO

Stirrup, P. (1984), 'Recent developments in superannuation arrangements for United Kingdom academic staff', *Proceedings of 22nd International Congress of Actuaries*, p. 40

Wilkie, A. D. (1983), 'Notes on equal treatment for men and women in occupational social security schemes', *Journal of the Institute of Actuaries*, Vol. 111, p. 15

Wilkie, A. D. (1985), 'Some experiments with pensions accrual', *Journal of the Institute of Actuaries*, Vol. 112, p. 205

Wilson Committee (1980), *Report of the Committee to Review the Functioning of Financial Institutions*, Cmnd 7937, London: HMSO

Wilson, G. R. G. (1984), 'Pensions and benefits in a reward strategy', *Journal of the Institute of Actuaries' Students Society*, Vol. 27, p. 128.

5 Funded Pension Schemes – Macroeconomic Aspects

DAVID WILKIE

Introduction

This chapter discusses certain macroeconomic aspects of funded pension schemes, and how they fit into the total economic framework of the United Kingdom. It is based on a talk given at a seminar on pensions held by the Institute of Actuaries and the Faculty of Actuaries in Staple Inn in November 1983, but with some revisions and alterations. In particular, 1982 figures have been replaced by those for 1984.

Economic identities

It is helpful to restate some very elementary economics, in order to emphasize the identities shown in Table 5.1. We see from this that the total production of goods and services in the economy equals the total incomes received by the factors of production – that is, the income from work, the income from capital, and the income from rent. Total income equals total expenditure, which can be split into spending on consumption plus savings – that is, the amount of goods and services consumed plus the amount that goes into capital formation – which in turn equals total production.

These identities apply to the world as a whole, or to any wholly closed economy. For a section of the world economy, such as the United Kingdom, there are adjustments to be made for external trade, income from overseas investments, and the purchase or sale of overseas assets.

Table 5.2 shows the figures for these items for the United Kingdom in 1984, in billion (i.e. thousand million) pounds. These are all very round numbers, and the residual error that arises when the figures are collected has been hidden away. We see that production of £277b was increased through our receiving income from overseas assets of a further £3b, giving a total available income of £280b. This was subdivided so that £207b was paid as income for work, that is, income from employment and self-employment and other items referred to below; £54b was paid in income for capital, that is, the profits of companies and of public corporations (in

Table 5.1 *Elementary economic identities*

TOTAL PRODUCTION
OF GOODS AND SERVICES

=

TOTAL FACTOR INCOMES

=

Income from work	+	Income from capital	+	Income from rent

=

TOTAL EXPENDITURE

=

Spending on consumption	+	Savings

=

Consumption of goods and services	+	Capital formation

=

TOTAL PRODUCTION

---

this case before allowing for depreciation); plus £19b in rent from land and property, a large part of which is the imaginary rent we pay to ourselves for living in our own houses. Of this total income, £226b was spent on consumption and £54b was saved, of which £53b was used for domestic capital formation and the remaining £1b in the purchase of overseas assets. This gives us total domestic consumption of £279b, which almost exactly matches the production of £277b, the difference being the £3b from the top line that provided the foreign currency for the £1b spent on purchasing overseas assets, and the £2b of other net current account expenditure (including, for example, overseas aid, contributions to the European Communities, and social security payments paid overseas, as well as the excess of imports of goods and service over exports, which in 1984 were about in balance).

The personal sector

What has been shown so far includes the personal sector, companies, and the whole of the public sector (that is, central and local government and

Table 5.2 *UK economy, 1984 (£b)*

Production 277	+	Income from overseas assets 3

Total Income 280

Work income 207	+	Capital 54	+	Rent 19

Consumption 226	+	Savings 54

Consumption 226	+	Capital formation 53	+	Net purchases of overseas assets 1

Domestic consumption 279	+	Current account surplus 1

Production 277	+	Income from overseas assets 3

nationalized industries). Table 5.3 shows data just for the personal sector, and for this purpose life assurance companies and pension funds are treated as if they were part of the personal sector, because their assets are held in trust for *persons* (at least those of pension funds are). Again the figures are in billion pounds. To wages and salaries and other employment income of £156b has to be added employers' contributions to the National Insurance Scheme of £11b and to private pension schemes of £13b, thus increasing the personal incomes of those in work to an extent that the individuals are probably quite unaware of. Income from self-employment of £27b is gross. Then we see that £13b of the income received by the

Table 5.3 *Personal sector, UK, 1984 (£b)*

Income from employment		156
Employers' contributions:		
National Insurance	11	
Pension schemes	13	180
Self-employment	27	27
Income from capital and rent:		
Life assurance and pensions	13	
Imputed rent	12	
Other	2	27
Total factor income		234

personal sector from capital and rent consists of the interest, dividend and rental income of life assurance and pension funds, a further £12b is the imputed rent for living in our own houses, and a mere £2b is direct dividends, interest and rent paid to the personal sector. The total is £234b. Of this, £26b (11 per cent) is received directly by the life assurance companies and pension funds, without passing through the individuals' hands. A further £11b, about 5 per cent of the total, goes directly from employers to the National Insurance Scheme.

Life assurance funds and pension schemes

Table 5.4 summarizes the accounts of life assurance funds and pension schemes (including funded, unfunded and notionally funded schemes) for 1984. We have to include individual life assurance here because a lot of pensions business is insured, and we cannot easily separate the investment income and the administrative expenses of life companies into a pensions part and a non-pensions part. We have already seen two items on the income side – the £13b of employers' contributions and the £13b of investment income. To these must be added £4b of employees' contributions and £9b of individual life policy premiums. This gives a total of £39b. The outgo of £22b is made up of about £18b of pensions

Table 5.4   *Life assurance and pension funds, UK, 1984 (£b)*

Income:		
Employers' contributions	13	
Employees' contributions	4	
Life policy premiums	9	
Investment income	13	39
Outgo:		
Pensions and other benefits	18	
Expenses and tax	4	22
Available for investment		17

and other benefits paid, mainly sums assured under life policies, and £4b of expenses and tax. This left life assurance and pension funds with £17b available for investment, and all of this contributed to personal savings.

Of course if an individual takes part of his pension scheme benefits as a lump sum, or receives the sum assured of his life policy, he may well invest it himself (or some of it may be used to pay Capital Transfer Tax if he is dead). But this is treated in the accounts as new savings.

Personal sector savings

Table 5.5 shows how the personal sector channelled its savings in 1984. Total savings were £54b, of which the personal sector provided £30b, the rest coming from companies and government. This £30b was split equally, with £15b going into fixed capital assets and the other £15b going into financial assets. The fixed capital assets were mainly housing, including both the construction of new houses and the purchase of council houses. The other fixed capital was plant and machinery and so on purchased by the self-employed, for example by farmers. Transactions in financial assets involve a lot of netting out, but in summary we see that about £6b was lent to the government; a net £4b was borrowed from banks, of which about half was for house purchase; £13b was deposited with building societies, which lent all and more back for house purchase; £3b was raised by the sale of ordinary shares and other company securities; and the £17b that went to life assurance and pension funds

Table 5.5 *Personal savings, UK, 1984 (£b)*

TOTAL SAVINGS			54
of which: personal sector			30
Fixed capital:			
Housing and land		12	
Other		3	15
Financial assets:			
Government		6	
Banks:			
Deposits	3		
Borrowing	−5		
House purchase	−2	−4	
Building societies:			
Deposits	13		
Borrowing	−14	−1	
Ordinary shares, etc.		−3	
Life assurance and Pensions		17	15

formed well over 100 per cent of the total net acquisition of financial assets. The figures have varied from year to year, but it has been true for very many years that savings through life assurance and pension funds have formed roughly 100 per cent of net personal financial savings.

Pension fund investment

Table 5.6 gives a summary of the way life assurance and pension funds invested their £17b in 1984. About £2b went into fixed capital formation, mostly property investment; £5b was lent to the government; £5b was used to buy UK company securities (but remember that the rest of the personal sector sold £3b); £1b went into the purchase of overseas securities; and there was a remaining £4b, mainly lent to banks as cash on deposit. Again, the proportions vary from year to year, but not so much as to make these figures unrepresentative.

Debt interest

The figures quoted are almost all taken from the National Income

Table 5.6   *New investments of life assurance and pension funds,*
UK, 1984 (£b)

Fixed capital (property)	2
Government	5
UK company securities	5
Overseas securities	1
Other	4
	17

and Expenditure 'Blue Book' for 1985, and the method of accounting in this has one serious failing. It treats the interest paid by the government on its debt as if it were all real interest, whereas it can be argued that debt interest at high nominal interest rates should correctly be treated only partly as real interest and partly as repayment of capital. The total government debt interest paid in 1984 was over £16b, and only about £11b of this was real interest, the remaining £5b serving to reduce the real value of government debt. In years of higher inflation the reduction in the real value of the debt has been much greater. In fact the real value of the national debt has reduced as a proportion of the GNP fairly steadily since the Second World War, and is now at about its lowest level, even though in nominal terms it is higher than ever before. If we adjust the government's accounts for this, we find that it has been running a surplus practically every year for the last twenty. In round terms, anything less than a £10b borrowing requirement in recent years has meant that the government may have been reducing the real value of its debt.

A large fraction of this debt interest is paid to insurance companies and pension funds, and to individuals in the personal sector. It has therefore been added to their income, to their savings, and to the net increase of the assets of life assurance and pension funds. To the extent that it is lent back to the government again, it should really be cancelled out on both sides. If all debt were index-linked we would be able to see the accounting done properly, but it has not been possible to make the necessary adjustments all the way through.

Depreciation

The figures so far have allowed for gross fixed capital formation without any allowance for the fact that the capital stock is always wearing out.

Thus no allowance has been made for depreciation. Earlier a figure of £53b in 1984 for capital formation was quoted; in fact this was a figure at factor cost, roughly excluding VAT, and the corresponding figure at market value was about £55b. Against this must be set an estimate of £38b of capital consumption, giving a net capital formation of only £17b.

Table 5.7 *Capital formation at 1980 prices, UK (£b)*

Year	Gross	Depreciation	Net
1972	40	21	19
1973	43	22	21
1974	41	22	19
1975	42	24	18
1976	42	24	18
1977	41	26	15
1978	43	27	16
1979	44	28	16
1980	42	29	13
1981	38	29	9
1982	40	30	10
1983	42	31	11
1984	45	31	14

It may be helpful to see the trend of these figures, and Table 5.7 shows gross capital formation, depreciation (which is an estimate of capital consumption), and net capital formation from 1972 to 1984, all at 1980 prices. Gross capital formation has remained about steady, the estimated depreciation has grown substantially as the capital stock has grown, and the net increase in the stock of capital assets has declined quite severely.

Capital formation

Table 5.8 shows gross capital formation subdivided according to which part of the economy does it. We can see how the private sector – both persons and industrial and financial companies – has increased its capital formation over the years; public corporations – mainly nationalized industries – have been pretty static; general government – central and local – has reduced its capital formation very substantially, at least until 1982. It is not difficult to see who has not been pulling their weight.

Capital stock

Table 5.9 shows the value of the net capital stock at current replace-

Table 5.8   *Gross capital formation at 1980 prices, UK (£b)*

Year	Private sector	Public corporations	General government	Total
1972	24	6	10	40
1973	26	6	11	43
1974	24	7	10	41
1975	25	8	9	42
1976	25	8	9	42
1977	26	7	8	41
1978	29	7	7	43
1979	31	7	6	44
1980	29	7	6	42
1981	28	6	4	38
1982	30	6	4	40
1983	30	7	5	42
1984	33	6	6	45

ment cost in 1984. The total is £939b, split up as shown. It is difficult to tell how reliable these figures are; they are mainly calculated by taking the original cost, allowing for depreciation, and adjusting the net result by an appropriate index. This may well reflect neither real replacement cost nor current market value, but whether these figures would be higher or lower it is difficult to say. However, the figures shown are reasonably consistent with the figures for income from capital and rent (£54b plus £19b), which excludes income from overseas assets. If the estimated depreciation of £38b is deducted, a net return on the capital stock of £35b is obtained, which is a return of 4.0 per cent, not an unreasonable real return on the assets. Not all this capital stock is owned by pension funds. In fact they, and insurance companies, generally own financial assets that usually represent claims on this income from capital. As has been seen, they received some £13b of money payments during 1984 from their financial assets.

National Insurance

Little has been said so far about the National Insurance Scheme. Pure pay-as-you-go pensions are simply transfers of purchasing power from one section of the population – those with factor incomes – to another section – pensioners. I give some of my money to Granny to spend as she wishes instead of spending it myself.

Table 5.9 *Net capital stock at current replacement cost, UK, 1984 (£b)*

Personal (mainly houses)	267
Companies	308
Public corporations	133
Government (central & local)	231
Total	939
Income from capital	54
plus Income from rent	19
less capital consumption	− 38
Net profit	35

Net profit equals 4.0 per cent of capital stock

In 1984 some £17b was transferred to pensioners through the National Insurance Scheme (and a further £18b in other social security benefits). Such transfers in themselves do not affect anything in the figures shown above, though of course they may have secondary consequences.

I may reduce my savings rather than my consumption in order to give money to Granny. She may consume it rather than save it. This will affect the total savings in the economy. If I have too many elderly relatives to support, and collectively they demand more than I am willing to give, there may be problems. In particular, if the government increases national insurance contributions and employees seek higher wages to compensate so as to keep their net income the same, this may lead to inflation, or to higher wage costs and higher unemployment. This is clearly the sort of problem that may arise if the state pension scheme promises improving benefits for future pensioners, which will necessitate increased contributions from the then current workforce.

Funded schemes

Fully funded schemes are different, in that the contributions *are* an addition to savings, which *may* then be used for additional capital formation, which will create the capacity for higher production in future years. The pensioner of the future gets his entitlement, not from a current transfer, but by receiving the investment income on the funds (part of the factor income from capital), and possibly by selling or passing on part of his capital to future generations.

However, it is quite possible that increased savings *may not* result in higher capital formation. In the very short term, savings can be increased only if expenditure on consumption is reduced; reduced consumption may mean that there is less incentive to invest in new plant, new machinery, new shopping facilities, and so on. So an excess of savings may just result in lower production and higher unemployment next year. One mechanism for getting savings and capital formation into balance is reduced interest rates, but interest rates seldom seem to come down fast enough or far enough to act as a stimulus. Another mechanism is for the government to borrow the excess savings and engage in capital formation itself.

Many actual schemes are somewhat less than fully funded, so they involve a mixture of the pay-as-you-go and the fully funded structure.

Savings for retirement

In one sense it does not matter whether savings for retirement are organized through group pension schemes of any type, by individual life policies or by individual private savings. All are treated in much the same way in the tables above. But, of course, the way in which the saving is done may well affect the quality as well as the total quantity, in that many individuals, if they were free to spend or save their incomes, would spend a higher proportion of it; they might then beg for charity in their old age.

On the other hand, pension schemes provide an efficient method of saving, and the prudent individual might feel that without them he has to save *more*, because of the greater uncertainty about the particular investment returns he would get and about how long he might live. The existence of insurance allows individuals to acquire a particular level of security for the future at a lower present cost.

Pensions paid for by employees

It can also be seen from the above tables that in an economic sense the total cost of pensions is paid for by employees. It is seen by the employer as part of his total wage cost, and he would have the alternative of paying higher salaries instead of making contributions to the pension scheme. If the employer is in a competitive market he cannot afford to pay more than the going rate for his total wage bill, and if he pays sufficiently much less than the going rate he cannot attract or retain staff.

It can be seen also that the assets of pension funds are, also in an economic sense, owned by the members of pension schemes. Pensioners and prospective pensioners are the new capitalists. They lend to government, they construct properties for investment, and they own a large part of the ordinary shares of most companies. In aggregate nowadays *the pensioners are the shareholders.*

When pension fund contributions and assets are seen as being attributable to the members in aggregate, then there is something to be said for attributing them to the members individually. The pension scheme has no purpose other than to provide benefits to its members, unlike a charity, so there is no need for it to have unattributable funds. It is possible that the failure of those who manage pension funds and those who advise the managers to attribute assets on an individual basis has helped to lead to the problems about early leavers, who do not really know whether they are being cheated or not, but suspect that they are, and to the proposals for portable pensions, which could more explicitly recognize the individual's entitlement.

It is actuarially quite possible, though administratively complex, to unitize pension funds, so that individuals do know exactly how much of the assets are attributable to them. Unitization would provide an immediate way of calculating transfer values unambiguously either to another scheme or to a portable pension, and leavers would neither be cheated nor feel that they were. Individual attribution of contributions does not of course mean that it is appropriate to allocate the same percentage of salary to each member.

The allocation of the present employer's aggregate contribution might well need to be done on the basis of percentages that vary considerably by age, sex (if one is permitted to do this) and salary level. Indeed, it might even be necessary to do this in order to satisfy the proposed EEC directive on equal treatment in occupational pension schemes, to show that contributions for higher-paid older employees need to be larger than those for lower-paid younger employees, whether or not the former are mainly male and the latter mainly female.

Uncertainty about the future

Although the existence of insurance and pension schemes allows us to spread individual uncertainty across whole groups, it does *not* reduce the *total* uncertainty about the future. Mortality rates change very slowly, but even the most careful projections may turn out to be wrong; the pensioners of any pension scheme may live for a longer or shorter time than the actuary has predicted. There is much greater uncertainty about future investment returns, even if we try to estimate these on a real terms basis. All we really know with certainty in aggregate for all schemes are the present assets and the current contributions. In aggregate, defined benefit schemes provide no more security to members than defined contribution schemes.

If the benefits of the scheme are defined, then future contributions are uncertain, and indeed, if there is uncertainty about the continued ability of the employer to pay contributions, then defined benefits are only conditional ones. There is much to be said economically and in accounting terms for calculating the liability of the firm for a defined benefit scheme regardless of how much is actually funded. If the firm actually remains in business, it is indeed a liability. It is only if the firm goes into liquidation that the status of that liability is in question – the part of the liability covered by the assets of the fund is absolutely secure, while the members have no claim at all for the unfunded part. The same applies to the government's unfunded and notionally funded schemes, which should appear in the national accounts as a liability of the government. The amount of this liability is not published; a possible estimate is around £100b.

A defined contribution scheme makes more sense economically and for accounting purposes than a defined benefit scheme, since wage costs are defined at the time the work is done, rather than leaving an uncertain liability hanging over the firm. However, the future level of benefits is more obviously uncertain, and dependent on the return on the assets. It may be seen to be an advantage for scheme members to be aware of the risks, rather than imagining that they can be spirited away.

Economic development

Once a fully funded scheme has been in existence for long enough in stable conditions a stationary position may theoretically be reached in which the total income from the funds plus the current contributions exactly equal the benefits being paid. In macroeconomic terms, this means that the total stock of fixed capital has reached a stationary position, total output is stationary at a higher level, and so higher pensions and also higher incomes for those working are available. The split between employees and shareholders, or rather between employees and pensioners, still depends on mutual agreement or on some form of bargaining process. If those in work demand higher incomes, then company profits may be reduced, hence company dividends, pension funds' income, and their ability to pay pensions.

It must be admitted at this point that this chapter has not been able to carry forward projections into the future in the same way as Chapter 8 on demographic forecasts, and Chapter 11 on the development of potential benefits under present schemes. To do this would require us to make complex forecasts of the contributions that might be paid into pension schemes, the return on their investments, the way in which the net increase in funds was invested, the rate of return that might be obtained on those assets, the increase in total production made possible by an increase in the capital stock and apportionment of that increased production between the owners of capital and the providers of labour. This would take us into the field of economic forecasting for the more distant future that has not generally been attempted. All that can be done at this stage is to emphasize the relationship between capital formation, financed by savings, and increases in total production. The rest of this chapter discusses some particular topical aspects that relate to the position of pension schemes within the economy.

Index to earnings or prices
One such topic is whether one should consider linking pensions to current earnings' levels or current price levels. On the whole, linking to earnings may seem to be fairer, since pensioners then get some of the benefit of increased production, and take some of the loss if production falls. But one must be careful not to destroy the incentive to increase total production: if I agree to give one-fifth of my income to Granny, then I can keep my agreement whatever level of income I have; but we are both better off if my income is higher. However, neither form of index-linking of pensions can be warranted absolutely. All we have is a starting point for a future bargaining process.

The present depression
Whether the savings that are channelled through pension funds can be productively employed depends on a great many factors in the economy outside the pensions industry. But it is regrettable that the spare resources of labour that at present exist in the form of more than 3 million registered as unemployed are not being used to contribute to additional capital formation. One cannot be sure what the effects would be if life offices and pension funds, which do have *some* choice about where to invest their money, were to make sure that it was channelled into real capital formation – property development, direct lending to companies for expansion, taking up new company securities, even direct lending for new housing – rather than lending to the government. Would this simply put up the price of shares further, and also put up the yields on government stocks, so that other investors would switch their funds and so cancel out this whole operation? Or would it actually stimulate a desirable economic recovery?

There is an oddity that results from the way pension funds are costed. If investment returns are expected to be high, then the contributions required to produce a particular future benefit are smaller. High interest rates – and in this context is meant higher real interest rates – may therefore result in lower pension contributions being required, and hence lower savings. This contradicts the usual economic assumption that an increase in interest rates will increase the supply of savings. It could mean either that there is no equilibrium between savings and desired capital formation at any interest rate, or that there are several different equilibrium positions, some of which may be unstable.

Actuaries do not know the rate of return that will be obtained on investments, but can only estimate it. It is worth considering what might happen if actuaries decided to assume a somewhat higher real rate of return than they have been doing. Pension funds would appear to be in a financially stronger position. It would be possible to reduce contributions. Employers would have available more funds for investment in their own businesses, and they would find that their wage costs had been reduced. They might therefore be more willing to engage in direct capital formation. This in itself might stimulate the economy and generate the higher real returns that the actuaries were assuming. Economic prophecies are not necessary self-fulfilling – otherwise we would all be living in the lap of luxury – but they may very well affect future economic events, either favourably or unfavourably.

Another way in which different actuarial assumptions about interest rates could influence the economy would be if the apparently better financial position of pension funds persuaded those responsible for managing them to pay substantially higher pensions to existing pensioners, perhaps index linking them fully from commencement, thus putting more money in pensioners' pockets, which could then be directly spent. This too would have a beneficial effect on the economy by stimulating consumer demand.

Recent events suggest that these two responses to apparent pension scheme surpluses are indeed occurring. Is this contributing to the economic recovery now under way?

Overseas assets
There has been a fair amount of criticism of the acquisition of overseas assets by life offices and pension funds. The rate at which this has happened has now somewhat diminished, and it should in any case be considered as complementary to the acquisition of UK shares by US pension funds, as part of a desirable diversification of investments by both parties. But it was also from 1980 to 1983 mainly just the counterpart of Britain's current account surplus. If we export more goods and services than we import, then we acquire foreign currency, which we have to do *something* with. We could, of course, spend this currency on increased imports, thus getting rid of the current account surplus. Otherwise, we have to use it to acquire overseas assets. Whether it is used by the Bank of England in building up foreign currency reserves in the form of deposits with other central banks, or by British industrial companies to finance direct capital investment abroad, or by British financial

institutions to acquire financial assets is a matter of detail. All these forms of investment provide future investment income, which adds to our national income in future years, and if we wish they can be sold (at some price or another) in the future. This is the way the proceeds of North Sea oil have been invested.

Those who argue that pension funds should invest in British industry must in effect be suggesting either that we spend the surplus foreign currency on importing machinery with which to equip new factories here, or else that we employ people in Britain to build those factories or make that plant, paying them in such a way that they will spend some of their income on imported goods or services. In either way we would get rid of the current account surplus, and we would not be able to acquire the overseas assets. Yet another possible solution would be to produce less and export less, but I can hardly imagine this being a useful stimulus to British industry.

Retirement age

Finally, it is worth considering the macroeconomic effects of the suggestion that the male normal retirement age be lowered, for example to 60, from its present 65. Usually the discussion has considered the direct costs to pension schemes. But the total macroeconomic effect includes the loss of production. To reduce the male retirement age by five years would transfer some 1.3 million males out of the potential workforce (some 6 per cent of the total workforce). There is no obvious reason to assume that males of this age are on average less productive than younger males; some may be failing but others may be at the height of their powers. It therefore seems reasonable to assume that total personal incomes would fall by some 6 per cent, or £14b on the basis of the figures shown above. There might also be a reduction in income for capital because of reduced capital utilization.

The main loss would, of course, fall on the newly retired, who previously had been earning a full income, and now were receiving only a pension. But some of the cost would fall on the rest of the working population, who in the case of pay-as-you-go schemes would have to pay these extra pension costs out of their own incomes, or in the case of fully funded schemes would have to increase their contributions so as to accumulate enough themselves in five years' less working lifetime to pay themselves pensions for a further five years of retirement.

It may be suggested that the lost production would be made up by employing those who are at present unemployed. This might well happen, but in effect we would just be accepting the present level of unemployment as permanent, and shifting the burden of it on to the 60–65 year olds. It would be quite different if we had such a rising standard of living that people were happy to take some of the excess in the form of increased leisure, and were earning so much during their working lifetime that they were happy to stop working sooner and live off their accumulated savings. But we need a real boom to create these conditions, and it would then be best for early retirement to be an individual option, so that the early retirer has to use some of his own pension or savings to fund it.

Conclusion

It is unfortunate that the way in which pension funds, both state and private, operate tends to conceal from people the reality that present prosperity comes from present work, assisted by the accumulated capital that has been inherited from past work, which we have a duty to maintain and, if possible, increase. There is no one to pay for our own pensions except ourselves.

6 Pension Fund Investment

GEORGE HELOWICZ

Introduction

Until recently, the question whether pension funds have been invested in ways that have benefited the national economic need has generally not arisen. However, this topic has been placed on the pensions agenda by those on the political left, by the trades unions and indeed the question was investigated by the Wilson Committee. The Trades Union Congress, for example, believes that the present investment policies of pension funds are

> reinforcing the long-term decline in UK industry and starving new growth sectors of investment capital. By increasingly investing overseas they are ensuring that their pessimistic assessment of the future of the UK economy is self-fulfilling . . . . The TUC believes that this approach is not in the best long-term interests of pension scheme members, pensioners and the economy as a whole. (Trades Union Congress, 1983, p. 4)

This was a belief shared by Arthur Scargill, the leader of the National Union of Mineworkers, when in his role as a trustee of the Mineworkers' Pension Fund he refused to endorse the 1982–84 investment plan.

By looking beyond the confines of individual schemes, Scargill and those of similar views would argue that they were seeking investment strategies that would benefit all sections of society and the national economy. They are in effect challenging established investment practices and the unrestricted freedom of investment managers to invest in ways that can ignore national needs. With increased overseas investment, 'British Industry and British Jobs' is a frequent slogan that has much appeal at a time when there are 3.3 million registered unemployed and probably a further million seeking work but not registered.

But do those who are responsible for pension fund investment need to consider national economic needs? Lord Richardson, a former Governor of the Bank of England, clearly did not think so, a view no doubt shared by most of the City establishment.

> The primary duty of pension funds . . . is to ensure the best return

on the money entrusted to them, for the individuals whose interest they represent. It is desirable also that they should provide adequate finance for industry. There should not in principle be any conflict between these two objectives provided that profitable investments can be identified. (Richardson, 1983, p. 510)

There is a clear absence in Richardson's statement of any reference to whether such investment is compatible with the needs of the general population or of the economy. The sole criterion appears to be profitability, and investment in UK industry will take place only if it conforms to an investment manager's perceptions of profit. Critics of pension funds see this as rather a short-sighted view of what is likely to be in the best interests of beneficiaries. Typical of these critics is the Labour Party's Financial Institutions Study Group, who have called for a reassessment of investment practices

> to make clear that the institutions have a responsibility not just to maximize the financial return on investments, but to ensure that their investment contributes to the long term economic prosperity of the country. That prosperity provides the only real security, both in work and retirement, for the workers whose savings they are entrusted with. (1982, p. 55)

Disquiet with the way in which pension fund money is invested is not purely a British phenomenon, but is paralleled in other European countries and also in the United States. The common catalyst appears to be slow economic growth and rising unemployment. Emerging from the debate is the question of whether changes in investment policy to incorporate 'social' criteria could help regenerate and restructure the economies of the countries involved. The debate surrounding the investment of American pension fund money has been summed up as relating to

> the control and direction of this massive, and rapidly growing, pool of investment capital. Weaving through this debate are questions about industrial policy, local development, job creation, housing, legal constraints, high interest rates, relative risk of different investments, union versus non-union companies, South Africa, market 'failures', productivity, economic efficiency, growth and scarcity, capital allocation, new investment mechanisms, social justice and economic as well as political power. (Barber, 1981)

This statement would also be an accurate summary of the debate taking place in the United Kingdom.

The aim of this chapter is to investigate these social and political issues. This will involve a discussion of:

- the type of assets held by pension funds;
- the role of investment managers;
- what is meant by socially responsible investment;
- the criteria that apply to pension fund investment and how these are affected by the 1984 Megarry judgment;
- local enterprise boards, a National Investment Bank, venture capital and government direction of pension fund investment.

Assets held by pension funds

Information relating to the assets held by all pension funds is not available. The information covering pension funds in the Central Statistical Office's *Financial Statistics* covers only non-insured schemes, and the data presented for life assurance offices does not separate out their pensions business from their ordinary life business. The tables that follow originate from *Financial Statistics* and will therefore relate only to non-insured schemes.

The enormous growth in the assets held by pension funds is clearly demonstrated by Table 6.1.

Table 6.1 *Market value of total pension fund assets, UK, 1963–1983 (£b)*

	1963	1971	Year end 1979	1982	1983
Private sector	2.8	6.2	22.4	46.8	58.9
Local authority	0.7	1.9	5.4	11.3	14.7
Other public sector	1.0	2.5	12.1	23.1	29.6
Total	4.5	10.6	39.9	81.2	103.2

Source: Phillips and Drew (1984).

This growth has been the result of a substantial increase in the numbers of working people covered by occupational pension schemes and the widespread introduction of final salary schemes. An increase in contributors has coincided with an increase in contributions required to fund these types of scheme. In addition, as salaries have risen so have the earnings-related contributions. Many of these schemes are some years from maturity and as a consequence their outgo has been relatively small compared to the inflow of income from contributions and investments. These schemes have therefore been faced with the task of investing large cash flows, and hence accumulating large amounts of assets.

In final salary schemes, retirement benefits are related in some way to salaries close to retirement. Any increase in salaries will therefore cause a related increase in the schemes' liabilities for active members. Pensions in payment may also be subject to increases. These may be in the form, for example, of funded 4 per cent per annum compound increases. Alternatively, increases may be granted from time to time to compensate for price inflation, being paid for either by additional contributions from the employer or out of surplus investment earnings. Whichever type of system operates, the effect is to relate pension increases in some way to price inflation. Table 6.6 (p. 91) indicates that the latter has averaged about 2 per cent below salary inflation.

Valuation bases normally assume that future investment returns will exceed salary increases. In these circumstances investments are sought that are expected to provide an overall return from capital and income combined that meets this assumption. Failure to achieve returns in excess of salary inflation has required an increase in contributions. There is in fact no need to make the above assumption and it is perfectly possible to fund in advance taking an opposite view. Essentially the aim is to obtain the maximum possible investment returns in order to minimize the cost of providing a given level of benefits.

Tables 6.2, 6.3 and 6.4 give market value details of the assets held as a proportion of total assets for private sector, local authority and other public sector funds respectively. In all cases there has been an increase in the proportions held in equities and property, and a decrease in the proportion held in fixed-interest investments. The increase in equities has been mainly caused by a significant increase in overseas equity purchases following the removal of exchange control regulations in 1979. The fall in fixed-interest holdings is a result of the reduction in gilt holdings and a dramatic fall in debenture holdings, the latter reflecting the decline of the private sector fixed-interest bond market. Whilst property investment has increased for the three types of fund, the total proportion held for other public sector funds is significantly greater. This may arise from the fact that other public sector funds are dominated by a very small number of very large funds for which property is a suitable investment to absorb their large cash flows.

Whilst these tables show the result of past investment decisions, Table 6.5 indicates the direction of new monies for the years 1981–83 inclusive. What stands out is the large proportion held as cash for 1983 as compared with the previous two years; 1983 also saw a reduction in equity investment both overseas and in the UK, together with an increase in gilt investment.

Table 6.2 Distribution of assets held by private sector pension funds UK, 1962–1983 (%)

	1962	1966	1970	Year end, 31 December 1973	1974	1979	1980	1981	1982	1983
Gilts	33	26	15	13	14	26	24	21	23	21
Debentures	18	22	17	13	12	4	3	3	2	2
Total equities	47	49	53	53	37	49	53	55	58	62
UK equities	–	–	–	48	31	46	46	45	45	47
Overseas equities	–	–	–	5	6	3	7	10	13	15
Cash	2	3	4	7	20	6	4	3	3	3
Property*	–	–	11	15	17	15	16	17	14	12

* No figures available prior to 1967.
Source: Phillips and Drew (1984).

Table 6.3 Distribution of assets held by local authority pension funds UK, 1966–1983 (%)

	Year end, 31 March						Year end, 31 December		
	1966	1970	1973	1974	1979	1980	1981	1982	1983
Gilts	39	28	21	22	30	30	23	27	24
Debentures	7	10	9	8	2	1	1	1	1
Total equities	49	58	62	53	57	54	64	61	65
UK equities	–	–	–	–	54	51	57	50	52
Overseas equities	–	–	–	–	3	3	7	11	13
Cash	4	4	5	13	4	5	3	2	3
Property*	–	1	2	3	8	9	9	9	7

* No figures available prior to 1970.
Source: Phillips and Drew (1984).

Table 6.4 *Distribution of assets held by other public sector pension funds UK, 1963–1983 (%)*

					Year end, 31 December					
	1963	1966	1970	1973	1974	1979	1980	1981	1982	1983
Gilts	25	19	10	9	9	18	18	17	21	19
Debentures	32	34	23	12	12	7	2	2	2	2
Total equities	36	36	50	52	31	46	49	53	52	56
UK equities	36	36	50	52	31	41	42	43	42	44
Overseas equities	–	–	–	–	–	5	7	10	10	12
Cash	1	1	3	6	15	4	3	4	3	4
Property	6	10	14	21	33	25	24	25	22	19

Source: Phillips and Drew (1984).

Table 6.5   *Net acquisitions of pension funds, UK, 1981–1983*

Year	Total net acquisitions (£m)	Cash	Gilts	% of net acquisitions UK equities	Overseas equities	Property	Others
1983	7480	14	34	20	16	7	9
1982	6646	5	19	28	25	11	12
1981	6841	2	27	27	22	11	11

Source: Financial Statistics, CSO, February 1985, Table 7.15.

The proportions shown in Tables 6.2, 6.3 and 6.4 obviously vary according to market conditions and the type of fund being considered. But it is possible to detect a uniformity of purpose that might be interpreted as some kind of norm. One writer has, however, commented that whilst this spread of investments might be

widely accepted as an appropriate asset distribution for a pension fund, there is little evidence to substantiate the asset distribution other than qualitative statements of support. Does it give the best chance for a fund to achieve the highest rate of return commensurate with an acceptable level of risk? (Hager, 1983)

A starting point for considering this question would be to examine the yields obtained from various categories of investment and compare these with salary and price inflation. Table 6.6 does this together with a comparison of the yields obtained by the average private and local authority fund.

Over the short to medium term, both United Kingdom equities and gilts have performed satisfactorily in relation to salary inflation. It is, however, over the medium to long term that the returns from gilts are below both salary and price inflation. Since pension funds are long-term investors, this must cast doubts on the suitability of such investments. Yet, as Tables 6.2, 6.3 and 6.4 indicate, gilts form about 20 per cent of their portfolios by market value. An investment strategy weighted more towards equities would seem more appropriate. In fact, over the longer term, cash on short-term deposit has performed better than gilts.

Property is an investment that is considered similar to equity investment in that rental income and hence capital values will increase at least in line with price inflation. Whilst this has been true over a five-year term, it has not occurred over a ten-year term. Over both periods of time

Table 6.6 *Annual rates of return and salary and price inflation, UK, period ending 1 January 1984 (%)*

Period in years	Average private pension fund	Average local authority pension fund	Salary* inflation	Prices* inflation	UK equities[a]	Overseas equities[b]	Gilts[c]	Property[d]	Cash[e]
5	19.4	20.2	12.8	10.9	23.1	12.9	18.0	14.6	14.2
10	15.8	16.6	14.5	13.3	18.3	11.0	15.8	10.3	12.5
15	11.3	11.2	13.6	11.5	12.4	N/A	10.9	N/A	11.0
20	10.7	N/A	11.8	9.7	13.1	N/A	8.2	N/A	10.0

* December on December.
Notes:
(a) FTA All-share index.
(b) Composite index for representative overseas markets adjusted for exchange rate and dollar premium changes.
(c) FTA over 15 years index (Phillips and Drew 25-year index up to 1975).
(d) Phillips and Drew property unit trust index.
(e) Local authority 7-day rate.

Source: Phillips and Drew (1984), tables 6 and 7.

the return has not even matched that obtainable on gilts. However, property should be viewed as a long-term investment and it is perhaps over a much longer time horizon that expectations will be fulfilled.

The justification of overseas investment is that it allows access to investment in economic sectors that are not available in the UK and also exposure to economies with greater growth rates. The figures in Table 6.6 indicate that the overall return has barely kept pace with salary inflation for the five-year period and is substantially below for the ten-year period. However, this hides the fact that returns were higher than those obtainable from United Kingdom equities over the period 1981–83, a fact shown in Table 6.7.

Table 6.7   *Annual returns from UK and*
overseas equity investments, 1981–1983 (%)

Year	UK equities	Overseas equities
1981	13.5	21.1
1982	28.9	30.7
1983	28.8	37.2

Source: Phillips and Drew (1984).

The return from overseas equities is the product of the return in local currency and a change in the currency value against sterling. A breakdown for 1983 is given for four markets in Table 6.8. Compared with the local currency return from American and Japanese equities, the return obtained from United Kingdom equities has been better. What makes the overall return better is of course the currency change, and this factor is perhaps the big difference between overseas and United Kingdom equities. As Phillips and Drew (1984) comment, 'it offers both risks and opportunities'. The short-term gains are therefore attractive, but whether the long-term return will be any better than investment in United Kingdom equities remains to be seen.

The question under investigation is whether the present asset distribution of pension funds is appropriate for the liabilities they have to meet. Consideration of the latter would suggest that investments were required that gave returns at least as good as salary inflation. Investment in gilts, over the medium to long term, has not met these requirements. Why then do these investments form such an important part of current portfolios? One reason perhaps is tradition, but as has been previously shown the proportion held is declining. Secondly, they may be used to match fixed liabilities such as frozen pensions. Thirdly, investment in gilts provides an outlet for the large cash flows that have to be

Table 6.8 *Components of overseas equity return, 1983 (%)*

Market	Income (gross)	Capital change	Total return (local currency)	Currency change (vs. sterling)	Total return (sterling)
USA	5.3	17.3	22.6	11.4	36.6
Japan	1.9	23.3	25.2	12.9	41.4
Germany	3.7	38.4	42.1	− 2.8	38.1
Australia	7.2	63.1	70.3	2.0	73.7

Source: Phillips and Drew, 1984.

invested. The gilts market is one market where large amounts of securities can be readily traded. A much more obvious alternative to the conventional gilt is the index-linked variety, which in mid-1985 were providing real rates of return of about 3.5 per cent per annum. United Kingdom equities, overseas equities and property are the types of investment that are likely to match the salary-related liabilities of pension funds. Of these, the first have demonstrated their suitability. The other two have a relatively short history as pension fund investments and have yet to demonstrate their expected advantages over the long term.

Hager's suggestions for a suitable long-term investment strategy are contained in Table 6.9. He further suggests that conventional gilts would be held on a short-term basis only if the market appeared temporarily favourable. If adopted by pensions funds, such a strategy would require a greater volume of index-linked stock to be issued. Clearly the emphasis is on investments that offer hopes of a positive real return, by which other investments should be assessed.

However, Table 6.6 does not distinguish between realized rates of return and yields at which new money is invested, which may reflect an estimate of future rates of return. For example, fixed-interest investment has shown a poor rate of return in the past, mainly because inflation was higher than either borrowers or lenders expected at the time the loans were arranged or the stock was issued, but at present long term gilts are yielding about 11 per cent per annum compared with a real yield of about 3.5 per cent per annum for the index-linked variety. If inflation is at or below 7.5 per cent per annum over a long period then long term gilts will turn out to be as good or better than index-linked stocks.

Table 6.9   *A long-term investment strategy*

	Proportion of fund's total assets %	Target real return above price rises %
Index-linked gilts	30–40	3
Conventional gilts	0	–
UK equities	35–45	4–5
Overseas equities	15–25	5
Property	0–10	4

Source: Hager (1983).

Pension funds and British capitalism

This section looks at some of the work by Richard Minns (1980) on those responsible for investment, namely the investment manager. Minns' work was based on a survey of pension funds and their shareholdings for the years 1972, 1974 and 1977. This involved interviewing managers or trustees of forty pension funds in the public and private sectors and representatives of thirty-three banks, stockbrokers and other financial institutions. Whilst time may have outdated the statistics. There is no reason to suppose that his conclusions have been invalidated.

One aspect that Minns was interested in was identifying the extent to which pension funds were externally managed: for the period mid–end 1978 he estimated that it was about 67 per cent. The percentages for private sector and public sector funds were 72 per cent and 60 per cent respectively. Over a similar time period, he calculatd that about £17.25b of pension fund money was externally managed and that about £13b of this was managed by twenty institutions, with each responsible for at least a minimum of £250m (1980, pp. 30–4). What stands out from these figures is, first, the extent to which the funds are externally managed and, secondly, the concentration of investment management in a relatively few institutions. A consequence of this is that the direction of investment will depend very much on the policies and ambitions of the managing institutions. This, as will be indicated at a later stage, can produce conflicts of interest.

Minns investigated the manner in which pension fund money was invested in quoted company shares by carrying out a survey of sixty-six pension funds of varying sizes from the public and private sectors. These funds at the time represented about 40 per cent of the market value of all pension funds. He concluded that 'there is no doubt that all funds and managers tend to concentrate on the larger companies. The large institutions nevertheless invest more of their funds in sectors dominated by large companies than other funds' (1980, p. 67). Whilst differences emerged between the public and private sector funds as they grew in size, all were likely to move towards the investment pattern of the larger public sector funds.

The emergence of such a trend is really not surprising given the maximum percentage limits for the amounts of a company's capital held or the amount of a fund that should be invested in one company. With the former restriction, large funds with large cash flows to invest would have no choice but to spread small-company investment over many such companies. Investment in bigger companies, in contrast, would mean that large amounts could be invested before coming up against the limits. With a consequent saving in time, effort and money, it is not difficult to understand why large-company investment is the preferred investment strategy.

Minns discovered that similar constraints applied to the managing institutions, and they in turn set limits on their own activities. The difficulties that arise are very much related to the size of funds under the manager's control. He notes that some of the managing institutions

have more total assets under management than many of the largest pension funds . . . The pressures of cash flow apply as much to an institution managing the pension funds as they do to each pension fund. The institution will therefore tend to buy the shares of the larger companies because the size of funds it has to invest prevent it, more than any single one of the funds under management from doing otherwise while at the same time keeping the management fee competitive. (Minns, 1980, p. 61)

For reasons similar to those for individual pension funds, a managing institution would not want a large portion of the funds in its care to be dependent on the fortunes of one company. The problem encountered can be simply illustrated by considering three funds of £10m each, which have a limit of 5 per cent operating on both the limits mentioned previously. Treated individually, each fund could invest up to £500,000 in a £10m company without infringing either limit. Suppose that the funds are managed by a single managing institution operating similar limits. Although £500,000 could be invested in the company by each fund, the managing institution would be in a position where it was responsible for 15 per cent of the equity of the company. This can be avoided either by reducing the percentage invested by each fund in the company and investing additional amounts elsewhere, or by adopting a strategy of investing in larger companies. From the viewpoint of economies of scale the latter would be the preferred strategy.

The preference for investment in larger companies was, Minns found, accompanied by a move towards investment in the financial sector at the expense of the capital goods sector. This was a natural consequence of the fact that the financial sector at that time had a greater number of large companies and a higher percentage of large companies than other groups. The capital goods group, in contrast, contained about 25 per cent of small quoted companies as well as a lower percentage of large companies than any other group (1980, pp. 49–53). Minns concludes that what emerges from his work 'is a structure of pension fund management which is predominantly under the day to day control of large institutions in the financial sector and which is invested more heavily by these large institutions in the shares of the same financial sector' (1980, p. 67).

Pension funds and financial institutions in general have been criticized over the years for their lack of support for unquoted small companies. The response has been to avoid state direction of investment funds at all costs and at the same time to be seen making a positive contribution to small-company finance. For the latter purpose a number of organizations have been created. The first of these was the Industrial and Commercial Finance Corporation, which the government and the banks set up in 1945. This, as the *Financial Times* comments, was 'somewhat reluctantly, however, as a sop to nagging but persistent lobbyists' (Dickson, 1984). Since that time a number of small-company investment vehicles have been set up that are financed by pension fund money. These have included Equity Capital for Industry and a number of joint ventures between various funds and the clearing banks, and a number of small business unit trusts. This was not only a response to the criticisms mentioned but also a recognition of the above-average returns that could be obtained from small company investment. An advertisement for the Arbuthnot Smaller Companies Fund explained that this was possible:

because [small firms] are not wholly dependent on world trade, smaller companies will benefit quickly from the anticipated upturn in the UK economy, particularly with North Sea Oil revenue and the internal reflation expected in the Chancellor's budget.

There is also the posibilty of take-over; most take-overs are between medium-sized and smaller companies, with consequent gains for unit holders.

Smaller companies can adapt to changing conditions much more quickly than larger corporations. Lines of communications are short, leading to improved labour relations, less disputes and higher productivity. (Minns, 1980, p. 83)

Minns found one feature that was common to nearly all the schemes with which the pension funds in his survey were involved: their considerable underspending or low spending targets. He explains this in terms of both the restrictive selection criteria adopted and the short time horizons within which a return was required. The return was expected to come from a public flotation, from a take-over or from some profit-sharing device. Finance was only directed to companies that could meet such criteria as 'outstanding growth prospects', 'a sound earnings record', 'a growth in profits record', etc. (1980, pp. 100–1).

It does therefore seem that small-company investment criteria are at least as stringent as those adopted for normal equity investment. Whether or not the various schemes can be referred to as risk-taking venture capital is by no means certain. In many respects, the caution adopted suggests an approach closer to the more traditional investment strategies of pension funds. There is no precise definition of what is meant by the term 'venture capital'. However,

there is general agreement that portfolio investment of purely a passive nature, where the investor has no involvement at all in the affairs of the company in which he invests, is not venture capital . . . Venture capital is used to describe a way in which investors support entrepreneurial talent with finance and business skills to exploit market opportunities and thus obtain long term capital gains. (Shilson, 1984, p. 207)

In recent years there has been a growth in the supply of venture capital through the formation of venture capital organizations. As profitability in more traditional industries has deteriorated, investors have become attracted by investment in riskier ventures. By direct involvement in an enterprise, investors are in a position to influence the way capital is used and the direction of the venture. This hopefully reduces the higher risks involved. The extent to which pension funds have become involved with venture capital is difficult to establish, although research is taking place on the matter at Nuffield College, Oxford. Is, for example, the setting up of a venture capital division called Pruventure by the Prudential in June 1984 an indication of future investment strategies by both insurance companies and pension funds? The expansion of the venture capital market is considered by many people to provide an impetus to both technological advance and economic growth. What may hinder this development and the expansion of venture capital in general is 'a shortage of specialists combining the financial, technical and management skills required both by venture capital companies and the entrepreneurs in whom they invest' (Shilson, 1984).

A further factor that may inhibit the growth of venture capital is the reluctance of financial institutions such as pension funds to become actively involved with a company, whether it be small or large. Investment managers do not have the training or experience or time to meet the demands of such involvement. As a consequence, small-company and venture capital investment form only a tiny proportion of the cash flows invested by pension funds.

Pension funds are a member of the group known as institutional investors. Harford Thomas, writing in the *Guardian* (1981), refers to this type of investor as 'a risk avoider . . . looking for the maximum return with the minimum risk' and as a consequence he considered the institutional investor to be 'exceedingly conservative', lacking any kind of entrepreneurial spirit. This he sees partly as a function of the kind of person in charge: 'Those who rise to the top of the institutions are the sound and the safe. The shrewd and ambitious play it safe too.'

Thomas' article develops an idea advanced by Professor David Cadman, that 'the investment institutions are not primarily concerned with the use to which their money is put. They are concerned with its return . . . its future exchange value'. Institutional investors, including pension funds, therefore seek prime investments whether they be property, equities or whatever. Given the huge cash flows generated by the funds, there is obviously a great deal of finance chasing the limited number of such prime investments. The effect is to maintain market values and hence exchange values. This may partly explain why equity price levels are buoyant at a time when the state of the economy is at a far from healthy level. 'Looked at in this sense, an investment becomes simply an alternative to money rather than a means to developing new wealth. And that is the direction the bulk of new investment money is taking'. In general, financial institutions do not have any expertise in the business of, or a commitment to, the companies in which they invest. Shares will be bought and sold on the basis of the potential financial return. It therefore follows that the potential social and economic implications of an investment decision have little influence on that decision.

Given Minns' findings, it is natural to ask what is their relevance and whether they alter our perceptions of pension fund investment. The work is important in that it seeks to place pension fund investment within some framework. We cannot begin to understand and explain pension fund investment without what sociologists refer to as a frame of reference. Thus, for example, he demonstrates the domination of external investment management by a relatively small number of external investment institutions and seeks to place this apparently unrelated activity in the context of their overall corporate strategies. Pension fund investment should therefore be seen as one of a number of profit-making activities. As such it would be expected to make a contribution to profit and be complementary to the institutions' other activities. An investment strategy that involves a minimum of effort and expense and that supports these other activities is likely to be favoured. But this may provide potential sources of conflict. These are illustrated in Figure 6.1, which details Kleinwort Benson's activities in unit trusts, investment trusts and pension fund investment, and how these are linked. The diagram shows clearly how neatly control of pension fund investment fits in with the bank's activities in unit and investment trusts. It is tempting to ask whose interests are served by such an arrangement. Minns refers to this type of situation as the use of captive funds and remarks that whilst a pension fund

> may decide that its individual investment in a bank's investment trust is unexceptional . . . when the total picture of institutional fund and trust management in certain financial groups is considered, then the aggregate situation is different. The structure of inter-related holdings and investments in a group must raise questions about the diversification of investments, and the strength of the group's structure if one part of it is threatened. (Minns, 1980, p. 109)

Socially responsible investment (SRI)

It is often assumed, without firm evidence, that an SRI policy is incompatible with the aim of obtaining a high financial return when compared to the more normal investment practices of pension fund investment managers. The debate taking place reflects the political and economic environment of the times. Unemployment continues to rise whilst money is exported overseas; large parts of the economy are dependent on continued defence expenditure; companies continue to invest in very politically sensitive countries; the economy stagnates. It is therefore not surprising that pension fund investment should come under scrutiny. In many ways, the debate in political terms is a left/right issue from which emerge two very important questions:

1 Should investment managers have complete freedom to invest, irrespective of the social, moral and economic implications?
2 Should pension fund investment be subject to some form of control and directed into geographical areas and economic sectors that meet the national economic and social priorities as defined by the government of the day?

An SRI policy can mean different things to different people. It can vary

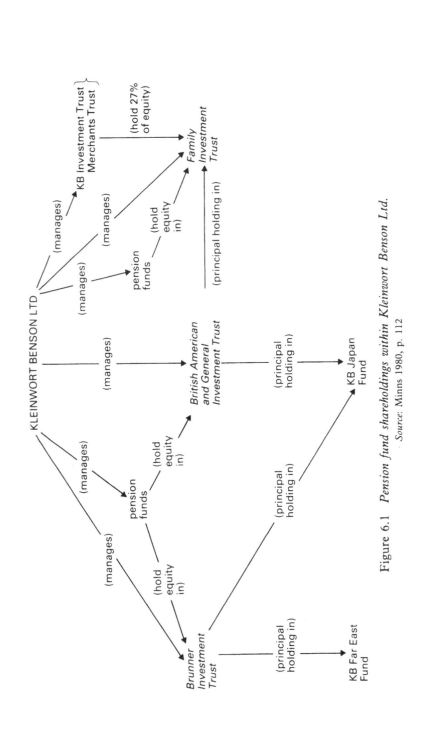

Figure 6.1 *Pension fund shareholdings within Kleinwort Benson Ltd.*

Source: Minns 1980, p. 112

from the avoidance of investments that fail to meet the moral codes set by the investors concerned, to state direction of funds into, for example, deprived inner-city areas such as Toxteth. Robert Schwartz, in a speech to a local authority pension fund conference in June 1984, organized by the Greater London Council, suggests that SRI 'may be based upon moral, politial or religious criteria. It may include the avoidance of specific classes of investments or the search for positive investments, those that are considered constructive to society, that create worthwhile services or products and create jobs' (Schwartz, 1984).

Whilst SRI is in its infancy in the UK, it is a strategy that has existed in the United States for over a decade. Schwartz has been involved with SRI in the USA and described his experiences and work in the field. Describing the way in which pension fund money is invested when placed under the control of traditional investment managers, he comments:

> these funds have been invested without regard to the broader goals of the contributors whether political, social or ethical. While claiming the overriding importance of 'fiduciary responsibility' and citing 'the prudent man' . . . pension funds have been used to help finance run-away shops [industrial plants which move from a unionized to a non-unionized area], and environmental destruction, to cite the most obvious examples. (Schwartz, 1984)

In many respects the duties and responsibilities of trustees in the UK and the United States are similar. For example, trustees have to look after the best interests of the beneficiaries and to this end must not do anything that might reduce the potential return from investment. Much of SRI includes an element of investment exclusions, such as investment in South Africa and defence-related industries. In such circumstances the question then arises whether 'barring an investment by pension funds in corporations that do not meet the social, moral or ethical standards set by a responsible Board of Trustees prevents a fund from earning the highest return possible on investment' (Schwartz, 1984). Schwartz's own experience with both institutional and individual clients allows him to say no to this question. Traditional thinking on the matter would have expected the opposite to be true. He explains why this may happen and in what circumstances the opposite may be true:

> investment performance depends to a considerable extent upon the investment manager. Within certain limits, working from a smaller universe may require greater competence. However if those securities eliminated from consideration are those with less satisfactory performance, then narrowing the universe would be a process of positive natural selection. (Schwartz, 1984)

As an example of positive natural selection he mentions his decision not to invest in any nuclear power utilities, of which a number in recent times have run into deep financial trouble.

The obvious implication to be drawn from Schwartz's comment is that many investment managers may not have the skills to cope with the demands of an SRI strategy, and their reluctance to adopt SRI policies may be an attempt to hide this lack of competence. It may also be due to the fact that the time and effort researching SRI opportunities does not easily fit into the profit-oriented structures of external investment management.

Research has been carried out in the United States to examine the effect of excluding investments in companies with, for example, interests in South Africa (Schwartz, 1984). The work has shown that a portfolio that avoided such investments would have outperformed one that contained these investments. The results of this work need some qualification in that the alternative investments made were in relatively smaller companies than those with South African interests, and over the period of the research smaller companies had outperformed larger ones. It is possible that large pension funds, because of restrictions on investment in smaller companies, would not have been in a position to have considered these.

The discussion so far has emphasized the exclusion aspects of an SRI policy, and as a consequence there is a danger of seeing SRI solely in these terms. However, Schwartz's definition does indicate that the term should include positive investment for social and national economic purposes. The problem with this aspect is that new investment mechanisms (for example, local enterprise boards and perhaps a National Investment Bank) must be created to ease the transfer of pension fund money into the required areas. Further consideration of these is left until later in the chapter.

In response to a possible demand for SRI, Friends Provident Life Office set up their Stewardship Unit Trust at the beginning of June 1984. The fund is aimed at those for whom selection of an investment is not solely based on the potential return. Moral and social considerations will play just as an important part. Thus investments in tobacco and brewery companies and companies with South African interests will not be chosen. In drawing up a list of appropriate investments, the Friends Provident have made use of the services of the Ethical Investment Research and Information Service (EIRIS), which was established with the aim of assisting investors to find investments of positive social benefit. Using the FT-Actuaries All Share List, EIRIS came up with a list of 200 companies that would meet their own guidelines and the Friends Provident's and therefore be appropriate for the fund. The list excluded banks, merchant banks, insurance companies and insurance brokers as well as the more obvious sectors. The emphasis was on the relatively small company and only one company from the FT 30-Share Index, Associated Dairies, was included. This selection of investments has close parallels with the choice of smaller company investments for the SRI portfolios in the United States.

The *Financial Times* reporting on the Stewardship Fund (Short, 1984) compares the return over the last five years of the excluded sectors of investments with the FT All Share Index. The results indicated that the excluded sectors performed worse and consequently a unit trust that had excluded them would have outperformed the average. Up to 13 February 1985 the fund had exceeded all expectations and grown to just over £2.1 million. The return since the launch date has been 27.6 per cent and has exceeded the market return of 25.6 per cent based on the FT All Share Index.

The City's attitude to pension fund investment assumes that beneficiaries are unconcerned where their money is invested and that their only concern is with obtaining the highest possible return. If this is true then there is no need for investment managers to concern themselves with SRI and the extra skill and effort required. But this is far from proven, and very rarely have alternative strategies to the more traditional ones been discussed with beneficiaries How do we know that pension fund members would not want their contributions invested in ways that might create more jobs and regenerate inner-city areas?

There are, however, legal barriers to the adoption of SRI policies and these were clearly stated in a High Court judgment by Sir Robert Megarry.

The Megarry judgment

From a legal point of view a pension scheme is a trust. Trustees are appointed to administer the scheme on behalf of the members. The arrangement provides for financial benefits to be paid either to the members themselves or to their immediate relatives in the event of certain circumstances such as death or retirement. Trustees have certain duties, responsibilities and powers placed on them by law. For example, they must exercise their powers in the best interests of the present and future beneficiaries of the trust. A great deal of debate centres around what is meant by best interests of the beneficiaries, particularly in relation to how the monies of the scheme should be invested.

The most recent court case to examine this issue took place in April 1984 and involved the National Coal Board (NCB) and the National Union of Mineworkers (NUM). The case concerned the pension scheme provided for all the Board's industrial employees. Control of the scheme was the responsibility of a Committee of Management, which was a committee of trustees. There were ten trustees divided equally between the NCB and the NUM.

The NUM trustees had refused to endorse the 1982 investment plan submitted by the scheme's investment manager on 9 June 1982. Instead they sought an investment strategy that did not increase the percentage of overseas investment, that any overseas investment already made was to be withdrawn at the appropriate times and that investment should not take place in energies that were in direct competition with coal. In court the NCB claimed that such an attitude was likely to impair the investment performance of the scheme and therefore ultimately affect the financial interests of the beneficiaries, particularly those of current pensioners, because if 'investment income was impaired the Board might find it impossible to continue to pay additional contributions in order to finance cost-of-living increases to pensions' (Megarry, 1984, p. 12).

The NCB trustees had therefore decided on legal action to clarify a number of issues, in particular:

- whether the NUM representatives were in breach of their fiduciary duties in relation to the investments of the scheme in refusing to endorse the 1982 plan; and
- whether the 1982 plan could be adopted without the agreement of the NUM representatives.

The presiding judge Sir Robert Megarry began by explaining what he understood by 'best interests':

When the purpose of the trust is to provide financial benefits for the beneficiaries, as is usually the case, the best interests of the beneficiaries are normally their best financial interests. In the case of a power of investment, as in the present case, the power must be exercised so as to yield the best return for the beneficiaries, judged in relation to the risks of the investments in question. (Megarry, 1984, p. 20)

Referring to other legal sources, he went on to say that this duty also included 'a duty to "gazump" however honourable the trustees'. With regard to investments that had political, moral or social implications, Megarry was definite that 'trustees must not refrain from making investments by reason of the views that they hold'. In some cases Megarry could see that the best interests of the beneficiaries did not coincide with their best financial interests. This could occur when the beneficiaries held 'very strict views on moral and social matters condemning all forms of alcohol, tobacco and popular entertainments, as well as armaments . . . The beneficiaries might well consider that it was far better to receive less than to receive more money from what they consider to be evil and tainted sources'. (Megarry, 1984, p. 23).

The NUM's own investment strategy was based on the idea that, if pension fund assets were invested in the UK rather than overseas, this would help revive the economy, particularly if 'real' investment in physical assets and new ventures took place. Continued investment in competing energies, it was argued, would be to the detriment of coal and would be against the interests of the scheme's beneficiaries.

In arriving at his judgment, Megarry cited two American cases that, although not binding, were in his opinion 'soundly based on equitable principles' and 'accord with the conclusion [he] would have reached in the absence of authority' (1984, p. 31). The first concerned the Teachers' Retirement System (TRS). In 1975, faced with the impending insolvency of New York, the TRS together with four other New York pension funds agreed to buy unmarketable and highly speculative New York City bonds. Because the TRS was an unfunded scheme it was held that the trustees had in fact acted in the best interests of the beneficiaries in seeking to ensure the continuance of the city's contributions to the scheme. The aim had not been to protect teachers' jobs or for the general public welfare. This case was completely different from the second case cited (Blakenship v. Boyle), where the ruling was that a breach of duty had occurred because 'the trustees pursued policies which may incidentally have aided the beneficiaries of the fund but which were intended primarily to enhance the position of the Union and the welfare of its members presumably through the creation and/or preservation of jobs in the coal industry'.

Megarry felt that the strategy proposed by the NUM was similar to the situation in the second case and he went on to justify this further by dividing the scheme membership into current and potential beneficiaries, and then making assumptions about their expectations and opinions. Without explicitly stating the fact, he implied that they diverge: 'There are many beneficiaries who no longer have any financial interest in the welfare of the Coal Industry . . . they are not affected by the industry and its success.' This allowed him to avoid asking whether these beneficiaries would have sympathy with the NUM's proposals by suggesting that the only interest they have in the coal industry is 'a natural curiosity and concern abut the industry and the people in it' (Megarry, 1984, p. 38), and as a consequence he 'cannot regard any policy designed to ensure the general prosperity of coal mining as being a policy which is directed to obtaining the best results for the beneficiaries, most of whom are no longer engaged in the industry, and some of whom never were' (Megarry, 1984 p. 32). In arriving at this conclusion Megarry appeared to ignore the crucial fact that many of these beneficiaries may still live in mining communities and may well have relations working in the mines. They therefore cannot but have an interest in the future prosperity of the industry and for that matter the economy as a whole.

Having reduced 'best interests' to 'best financial interests', Megarry then explored the type of investment strategy that would achieve this aim.

Referring to section 6(1) of the 1961 Trustee Investments Act, he interpreted the need for diversification not only from a risk point of view but also as a means of increasing the financial returns from investment. Thus, in relation to the NUM's proposed restrictions, he found it

> impossible to see how it will assist trustees to do the best they can for their beneficiaries by prohibiting a wide range of investments that are authorised by the terms of the trust . . . It is the duty of the trustees, in the interests of their beneficiaries, to take advantage of the full range of investments authorised by the terms of the trust, instead of resolving to narrow that range. (Megarry, 1984, p. 36)

The implication of his statement is that restrictions on investment overseas or in competing energies can seriously restrict the potential yield. Megarry did not prove that this would be the case but assumed that restrictions must be detrimental, particularly if the opposite is advocated by investment experts. In adopting an investment strategy, he went on to say, it was not sufficient to show that restrictions were not financially harmful: 'Trustees must do the best they can for the benefit of their beneficiaries and not merely avoid harming them' (Megarry, 1984, p. 36).

The Megarry judgment is important in that it firmly establishes the restricted interpretation of best interests as meaning best financial interests. From a practical point of view this would mean an investment strategy that maximized the yield. Such a strategy is likely to be based on advice received from establishment investment experts and is therefore unlikely to be dominated, if at all, by elements of social responsibility. In fact such elements in Megarry's judgment should have no place in the deliberations of a trustee. A trustee has a duty to seek investment advice but is 'not entitled to reject it merely because he sincerely disagrees with it, unless in addition to being sincere he is acting as an ordinary prudent man would act' (Megarry, 1984, p. 25).

One of the difficulties for those advocating SRI strategies is the reference to exclusions. An SRI policy in many cases is based on these and Megarry has issued a warning that 'the burden would rest and rest heavy on him who asserts that it is for the benefit of the beneficiaries as a whole to receive less by reason of the exclusion of some of the possibly more profitable forms of investment' (Megarry, 1984, p. 24).

Robert Schwartz has managed SRI portfolios that have achieved performances superior to those of more traditionally invested portfolios. That has been a fact demonstrated over time. The difficulty is in predicting what will happen in the future. Given Megarry's attitude to exclusions and his emphasis on maximum yield, it is difficult to see how pension funds can adopt other than traditional investment policies, which only coincidentally may have elements of social responsibility –

although the performance of the Stewardship Fund is most encouraging. For those who would like to see pension fund money invested increasingly for social and national economic purposes, the judgment is a difficult legal obstacle. Perhaps one way round the difficulty would be to seek investment advisers sympathetic to socially responsible investment ideas, who would propose policies that would meet the needs of such trustees.

Investment vehicles for social and economic need

The control of pension fund investment is in the hands of a relatively few investment managers, who may themselves be responsible for the investments of several funds. Investment has tended to take place in the equities of larger national companies, in government securities, in large property developments, and overseas. A consequence of this has been that 'workers' savings have been diverted from localized capital markets into the national and global markets. Thus, savings that were once principally dedicated . . . to investment in local housing and small businesses are now both far more mobile and invested in a far more concentrated and centralized market' (Barber, 1981).

Whilst this was said in connection with American funds, it is equally applicable to the United Kingdom. One only has to know the attitude of investment managers to inner-city investment to appreciate the fact. Harford Thomas noted, for example:

> Some private savings are being made even in the rundown decaying inner city, but once these savings pass into the hands of the financial institutions, they will be invested in the most prosperous of our flourishing urban areas and the most fertile of our countryside or, for that matter, abroad. So this process of institutionalised investment enriches the rich and further impoverishes the poor. (Thomas, 1981)

After the urban riots of 1981, an attempt was made to divert institutional investment in the direction of the inner city. One initiative was the setting up of the Financial Institutions Group (FIG), a group of twenty-five people seconded for a year from various financial institutions and some leading companies. One of their proposals resulted in the formation of Inner City Enterprises (ICE), an independent company acting as broker or agent to seek out institutional investment for large inner-city projects. A *Financial Times* report commented that the results to date were far from encouraging and noted that despite 'the great hopes for persuading the institutions to accept some civic responsibility and replace lip service enthusiasm with cheques . . . not a single project has yet succeeded in attracting a funding agreement' (Pauley, 1984). One of the difficulties encountered by ICE has been that it has no funds of its own and has to devote large amounts of energy and time to chasing around for institutional funding.

Another type of organization, known as an enterprise board, has been set up in an attempt to attract pension fund money into the inner city. These are backed by local authorities alarmed by the decline of industry and commerce in their areas. So far, the Greater London Council, and Lancashire, Merseyside, West Midlands and West Yorkshire county council have established enterprise boards.

The West Midlands Enterprise Board (WMEB) was set up by the West Midlands Metropolitan County Council in response to the high levels of unemployment in the area. The function of the board was to identify opportunities for successful investment in the West Midlands, opportunities that the council felt had been ignored by pension funds and other financial institutions. The WMEB is interested in long-term growth investments that would cover a range of company sizes. Priority is given to investment in commercially sound firms with good opportunities for growth in employment through product development, diversification and investment in new plant and machinery. Whilst some of the board's funds would come from the West Midlands County Council by means of a levy on the rates, it was intended that funds should also come from pension funds based both locally and elsewhere. It was intended that pension funds would allocate finance over a specified period of time. This could be a fixed amount of finance or a sum linked to cash flow or increases in the fund or linked in some way to the total size of the fund. To date, five local authority funds have placed funds with the board.

The Greater London Enterprise Board (GLEB) was created later than the WMEB. It was set up by the GLC with social and employment objectives in mind and these are clearly stated in the board's publicity literature. Thus, whilst economic viability would be an important factor in determining whether an investment would be made, priority would be 'given to areas, industries and social groups most affected by unemployment and industrial decline'. Special consideration would also be given to 'projects that meet the particular employment needs of women and ethnic minorities who find it most difficult to attract finance'. In addition to the market and financial viability of a project, the board would also need to be satisfied about a number of social factors 'from the number and type of jobs which will be created to the level of work place participation and the social benefits which can be gained from a particular product or service'. It would also be necessary for an enterprise plan to be drawn up. This would set out 'the strategic framework for investment, covering policies on jobs, industrial relations, trades union recognition, equal opportunities and training, as well as the more usual content of business plans'. Finance for the GLEB was initially obtained by a levy on the rates, but the intention is that eventually pension funds should be invited to subscribe.

At a national level, a National Investment Bank (NIB) has been proposed by the Labour Party and the TUC in the belief that the United Kingdom financial system has failed to make available long-term funds for investment in industry. The intention is that the NIB would be jointly funded by pension funds, life assurance companies and government. This new source of finance would be 'part of a programme of economic expansion and planning designed to stimulate investment levels, which would ensure that investment is not held back through a lack of adequate finance on the right terms, and that funds go to priority areas' (Labour Party Financial Institutions Study Group, 1982, p. 57).

In a note of dissent to the Wilson Committee report, proposals were made for an NIB (Wilson Committee, 1980). Some of the main features were that:

- the institutions would make available £1,000 million as the Bank was set up, and as the fund became established this would increase to an annual flow equal to 10 per cent of the net annual funds for investment by the institutions;
- the return to the institutions would be guaranteed at a level equal to at least that available on gilt edged stock;
- the government would make a loan contribution equal to that from the institutions, to be allocated from North Sea Oil and gas revenues;
- loan finance would be allocated below the market rate of interest – but at a spectrum of different rates depending on the project under consideration; the criterion for choosing projects would be the expectation of long-term profitability.

The NIB would be funded by long-term deposits from the pension funds and life assurance companies. These deposits would probably take the form of a variety of special indexed National Investment Bank bonds. Lending to the NIB would therefore be very similar to existing lending to government.

Supporters of an NIB have recognized that 'There will be considerable pressure to restrict the bank's investments to conventionally defined "commercial propositions" and this could leave it with large funds sitting in idle balances' (Labour Party Financial Institutions Study Group, 1982, p. 62). As a consequence, existing investment criteria would be extended with the introduction of certain basic social principles. Investment would be guided by priorities determined within an overall economic planning framework, which might include priorities for investment in the regions and specific sectors. Decisions on investments would also take into account non-financial benefits – such as bringing jobs to an area of high employment – by carrying out a social audit of larger investment projects. The benefits obtained would be reflected in a subsidy on the investment rate. Additionally loans would be for a period of at least 10–15 years and current interest payments would be index linked. This would help overcome the difficulty in the early years of a conventional loan where substantial cash flows may be required to meet large capital and interest payments.

There are a number of lending institutions already in existence that partially fulfil some of the functions proposed for the NIB. The oldest are perhaps the Industrial and Commercial Finance Corporation (ICFC) and the Finance Corporation for Industry (FCI) which were founded in 1945. ICFC provides finance for small and medium-sized companies, whilst FCI provides finance for larger companies. Finance for Industry (FFI), which acted as a holding company for both those organizations, has now been reorganized and renamed Investors in Industry. Finance for their lending activities comes in the form of fixed-term deposits. This means that any lending must be made at commercial rates of interest. The NIB proposals, in contrast, envisage a continuous flow of funds from the institutions and the interest rates on loans will be below commercial rates.

Equity Capital for Industry (ECI) was set up in 1976 to provide equity capital for firms that have difficulty raising it from other sources. The total capital of £41m has been subscribed by 365 financial institutions and only about a quarter has been invested in companies, with the rest on deposit. 'It has done very little to seek business and its impact is barely perceptible' (Labour Party Financial Institutions Study Group, 1982, p. 59). ECI did, however, play an important and leading role in the attempted rescue of Stone Platt, only to be thwarted by the banks calling in a receiver a year after a rescue package was introduced.

The creation of an NIB would be an attempt to direct pension fund and institutional investment into sectors that are considered to meet national economic and social needs, rather than depending upon institutional investment managers to carry out this task. The proposals are, by their very nature, political and evoke both a political and self-interested response. For example, the City Capital Markets Committee (1982) thought that 'the idea of a National Investment Bank . . . will create extra bureaucracy and tend to direct resources in uneconomic directions, which is not only wasteful in iself but also directs real resources away from successful enterprises'. This of course begs the question of what is meant by the non-neutral terms 'uneconomic directions' and 'successful enterprises'. It also ignores the social aspects of the NIB proposals and presupposes that in some way current institutional investment practices result in an allocation of funds that, from an economic view, benefit the country as a whole. Although frequently assumed to be the case, this is far from proven.

It is difficult to see how the pension funds and other financial institutions can possibly obtain an overall picture of national economic and social needs. Perhaps the answer to this question is that they cannot. Social aspects have rarely if at all been considered. As for national economic needs, these would take second place to the search for 'prime' investments that sustain their 'exchange value'. A cynic would therefore argue that the City Capital Markets Committee's reaction is no more than a response seeking to protect vested commercial interests. In fact, the Committee believes that there are sufficient funds available for venture and development capital from the institutional participants in this field, the only problem being a lack of suitable projects.

It therefore seems unrealistic to assume that there are any great number of profitable opportunities open to pension funds which so far have remained undiscovered by these active bodies. What seems more likely is that the proposed National Investment Bank and Local Enterprise Boards would adopt investment criteria which would lead to inferior performance in the long term on the part of investing pension funds. (City Capital Markets Committee, 1982)

Conclusions

This chapter has examined some of the criticisms made of pension fund investment and also briefly described some of the initiatives by local authorities to increase investment in their areas and thereby to reduce unemployment. It is the rising trend of unemployment that has caused attention to turn towards long-term investing institutions like the pension funds. With 3.3 million registered unemployed and the inner cities fast decaying, surely, the argument goes, the pension funds can invest in the UK economy in ways that will help to tackle these problems? In theory, they could of course do so, but from a practical viewpoint they are unable to invest in ways that meet social and economic needs.

They operate within a set of assumptions which belong to an era of rapid economic growth which is now past. They are stuck with conventional criteria which do not apply to the reality of economic decline, low economic growth, rising energy costs, an ageing population and rundown cities with increasing numbers of old and even derelict buildings. (Thomas, 1981)

Pension fund trustees would, however, argue that they should not be accused of failing to meet national social and economic needs as these do not form part of trustees' responsibilities with regard to investment. They will point to the Megarry judgment which makes it quite clear that the purpose of an investment strategy must be to obtain the highest possible financial return. The only question that can arise, therefore, is whether or not pension fund investment managers, adopting conventional criteria, do in fact achieve the maximum possible returns for the funds under their control. This is a difficult question to answer. The average return from investment has been less than salary inflation over a twenty-year period. If this were to persist, the relationship between the rate of return and the salary growth rate assumed in the actuarial basis would be invalidated. Such a situation would not necessarily be the fault of investment managers, who might argue that they had been set an almost impossible task and in the circumstances had achieved the best possible investment returns. It is the assumption in the actuarial basis, they might claim, that is at fault.

In respect of individual categories of investment, equities were the only investment to perform satisfactorily when compared with the growth in salaries. Does this imply that the mix of pension fund portolios has been wrong and that there should have been a much larger equity element? It might be claimed that the large proportion of gilts was in fact evidence of socially responsible investment. It could also be claimed that it merely represented a respectable and convenient investment to absorb large cash flows.

The debate about pension fund investment should not be divorced from the main economic debate taking place amongst the political parties. The current Conservative government's 'free market' philosophy is one that investment managers in general have found acceptable and in investment jargon is often referred to as 'capital market efficiency', This holds that

> the capital markets are, and should be, the autonomous and self-regulating allocators of societal resources. The criteria for this process are determined by what is in the best interests of capital, as defined by those who are its intermediaries in the market place. And the capital markets are presented as independent and neutral enforcers of economic efficiency and of the supremacy of financial considerations over social or political concerns. In fact, social good is derived from, and even defined by the efficient functioning of these markets. (Barber, 1981)

As a consequence, the national income – whether it comes from internal or overseas investment – will be maximized, thus in theory benefiting everyone.

There is no doubt that financial institutions do make funds available for real investment. But this is really a response to demands for finance made upon them at prevailing market rates. In no way can it be described as a promotional role that actively seeks out real investment opportunities. This would require a much closer relationship between the institutions and industry than prevails at the moment. Unfortunately this is a role that the institutions, including the pension funds, are not necessarily keen to take on.

It should also be appreciated that the City's historical development has been geared towards the provision of international finance rather than to financing the development and reconstruction of domestic industry. In general, large companies and multinationals have usually been able to provide their own finance and attract sufficient resources, and institutional money such as pension fund money has been channelled into the largest companies, particularly in the financial sector. However, a very large part of British industry remains untouched by City finance – industries that perhaps need funds for research and development, or for reorganization and investment.

As indicated already, the historical development of the City has tended to orientate the financial institutions towards overseas investment and international currency dealings. Even in 1933, foreign government and railway stocks represented 80 per cent of all quoted securities on the Stock Exchange. So far as investment in United Kingdom securities was concerned, the appearance of institutional investors on the scene shifted the balance towards the stocks of larger companies. This was one of the reasons for the discovery of the famous 1930s 'Macmillan gap' in the finance available for smaller and medium-sized companies, in this case because of the preference of the stock market investors for larger issues in the shape of foreign stocks and large companies.

The stock market is much more active as a secondary market than as a primary one. The increasing institutional domination of the stock market, particularly by pension funds and insurance companies, has seen a transfer of share ownership from private individuals to the institutions. To the limited extent that the Stock Exchange does function as a primary market by means of 'rights issues', the finance raised will be substantially aimed at multinational corporations and the financial sector, which can, for the most part, restructure themselves. In the five years 1979–83, £7b was raised on the Stock Exchange in the form of capital issues (rights issues and new issues) for UK industrial and commercial companies. Only 40 per cent of this was for manufacturing companies. This figure also includes round £3b raised from the government's programme of public sector privatization. The total issues in these years are equivalent to less than 10 per cent of the total new money invested by pension funds and insurance companies world-wide in the same period. Over half the £6.7b raised by rights issues in these five years went to fewer than thirty companies, including ten financial institutions (one twice), property companies and oil companies, and also major internationals like Rio-Tinto Zinc (twice) and Consolidated Goldfields (the last two engaged in financing and developing international mining interests), and Harrisons and Crossfield (overseas traders). A large part of the finance raised has tended to be for non-manufacturing companies or companies looking to spend money on foreign acquisitions. The evidence therefore lends support to those who argue that there is an absence of long-term finance and mechanisms for investment in domestic production, especially linked to industrial reorganization. As we have seen in the previous section, there have been some attempts under political pressure to recognize this.

Pension fund investment, like all institutional investment, has become centralized and it is difficult to believe that from such a position the funds are sensitive enough to identify investment opportunities at the local level. The way forward may be to decentralize the investment process through the creation of local enterprise boards. Local enterprise boards offer the prospect of local information about investment opportunities and would be involved in an active way in promoting investment. A network of such local boards would offer pension funds a range of investment opportunities in British industry that could lead to the promotion of economic growth and employment opportunities.

The chapter has also examined the idea that pension funds should invest within a nationally defined economic and social plan. Central to this plan would be a National Investment Bank. As well as considering the financial return from a project, the plan would concern itself with the social implications of an investment decision. It is possible, although by no means proven, that in terms of an individual pension fund an SRI strategy seeking to create jobs in the United Kingdom might result in a lower financial return than that available on more conventional investments; in terms of the whole economy, however, the alternative cost of unemployment needs to be brought into any calculations. Pure reliance on the efficiency of the capital markets is unlikely to meet social and economic needs.

> In a market economy it is not realistic to expect the financial sector to change its conventional criteria. Short of the direction of funds or substantial public sector investment, . . . we have to rely upon market forces, and we should not delude ourselves as to their nature. (Thomas, 1981)

The debate surrounding pension fund investment is essentially part of the much wider debate about reducing inequality. It is about society's collective responsibility to the people and about individual freedom. Until social and economic needs have been fulfilled it is not obvious what economic and financial freedoms an individual should enjoy. Inequality is endemic throughout the United Kingdom. Recent research from the Child Poverty Action Group and the Low Pay Unit confirm the increasing trend of poverty. The redirection of pension fund monies in ways that can redistribute wealth on both a regional and individual level can help towards reducing this. At the very least, it has been suggested, pension fund money 'should be "recycled" in ways that have a beneficial direct present impact on pension fund owners (workers) through job creation and community stabilization . . . [and] should not be invested in ways that work counter to the interests of pension fund participants' (Barber, 1981).

It remains to be seen whether pension fund investment will come increasingly under state control. This will, however, be highly dependent on any government's determination to institute control and on the resistance that can be mounted by the pensions industry.

References

Barber, R. (1981), 'Pension funds in the United States: Issues of investment and control' unpublished paper, Arbetslvscentrum Stockholm

City Capital Markets Committee (1982), 'Pension fund investment and trusteeship', paper published in response to the TUC's *Report on Pension Fund Investment and Trusteeship*, November

Dickson, T. (1984), The problems of success, *Financial Times*, 28 April

Hager, D. P. (1983), 'Investment in the 1980s – Is a new approach needed?' paper presented to the Institute of Mathematics and its Applications

Labour Party Financial Institutions Study Group (1982), *The City. A Socialist Approach*, London: Labour Party

Megarry, Sir R. (1984), Judgment (revised) in the matter of the Trusts of the Mineworkers' Pension Scheme, CH 1983 M. No. 5498

Minns, R. (1980), *Pension Funds and British Capitalism*, London: Heinemann

Pauley, R. (1984), 'The City's unfilled promises over fighting urban decay', *Financial Times*, 25 July

Phillips and Drew (1984), *Pension Fund Indicators*, London: Phillips and Drew

Richardson, Lord (1983), 'The provision of pensions', *Bank of England Quarterly Bulletin*, December, pp. 502–12

Schwartz, R. J. (1984), 'Socially responsible investment – the American experience', paper given to the 3rd Local Authority Pension Fund Conference, June

Shilson, D. (1984), 'Venture capital in the United Kingdom', *Bank of England Quarterly Bulletin*, June 1984, pp. 207–11

Short, E. (1984) 'The knotty problem of bringing ethics into investment', *Financial Times*, 2 June

Thomas, H. (1981) 'Conventional financial institutions will not – and cannot – help the Toxteths' *Guardian*, 8 August

Trades Union Congress (1983), *Pension Fund Trusteeship and Investment*, London: Trades Union Congress

Wilson Committee (1980), *Report of the Committee to Review the Functioning of Financial Institutions*, Cmnd 7937, London: HMSO

7 Taxation of Occupational Pension Schemes

GERALDINE KAYE

Introduction

Over the past forty years in the United Kingdom three forms of personal saving have received particularly favourable tax treatment – pension schemes, individual life insurance, and the purchase of owner-occupied houses financed by mortgages. Not surprisingly, these have come to dominate the structure of personal savings. Direct personal saving, for example by direct investment in ordinary shares, has not in general received the same tax advantages, and indeed through investment income surcharge (only abolished in April 1984) and its predecessors has received distinctly unfavourable treatment. If a particular form of financial transaction receives more favourable tax treatment than another transaction that otherwise has a similar effect, it is not surprising to find that investors prefer to enter into transactions of the former kind and that such transactions thus flourish.

The 1984 Budget took two steps towards a more uniform treatment of different forms of savings – the abolition of life assurance premium relief (LAPR) and the abolition of investment income surcharge. Thus savings through individual life insurance are now taxed on a basis roughly equivalent to that for direct investment by individuals. It is too soon to say how quickly this will affect individual life insurance, but it is almost certain that it will, in the long run, have a very substantial effect in diminishing the attraction of life insurance for individual savings. Life insurance companies do, however, remain unique in being able to offer life insurance cover as such.

The withdrawal of LAPR from policies taken out after the 1984 Budget has led many to speculate that the Chancellor will consider that the removal of some of the tax advantages from pension funds would be a logical consequence. The two situations are fundamentally different and must therefore be considered completely independently of each other.

Life insurance contracts were not originally introduced as a savings medium. Their function was purely to provide protection against the contingency of death. Death is not a popular subject. There has long been a superstition amongst many people that to discuss death or plan for its coming will in some way hasten its arrival. Relevant contracts are therefore contracts of life cover, not – as would be far more logical – death cover; they provide protection and, more recently, savings. Life insurance contracts have always had to be sold rather than bought and their sales presentations will go to great lengths to prevent the salesman needing to mention death. As early as 1799 it was considered socially desirable for people to have life insurance cover and tax relief was introduced as an incentive for people to buy a contract. Tax relief provided the salesman with an additional means of selling a policy without directly mentioning death; for example, as a tax-efficient vehicle to provide for one's dependants. Unfortunately, over the years the tax relief aspect was developed and the death cover aspect diminished to such an extent that many policies were designed purely as savings media, containing only sufficient death cover to make the policy eligible for LAPR. By the date of the 1984 Budget that removed LAPR there were over fifty pages of legislation dealing with this abuse. Tax relief was no longer being used as a means of encouraging the provision of death cover, that is, the purpose for which it was intended. If it is found that the removal of tax relief greatly reduces the new business figures of life insurance companies in terms of sums insured at risk (as well as in terms of premium income, which is after all only a consequence of introducing fiscal neutrality), then it could be that the government will need to reconsider the matter. There is a precedent: LAPR was removed in 1842 and reintroduced in 1853.

Each of us will need an income on which we can live in retirement and if our savings are insufficient then the state will need to assist. Funded pension contracts have always been considered a desirable way of saving for old age because of the commitment involved. Encouraging such long-term saving was the objective of the various governments that introduced and continued the provision of tax reliefs for pension fund saving. Although tax relief did not achieve its objective for life insurance, it does appear to be achieving its objective well in the case of occupational pension schemes. A further difference between life insurance and pensions is that, whereas in the former case there was much abuse of the reliefs available, this is not the case with pensions, as will be shown in the body of this chapter. Indeed there is a strong case for liberalizing the regulations surrounding the granting of tax relief to pension funds.

There is little doubt that the tax relief on saving for retirement via pension fund contributions has had a considerable influence on the volume of savings channelled through them both by employees and employers. That this is so was acknowledged by members of the actuarial profession as long ago as 1954 during the discussion on a now classic paper (Bacon, Benjamin and Elphinstone, 1954a). In his opening speech to the Faculty of Actuaries in Scotland when the paper was discussed there, a leading actuary of that time included in his speech the remarks:

> It is known that many schemes are being set up more for the purpose of spreading the employer's tax burden than through any solicitude for the well-being of, or any particular demand on the part of, the employees. (Bacon, Benjamin and Elphinstone, 1954b, p. 352)

This was an extreme view but, less forcefully perhaps, the point was taken up by various other members both in England at the Institute of Actuaries and in Scotland at the Faculty of Actuaries. The advantage taken by the employer is acceptable if one also acknowledges the desirability of encouraging individuals (in this expression is included employers on the behalf of individuals) to make provision for their retirement. However, there is clearly the possibility that the form of the schemes that are being encouraged could be different in the presence of different types of tax relief. With different types of tax relief, different types of schemes would have been and possibly still could be, encouraged to exist. Individuals wish to make provision for their retirement by one means or another, but if organizations other than individuals choose to take responsibility for the financing of retirement benefits the method selected is psychologically very important because the individuals may be more willing to pay in one way than in another. The provision in advance for future liabilities by the accumulation of assets, normally external to the employer's business (commonly referred to as funding) may, for example, engender a greater degree of financial responsibility than provision purely on a pay-as-you-go basis.

The Inland Revenue has been given wide powers of discretion with regard to the requirements that they can impose as a condition for a grant of approval. These requirements, initially simple to operate, have in recent years become increasingly extensive and complex as the Inland Revenue has sought to close gaps where, as it sees it, there might be scope for possible abuse, by imposing progressively more onerous requirements upon schemes generally, an understanding of the detailed contents of which is beyond all but a small body of specialists who have been required to exercise their skills in this way. Thus not only do the current methods of granting tax relief via Inland Revenue approval dictate the general form of schemes, but they also have a tendency to eliminate flexibility. For example, the present practice of placing a special restriction on the amount of benefits for late entrants to schemes who only have a short period of service to normal retirement age discourages mobility of labour in the later years of a working lifetime when an employee's experience might be invaluable to a prospective new employer and hence to the national economy. Another undesirable effect of the restriction is on the early leaver who leaves before five years of service, so that his occupational pension is not preserved. Because such a person has been in pensionable employment, he has not been permitted to make his own pension provision, and so on leaving service he may find himself in a far worse position than a comparable employee who had throughout the period been in non-pensionable employment and had had the same money applied to an S226 contract (a person who is self-employed or an employee not in an employer's pension scheme can effect a savings plan by what is technically a retirement annuity, approved under section 226 of the Income and Corporation Taxes Act 1970 – commonly referred to as a S226 contract).

The deployment of skilled specialists to unravel the complexities of the Inland Revenue's latest practice notes deprives the community of the best use of their skills. It is the combination of all the above drawbacks that has caused many to question not only the cost of pension fund relief, but also whether it should exist at all. For example, the Wilson Committee report (Wilson Committee, 1980) made the general recommendation that consideration should be given to putting the tax treatment of interest payments by all deposit-taking institutions on to a common basis, and that the tax arrangements for government borrowing and those that apply to other borrowers should be brought into line.

General principles of the taxation of savings

Two logical and consistent methods for taxing personal savings are frequently discussed:

● comprehensive income tax
● comprehensive expenditure tax.

The system we have at present is broadly speaking a system based upon tax on income, but because we live in a practical rather than theoretical world it is far from comprehensive and we find many exceptions. In broad terms, though an individual's personal income is taxed, he may then save out of net income. Any investment income on his saving is taxed, but he can withdraw the original capital free of tax, paying capital gains tax only on any (indexed) capital gain.

Expenditure tax has been discussed very fully in the Meade Committee report (Meade, 1978). With the exception of the anomaly that lump-sum benefits are tax free, we find that the system of taxation of pension funds in the UK follows very closely the principles of an expenditure tax.

Two important and very different questions with regard to pension funds are:

1 whether all savings should be taxed under an income or expenditure tax structure;
2 whether to continue the privileged treatment of pension funds under our present income tax structure.

It would clearly be possible for a government that wished to do so to put many different forms of individual savings on to an expenditure tax basis. Mechanisms would need to be set up to ensure that individual savings that were to qualify for this treatment were held through suitable trustee companies. These could authenticate the purchase of securities or other property as qualifying for tax relief in the year of purchase, could claim back tax on income from the assets (if indeed this continued to be deducted at source), and could then account for tax to the Inland Revenue when the assets were sold and the proceeds passed over to the individual. It is absolutely essential, however, that any such mechanisms that are introduced are not so complicated as to engender a feeling that the cure is worse than the disease. This is an important caveat and one that could prove to be a major stumbling block. If simple mechanisms could be introduced, such a system, which could presumably be run by many responsible financial institutions, would not in any way inhibit the individual's choice of investments within a suitable range. It is fairly clear that most financial assets could come within the expenditure tax rules, the boundary being drawn somewhere between current accounts and term deposits, and one side or another of works of art and investment in one's own business. Although a boundary would need to be drawn between permissible and non-permissible savings media, one distinction would fall away: that between income and capital gains, since both would be tax free until the proceeds were taken out of the system for use as expenditure.

If such a system of expenditure tax were adopted, any restrictions on the size of pension fund contributions or the amount of benefits would become redundant. There would be no need for pension funds to restrict themselves to providing pensions; benefits could be taken in any form, provided that tax were paid in the year they were transferred to the individual. (Of course, if he then re-invested the proceeds elsewhere, he would end up paying tax only on any net withdrawal.) It is hardly necessary to state that the anomalous tax-free lump sum would require to be taxed under such a system.

Alternatively a government might choose to go for a comprehensive income tax system, in which personal savings would get no preferential treatment. This would leave most savings as they are at present, but would have a substantial effect on pension funds. First, an employer would have to attribute notionally contributions to the scheme to each individual employee (not a practical proposition at the moment) and these contributions would then be added to the employee's income for tax purposes. The investment income of pension funds would also become taxable. Benefits from the pension funds would then be tax free, whether taken as a lump sum or as pensions, and therefore there would be no need from a taxation viewpoint to require them to be taken in any particular form. Any such change in the taxation system for pension funds would require consideration of the position of existing funds. Since they have not been taxed on their inputs, it would be over-generous to transfer them wholly to an income tax basis where the benefits could be paid free of tax, even if tax were to be paid on future investment income. One method would be to freeze the present schemes, making them all paid up, with no future contributions, but otherwise on the same tax basis as at present. At the other extreme they could be wholly transferred to an income tax basis, paying tax on their output at that time, but this would produce such a massive single tax levy as to be unacceptable. A compromise would be to require the transfer of the new basis to take place over a limited number of years, with tax being levied on the transfer as it occurred. Once the funds have been transferred (after tax) to the new basis, they would not be subject to further tax when benefits were paid, so tax would only be being paid early, and there would be no element of double taxation.

Any substantial change in the system of taxation would involve administrative expense, for those reponsible for administering the change, for those who have to comply with it, and perhaps for those who find that a route that they once thought was advantageous is no longer so, and who attempt to find another. On the other hand, the costs of change may be mitigated by simplifications in other respects, or in the long-term annual cost of running the system. Even if the net cost is positive, there may be advantages in a change if it promotes greater equity between individuals, or achieves some other objectives that the proposers consider desirable. It is not intended in this chapter to promote either of the views – that all savings should be taxed on an income tax basis or all on an expenditure tax basis. It is, however, appropriate to consider the possible effects on tax revenue and on the overall pattern of savings of the two methods.

Model: income versus expenditure tax basis
Let us assume a very simple model. The government wishes to raise a certain amount of taxation in order to pay for current public expenditure. It is not concerned with the distribution of taxation among individuals and there is a uniform single tax rate on *all* income or *all* expenditure (depending on whether an income or an expenditure tax is adopted). Let us now consider a pension fund that has reached maturity and is in stationary position, that is, the fund is not growing. In these

circumstances, income (contribution income plus investment income) and outgo (benefits) exactly balance. In our simple model, exactly the same tax rate is required whether an income tax or an expenditure tax is adopted. At first sight therefore it appears as if in such a situation the choice of tax basis makes no difference at all. However, under an expenditure tax basis the stated level of pension requires to be gross, whereas under an income tax basis the stated level of pension need only be the net equivalent. We must consider this point in more detail.

One proposal that has been reported fairly regularly in the financial press is that pension funds might be taxed on their investment income, possibly at a lower rate than the standard rate, in order to put them roughly into the same position as other forms of saving.

Let us consider simply the accumulation of £1 for a period of n years at a gross interest rate of i . Assume that the standard rate of tax is t , and that it remains unchanged throughout the n years. If the pension were also taxed at the same rate t, the net benefit for a gross contribution of £1 would be:

$$[1 + i\,(1 - t)]^n \times (1 - t),$$

whereas the private individual would be able to save a net $(1 - t)$ out of his gross income of £1, giving a final proceeds of:

$$(1 - t) \times [1 + i(1 - t)]^n$$

which is exactly the same as the first expression if the tax rates are the same. Thus, fiscal neutrality (at least for standard rate taxpayers) would apparently be achieved by taxing pension funds on investment income at the standard rate, and on capital gains on the same basis as private individuals (except that, since pension funds would be free to invest in authorized unit trusts, which are free of capital gains tax on their transactions, they would effectively defer payment of capital gains tax indefinitely just as in various ways private individuals can). However, this equality would be achieved only for the standard-rate taxpayer. The higher-rate taxpayer would, as at present though to a lesser degree, find it advantageous to put the maximum contribution into a pension scheme, achieving a standard rate roll-up, and drawing out benefit when his marginal rate would perhaps be lower.

With the exception of higher-rate taxpayers, therefore, the proposal that pension funds should be taxed on investment income would indeed achieve the objective of broad fiscal neutrality between pension funds and other forms of saving. There would then be no point in maintaining the Inland Revenue restrictions on the amount of pension fund benefits or of self-employed retirement annuity contributions, or in requiring that any of the benefits be taken in the form of pension, provided of course that they were all subject to tax in the year in which they were withdrawn.

Neat though this solution seems, its effect is somewhat different from that of a pure income tax. The contributions for a given level of net pension would be the same, but since tax is not paid on it immediately the government's tax revenue is lower during the period of build-up of the fund, and the capital formation is higher. The total funds build up to a greater amount than under a pure income tax position, since to achieve equilibrium we must have, in the pension fund case, that gross contribution (C) plus net income ($I_1(1 - t)$) equals gross pension (P), whereas in the individual case the net contribution ($C(1 - t)$) plus net income ($I_2(1 - t)$) equals net pension ($P(1 - t)$). That is:

For the pension fund:
$$C + I_1 (1 - t) = P \text{ so that } C - P = I_1(1 - t).$$

For the individual:
$$C(1 - t) + I_2(1 - t) = P(1 - t) \text{ so that } C - P = I_2.$$

Thus it is necessary to provide the same income net of tax from the pension fund as is needed to provide gross of tax for the individual. The total invested funds are therefore $1/(1 - t)$ bigger than they otherwise would be. In effect, the government's tax revenue forgone during the build-up of the fund is 'invested' in the extra assets. The immediate effect of altering the tax basis of pension funds to tax investment income would probably be a reduction in government tax revenues since some pension funds may wish to increase their gross contributions so as to maintain at least partially the present gross benefit, which would result in a greater amount of contributions receiving relief from tax immediately. It is difficult to forecast the longer-term effects since doubtless the revised tax basis would cause a number of funds to close.

Let us now return to more general matters in our simple model. So far we have considered only the stationary state. We have not considered how such a state is achieved, or what happens if a stable, steadily changing state is achieved. Clearly, if there were no interest income and all calculations were made at a zero rate of interest, then it would make no difference to a pension fund in any state whether an income tax or an expenditure tax basis were adopted, apart from the method of expressing the pensions. Tax on contributions in one case would exactly equal tax on pension outgo in the other, and even if these were paid at different times they would have the same value at zero interest both to the payer and to the receiver of tax. (At zero interest the government could presumably borrow whatever it wished to cover any cash flow shortage at any time, so it would equally be indifferent to when the tax was received.)

The difference between the two tax bases is thus seen to be entirely caused by the effect of tax on investment income. If it is desired to achieve a given level of net pension, then accumulation at a gross rate of interest allows a lower contribution than accumulation at a net rate of interest. Thus an income tax basis would require a higher gross contribution (since it would be calculated at a net rate of interest) than an expenditure tax in which the gross contribution can be calculated at a gross rate of interest. However, only the net contribution is in fact available for investment under the income tax system. Whether the amount available for investment is greater or smaller under an income tax than under an expenditure tax depends on whether $(1 - t)/[1 + i(1 - t)]^n$ greater than or less than $1/(1 + i)^n$ or n greater than or less than $\log [1/(1 - t)]/\log \{(1 + i)/\log [1 + i(1 - t)]\}$.

The critical values of n for various values of i and t are given in Table 7.1. It can be seen that whether the amount available for investment is greater or smaller under an income tax than under an expenditure tax depends on whether the average time between payment of contribution and receipt of benefit is greater than or less than the value of n given in the table. The value of n varies more with the rate of interest than with the tax rate, and is lower for higher rates of interest. If rates of interest are considered as being in money terms, then the income tax basis will probably produce a higher level of net investment (on the assumption that the net target benefit remains unchanged), whereas if interest rates are considered as being real rates (that is, capital gains are tax free or taxed only on 'real' gains), then the values of n are sufficiently high that it is likely that the amount of net investment would be lower under an income tax regime.

If the net contribution rate and hence the rate of capital formation is higher, then (for a given level of total national income) available salaries will be lower, and the rate of accumulation of capital will be higher; the rate of growth of national income may then be higher, and the funds may more quickly achieve their stable amount. Whether this is desirable or undesirable is not for this chapter to judge.

Of considerable significance is the question whether either a fixed level of pension or a fixed proportion of salary is in fact a target that would remain unchanged in the presence of a different tax regime. This remains a question, whether savings for retirement are carried out through a formal pension fund or by individuals, though the answer may be different in each case. Of course, if a scheme is expressed as having either defined benefits or defined contributions then it might appear that one or the other of these would remain unchanged under a different tax regime. But it is already clear that the defined level of benefit under an income tax regime should be the net of tax benefit, whereas under the present expenditure tax regime for pension funds it is the gross benefit. If the tax

Table 7.1 *Critical values of n*

i%	t =	0.2	0.25	0.3	0.35	0.4
3		38.2	39.4	40.6	42.0	43.6
4		28.9	29.8	30.7	31.8	32.9
5		23.3	24.0	24.8	25.6	26.6
6		19.6	20.2	20.8	21.5	22.3
7		16.9	17.4	18.0	18.6	19.3
8		15.0	15.4	15.9	16.4	17.0
9		13.4	13.8	14.2	14.7	15.2
10		12.2	12.5	12.9	13.3	13.8
11		11.2	11.5	11.8	12.2	12.6
12		10.3	10.6	10.9	11.3	11.7

regime were changed, one cannot assume that pension funds (or individuals) would not also change the target level of net benefit.

The various actions that might be taken by firms if pensions were placed wholly on an income tax basis are several. Employees' contributions could be raised; this might appear reasonable if at the same time the government had reduced the standard rate of income tax, but it would nevertheless be resisted by employees. If it were accepted, we do not know whether the higher contributions would come from reduced savings elsewhere, or reduced consumption. The firm could increase the employer's contributions; this might come either out of reduced retained earnings, that is, reduced savings, or reduced dividends to shareholders. Whether this would affect total consumption or total savings depends on the response of shareholders to a reduction in their income and on the proportion of dividends being paid to other pension funds. The firm might reduce the targeted level of net benefit, leaving the gross contribution rate unchanged. Since tax would now be being paid out of the gross contribution the amount of savings in the economy would fall from this cause (though the aggregate effect depends on tax changes elsewhere). The firm might keep contribution rates and benefits unchanged, and simply allow schemes to become less fully funded. This too would produce less total savings in the economy from this source, with a change towards a greater level of pay-as-you-go benefit in private pension schemes. We cannot tell the extent to which firms would choose any of these different responses, and so we cannot tell whether a change in pension scheme taxation to an income tax basis would or would not promote higher capital investment.

One has to consider also the fact that the level of contributions is only one aspect of the way in which interest rates and capital investment are determined in the market. The other aspect is the demand for investible funds to finance real capital formation. In general one can assume that the demand for investible funds reduces as the (real) rate of interest increases. Now, whereas for many commodities the supply of that commodity increases with the price, so that an upward-sloping supply curve has a unique point of intersection with a downward-sloping demand curve, in the case of savings for retirement the supply curve (that is, the contribution rate required at a given rate of interest to provide the targeted benefit) is also downward sloping. It is therefore not clear, unless a great deal more empirical evidence were available, whether a change from an expenditure tax basis for savings through pension funds to an income tax basis would result in a higher or lower level of saving, a higher or lower level of capital formation, and higher or lower interest rates. Equally, one cannot tell what the net effect on savings would be if other forms of saving received the same expenditure tax treatment as pension schemes at present do.

The current system of tax reliefs

An individual may obtain potential benefits within the general pension limits, including: a personal pension of up to two-thirds of their final salary (if they have been employed by their companies for ten years or more); the right to commute a portion of their pension up to a maximum of half their final salary, after twenty years' service; a widow's pension of two-thirds of the individual's pension; and, in the case of death in service life cover, four times their salary plus a widow's pension of 4/9 of their salary. This summary is necessarily brief and, as has been mentioned earlier in this chapter, skilled specialists are required to unravel the complexities of the Inland Revenue's latest practice notes. Many firms of such specialists publish guides aimed at individuals (for example, Kaye, annual).

The tax reliefs that arise in respect of approved schemes may more formally be summarized under the following heads:

- relief on contributions by employers;
- relief on contributions by employees;
- relief in respect of investment income;
- relief in respect of capital gains;
- relief in respect of lump sum benefits;
- treatment of pensions as earned income;
- relief in respect of VAT, etc.

We shall consider in detail tax reliefs under these seven different headings and in particular their apparent cost, that is, what would be the saving to the Exchequer if the particular relief were abolished and if the completely unrealistic assumption is made that, in the absence of relief, the pattern of pension arrangements would remain substantially unchanged. We shall comment on some of the likely consequences if the particular reliefs were abolished individually rather than being treated as a coherent whole.

Contributions by employers
Contributions to a pension fund by an employer are an expense to his business in the same way as is his payroll and other related costs and there is no obvious reason why they should not be entitled to relief on the same basis. In fact, contributions by an employer to a pension scheme that fails to obtain approval are nevertheless usually allowable as an expense of his business under the normal rules of Schedule D. Pensions paid directly to former employees (on a pay-as-you-go basis) and funds used to supplement pensions in course of payment by purchasing immediate annuities are similarly allowable.

If the tax relief on contributions to pension funds were abolished, employers might react in either of two ways. First, they might set aside internal reserves to meet their future pension liability, still obtaining relief; to prevent such a move to internal financing by abolishing even that tax relief would entail a fundamental amendment to company tax law, rather than to pension fund tax law, since it would prevent a company from obtaining tax relief on advanced provision for its specified future liabilities. It would not be difficult for companies to turn promises of pensions into contractual liabilities in these circumstances, although probably on a smaller scale than at present. Second, employers might react by increasing salaries in lieu of making contributions to the pension fund, and for the same contributions to be made explicitly by the employees. In such a case, pension funds would need to move towards a defined contribution basis, or at least a basis in which contributions were attributed to individual members, and away from the present system of aggregate funding.

The Inland Revenue's monitoring of contribuitions to approved schemes seems designed to ensure that contributions should not exceed certain limits or fluctuate unduly from year to year. As to the level of contributions, monitoring would seem unnecessary because competitive commercial pressures on employers will inhibit them from building up unnecessarily large funds in relation to the liabilities they are intended to cover. The Inland Revenue's concern about fluctuations also seems largely misplaced. There are far more extensive opportunities for a company to put aside money when profitability is high in other areas than pension provision and to obtain tax relief in respect of it. (Although admittedly these opportunities are fewer now than previously.) The possibility of abuse in the pension field is therefore insignificant in practice, except maybe in the case of small self-administered schemes. Small self-administered schemes have always been a law unto themselves in the field of pensions with additional requirements applicable and so it would not be exceptional for the Inland Revenue to continue monitoring their contributions, whilst ceasing to monitor the contributions of the remainder of the pensions industry. It is impossible to quantify the saving in money terms to the economy of such a move because the saving consists of a reduction of non-quantifiable clerical duties amongst such a multitude of schemes, but the saving must be considerable.

Contributions by employees
Tax relief on explicit employees' contributions does not confer any special advantage on the employers, nor is there any abuse that requires control by special regulation because the same result can be achieved whether or not part of the cost of financing a fund is met by employees' or employers' contributions. In recent years there has been a tendency for employees' contributions to be discontinued and for the whole cost of a scheme to be met by the employer. Clearly it would always be practicable and legitimate for an employee to sacrifice part of his salary and for the employer to apply that amount as a pension contribution without loss to the employee (whose net of tax income would be unaltered) and without gain to the employer (whose total net outlay on contributions and payroll would be unchanged), albeit that this would marginally affect the maximum non-taxable lump sums (and maximum two-thirds pensions). Similarly, if it were to be argued that there should be a limit to additional voluntary contributions by employees on the grounds that these in effect obtain a gross build-up of savings, then it can be counter-argued that the gross build-up could be achieved in any event by the employer contributing under a salary sacrifice arrangement.

At present, contributions paid by an employer on behalf of his employees are not usually taxed as any benefit in the hands of the employee. Under the current system of occupational pensions where most schemes are of defined benefit structure, it would in practice be very laborious to decide each individual's notional contribution and grossly unfair to assume it were the average funding rate. Simple calculations show that, under given assumptions, an average company lifetime funding rate of, for example, 15 per cent would represent a retrospective level contribution rate ranging from 10 per cent of salary for a 'low flyer' to nearly 35 per cent for a 'high flyer' (Wilkie, 1985; see Table 4.2, p. 62 above).

It is a purely theoretical exercise at present to consider what revenue would be raised by adding notional employee contributions to incomes and taxing them at the appropriate marginal rates. With the advent of portable pensions in which contributions are attributed to each specific individual, it becomes a somewhat more practical proposition. Under the present system, the Treasury is paying out large amounts of tax concessions on contributions and investment income, but its return from tax on pensions will not be reaching maturity for many years. A switch to taxing contributions and treating the ultimate benefit rather more favourably would reverse the position and in the short term ease the current burden of the Treasury. In practice, however, such a change would be likely to encourage employers to switch from external to internal funding and in the long term could produce a loss for the Exchequer.

According to the sixth Government Actuary's survey (Government Actuary, 1981), the total of employers' net payments and members' contributions for 1979 was £9,000m. Small self-administered schemes accounted for about 2 per cent of that figure. At that time, the basic rate of tax was 30 per cent and the highest personal marginal rate chargeable on income was 60 per cent. On the assumption that members of small self-administered schemes pay tax at the highest marginal rate and that all other occupational pension scheme members pay the basic rate, the cost of tax relief in 1979 was £2,754m. This figure is, if anything, likely to be an underestimate. Despite the vast increase in contributions in the intervening period, the official Inland Revenue estimate for 1983/84 is only £2,200m (Board of Inland Revenue, 1983).

Investment income
The cost of tax relief on pension fund investment income ought to be equal to the difference between the present tax charge (nil) and the charge under a system that is neutral between investment into pension funds and investment into alternative media. Here our conceptual problems really begin, since the current fiscal infrastructure of the UK is far from neutral, but which alternative medium should be chosen? Furthermore, there is the conceptual problem of whether to consider pensions as deferred pay or as savings out of income.

If pensions are considered as deferred pay (for the purposes of this exercise only, but this conforms with the current procedure of not taxing employee contributions) and are not directly attributable to individuals until payment at retirement, then they must be assumed to be taxable at some sort of rate that would be attributable to a company if they had invested in the identical assets in the absence of the pension fund trust. Companies are normally taxed at 30 per cent on capital gains and until the Finance Act 1984 were taxed at 52 per cent or at 40 per cent on investment income, depending on the size and tax status of the company and in the absence of any artificial means to reduce taxation. Available statistics on pension funds do not differentiate between investment income and capital gains since the distinction is a purely artificial one for the purposes of taxation and is therefore not applicable to pension funds at present. The figure given in the sixth Government Actuary's survey (Government Actuary, 1981) for investment income (including capital gains) is £4,140m for pension schemes; tax on this at 30 per cent would have amounted to £1,245m. In view of the above comments this would probably be a lower bound.

If, however, as is more likely in the absence of special tax concessions, funds are no longer invested in external assets, tax relief on the investment return on invested funds does no more than place these funds in a similar position to money invested in the company itself, with pension liabilities provided for in the company's accounts by way of book reserve. In this latter case the money could be invested in plant or other business assets of the company and could qualify for tax allowance on the appropriate scale; as long as the return secured from the additional investment is itself put back into the company, relief from tax can be achieved. Book reserves are far more common in countries other than the UK and have been described in detail by the Occupational Pensions Board (1982) in an appendix to its report on the security for the rights and expectations of scheme members.

It should be noted that, in suitable circumstances, an unfunded scheme or one funded by means of a book reserve in the company's accounts that qualifies for relief on allocations to it would be more advantageous financially for the company than a properly approved externally funded scheme (Langham and Sparks, 1976). Of course this method of pension provision by book reserves suffers from the obvious disadvantage of concentration of investment into one asset. Some form of credit insurance would appear to be necessary to safeguard the pension fund since, whilst the book reserve method provides the company with a flow of money from a captive investor (the pension fund), it does nothing to separate the pension fund from the fortunes of the company. It is also unlikely that investments that are suitable for the company will fall due with convenient timing to pay any appropriate pension benefits.

If pensions are treated as savings out of taxed income, then the investment income must be considered as directly attributable to individuals at their highest marginal rate. In practice this is not a viable possibility unless portable pensions become universal, and even then most of the money would probably be invested via life funds or unit trusts because of the more favourable tax implications. The current government intends to reduce company taxation to 35 per cent by the tax year 1985/86, but has not gone on record regarding any specific lowering of higher personal tax rates (The Chancellor, 1984). A tax rate of 30–35 per cent would therefore be the most appropriate to use in this case and the cost bounds would be between £1,245m and £1,453m as above.

Capital gains

Capital gains are treated in an exactly similar fashion to investment income under the present tax regime for pension funds. Similar considerations therefore apply to possible changes. It would be necessary either to attribute capital gains to individual members, or to the company, or to attribute a specific average tax rate that might be deemed to apply to the whole pension fund. However, since authorized unit trusts are at present relieved from paying tax on capital gains, the likely response of pension funds would be to invest through the medium of an authorized unit trust, thus deferring any payment of gains tax until the fund realized assets. Further, the present system of indexation allowance would give the advantage of, in effect, getting relief on losses calculated on an indexed basis, which are not individually allowable at present.

Lump-sum benefits

Although in general pension funds received only brief treatment in the Wilson Committee report (1980) and were not the subject of detailed tax recommendations, a complete section was none the less devoted to lump sums.

> If this view of pensions as deferred pay is accepted, the chief anomaly lies in the tax-free nature of the lump sum. It is difficult to justify this on logical grounds. But it has become such an accepted part of the present arrangements that its removal could not be regarded as equitable in its effects. It should also be noted that the relief of tax on the income and capital gains of pension funds contrasts markedly with the tax treatment of an individual who saves privately for his retirement instead of through institutional channels. There is no particular logic in the Inland Revenue limitations on the size of pensions, relative to pay, that can be allowed to qualify for the reliefs discussed above.

Under whichever conceptual framework one considers pensions, exempting lump sums is anomalous. Payments of lump sums on retirement in 1979 were £950m (Government Actuary, 1981); tax at 30 per cent would have been £285m. However, immunity from tax on lump-sum retirement benefits no longer depends solely on trust law but has been enshrined in legislation; reference should be made to section 14 of the Finance Act of 1973 as follows:

(1) A lump sum paid to a person on his retirement from an office or employment shall not be chargeable to income tax under Schedule E if –

(a) it is paid in pursuance of any such scheme or fund as is described in subsections (1) and (2) of section 221 of the Taxes Act or in section 24 (1) of the Finance Act 1970 and is neither a payment of compensation to which section 73 of the Finance Act 1972 applies nor a payment chargeable to tax under paragraph 9 of Schedule 3 to the Finance Act 1971;

or

(b) it is a benefit paid in pursuance of any such scheme or agreement referred to in section 220 of the Taxes Act or in pursuance of a retirement benefits scheme within the meaning of section 25 of the Finance Act 1970 and the person to whom it is paid was chargeable to tax under section 220 of the Taxes Act or section 23 of the Finance Act 1970 in respect of sums paid, or treated as paid, with a view to the provision of the benefit.

(2) This section shall be deemed always to have an effect.

If it were decided to amend the Finance Act 1973, and to tax lump sums, it might be felt desirable to introduce transitional arrangements so as not to penalize the expectations of current pension scheme members who are nearing retirement and who have made plans that take into account the receipt of the tax-free lump sum.

Further, if lump sums were treated wholly as taxable income in the year of receipt, some people would find themselves paying at higher tax rates in that year. It would therefore be desirable either to tax lump sums on a 'top-slicing' basis – for example wholly at the highest marginal rate on other income in the year of receipt or in the first full year of retirement – or to allow the lump sum to be taken in instalments over a small number of years as the individual desires, being added to his income nevertheless in any year an instalment was received.

Pensions in payment
If pensions are treated as deferred pay, with contributions being exempt from tax, pensions in payment should be treated as earned income. Such is the case at present. There is therefore no tax cost to the Exchequer on the pensions in payment.

If pensions were to be treated as financed by savings out of taxed income then contributions would be taxable and pensions should be treated as a return of those savings. Provided, therefore, that the investment income has been taxed throughout, pensions should be tax free. In 1979 occupational pensions in payment amounted to nearly £3,500m. If it is assumed that the basic state pension used up any available reliefs, the tax payable (which it would no longer be) would have been just under £1,200m. This should be compared with the current cost of not treating contributions as a tax exempt, which is just over double that figure. Complicated systems can be envisaged such as treating pensions as analogous to annuities and introducing the concept of capital elements (as has been done by the Inland Revenue; Board of Inland Revenue, 1983). This introduces unnecessary complications, as such schemes are themselves far from fiscally neutral.

Value added tax
Tax exemptions to pension funds have been restricted in only three fields – profits arising from property development, profits arising from trade, and VAT. The first two topics are in general beyond the scope of this chapter, belonging more to the province of accountants than actuaries. The third topic requires special mention because of the particularly capricious way in which it operates with regard to pension funds. The Pensions Research Accounting Group (PRAG, 1985) has produced the most complete analysis to date of the way in which pension funds become liable for VAT and what can be done to mitigate its effects.

Taxes on pension funds – current and proposed

Case VI tax on insured pension funds
It is often forgotten when discussing tax reliefs and pension funds that pension funds held by insurance companies are subject to Case VI tax. In the past it was unusual for pension funds to produce a Case VI profit and this aspect of taxation could have been ignored with impunity. There is now far more active management of the assumptions used when valuing the funds of life offices and it can result in large spurious profits arising in the pension fund with consequent large tax assessments. This is a particularly difficult problem for funds writing unit-linked business.

Proposed taxation of pension fund surpluses
Speaking in the House of Commons on 18 March 1986 when presenting his Budget, the Chancellor of the Exchequer, Nigel Lawson, said:

> The Social Security Bill now before Parliament proposes important and far reaching changes in pension provision, notably by encouraging the growth of personal pensions. Those changes, to which the Government attach the highest importance, have been warmly welcomed both for the greater freedom they will give to existing pension scheme members and for the new scope they will offer to the millions of working people who are not in an occupational pension scheme. In the light of these changes, I intend later this year to publish detailed proposals designed to give personal pensions the same

favourable tax treatment as is currently enjoyed by retirement annuities. Publication of these proposals will enable there to be the widest possible consultation prior to legislation in next year's Finance Bill. Meanwhile, I can assure the House that, as I made clear last year, I have no plans to change that favourable tax treatment.

But I do need to deal with the growing problem of the rules governing pension fund surpluses. The dramatic improvement in the financial climate compared with a decade ago, most notably as a result of the sharp fall in inflation, has seen a number of pension funds become heavily over-funded. This presents a double problem, both aspects of which the Inland Revenue is at present having to deal with through the exercise of its discretionary powers. In the first place, excessive surpluses, even if they arise unintentionally, represent the misuse of a tax privilege which was intended to assist the provision of pensions and for no other purpose. So the Inland Revenue requires from time to time that surpluses be diminished. But at the same time, the Revenue feels obliged to turn down many of the increasing number of requests from companies which, often for good reasons, wish to take refunds from their pension funds into the company itself. The absence of clear rules on how surpluses should and may be dealt with, and the consequent reliance that has to be placed on the exercise by the Inland Revenue of its discretion, have created considerable uncertainty and have unnecessarily constrained trustees' freedom of action. I therefore propose to replace the discretionary arrangements with clear and objective statutory provisions.

In future, the amount of any surplus in a fund will be determined for tax purposes in accordance with published guidelines based on a secure funding method and prudent actuarial assumptions as advised by the Government Actuary. Where a surplus is 5% or less of the total liabilities, no action will need to be taken. Where it is higher than that, action will be required to eliminate the excess. It will be entirely a matter for the trustees and employers to decide whether the reduction is to be achieved by increasing benefits, or by reducing contributions, or by making a refund to the company. If, and only if, they choose to make a refund, the employer will be liable to tax at a rate of 40% of the amount refunded so as broadly to recover the tax relief previously given. The effect of these new arrangements is likely to be a yield of £70m in 1986–87, and £120m in 1987–88. (The Chancellor, 1986)

These Budget proposals had the twofold objective of avoiding the accumulation of excessive assets in a tax-free fund and at the same time allowing greater freedom for surplus to be returned to an employer in certain circumstances. In particular, when surplus is returned to an employer he will automatically suffer corporation tax on it and not be able to set the surplus against trading losses. It was the practice of setting surplus against trading losses that was one of several aspects of concern to the Inland Revenue, providing – as it did in most of the publicized cases – an interest-free loan from the Revenue to the employer. If any surplus is retained by a company over and above that permitted by the Inland Revenue, it may result – where, for example, the trust deed prevents the return of any part of the pension fund to the employer – in the partial disapproval of the fund. In practice this will mean that a proportion of the fund's investment income will be taxable, as the fund is likely to be enjoying a 'contribution holiday'.

The Budget proposals raised many issues that at the time of writing this book have still to be finalized by the authorities. The prime question raised must be: what is surplus? The simplistic answer is the excess of assets over liabilities. There are, however, many different ways of valuing the assets and the liabilities as well as the combinations of both – albeit some combinations are more appropriate than others. It must always be remembered that surplus is a function of the valuation assumptions. Profit is a result of investing a higher contribution than the subsequent experience merits. Apart from saying it is independent of the valuation basis, it is difficult to say exactly what it is. To be able to say precisely what is the present value of potential profit it would be necessary to have precise knowledge of future experience. It takes an actuary many years of training to understand the concept of surplus. It might be appropriate at this point to question whether the government definition of surplus is appropriate. Much discussion is currently taking place within the actuarial profession on just that question.

Other related questions are:

- To whom does it belong?
- How much is it?
- Why don't we know about it?
- Why were the professionals allowed to hide the details of it for so long?

Unfortunately, owing to space constraints, these questions cannot be answered here. The interested reader is referred to a forthcoming publication on the subject by the Pensions Research Accounting Group, to be entitled *Pension Fund Surpluses*. At the date of writing this book their Working Party has not reached a working draft of its conclusion, but it is hoped that they will publish a report early in 1987 (PRAG, 1987).

Official Inland Revenue estimates

In September 1983 the Board of the Inland Revenue published a paper entitled *Cost of Tax Reliefs for Pension Schemes: Appropriate Statistical*

Approach. The object of the exercise was simply to produce a cost for the existing reliefs, on an *ex ante* basis. The report stressed that it would review several regimes that might apply if reliefs were to be withdrawn, but this did not imply that the reliefs would be withdrawn and that any results would therefore provide benchmarks for the costing and not definitive results. Despite the many caveats in the paper, the results were widely reported in the press out of context and without any reservations. This is particularly unfortunate because, although the paper exhibits much academic merit, its results, when presented in an unqualified form, have very little practical value. The alteration of any aspects of the existing tax reliefs would almost certainly result in a change in the pattern of investment into pension funds, thereby destroying the *ex ante* assumption. In particular, it cannot be assumed that the figures for the cost of tax relief would actually arise if tax were imposed and, because of the *ex ante* condition, no assumptions have been made as to the number of pension funds that would cease to exist if pension fund tax relief were withdrawn.

The estimates for the cost of specific reliefs include implicit assumptions that are not always obvious or unquestionable. For example, the figure given for the cost of tax relief on employee's contributions makes the implicit assumption that the employee's contribution is a fringe benefit of his employment. Following this assumption is the assumption that employees earning less than £8,500 would be exempt from tax by Inland Revenue concession. (This assumption is questionable since certain travel perks are not exempt and hence one cannot automatically assume that all fringe benefits are automatically exempt.) The Inland Revenue has then used its survey of personal incomes (Board of Inland Revenue, 1979) as a data base to derive a composite rate of tax that would be paid by employees on their contributions. The rate used is not stated in any official document, but is 25 per cent. When considering the cost to employees in respect of their employers' notionally attributed contributions, the paper takes into account only private sector funded schemes and completely excludes the taxing of public sector schemes. The composite rate derived is 31 per cent.

Conclusions

There is no specific answer to the question 'What do pension fund tax reliefs cost?' It all depends on what assumptions are made and little would be achieved by totting up all the individual figures calculated earlier. The size of the individual figures does, however, provide food for thought, in particular as regards the timing of tax reliefs.

The current system, as has been shown above, defers tax by giving relief on contributions rather than on pensions in payment. Hitherto this aspect appears to have escaped considered political scrutiny. Any political commentary seems to have concentrated on specific figures provided by the Inland Revenue, which take no account of the changes that would take place in pension funds if a different tax regime were imposed; nor do they take account of intergenerational differences. In most cases where figures have been quoted, the user has merely taken the difference between the costs of removing tax from pensions in payment and imposing it on contributions. This is a large positive figure, since, as most schemes are not yet mature, there are not yet many pensions in payment. As time progresses and more current members become pensioners, the position may stabilize and even reverse in certain circumstances.

The taxation of emerging benefits in pension form means that the Inland Revenue appears eventually to recover the tax that has been deferred from the contributions or from the investment return that has gone to build up the resources of the fund. Although there is deferment of tax, it will depend on the tax circumstances of the company and/or individual whether there is any long-term advantage in practice. Certainly, much of the detailed scrutiny by the Inland Revenue to prevent tax avoidance would appear unnecessary and even, in some cases, counter-productive when one considers the opportunity cost of the specialist time utilized by both the Inland Revenue and the involved professionals. In addition, there is often a lack of incentive to overfund because of competitive pricing pressures.

The administration of pension schemes could be greatly simplified both for the Inland Revenue and for pension practitioners if the privileged tax position for pension funds were to disappear by any of the changes outlined above. The detailed work of scrutiny of complex documents and control of benefits would fall away, although detailed monitoring might still be required in particular areas where the Inland Revenue may be most concerned about potential abuse, that is, controlling directors.

Lump sums payable on retirement represent the obvious place where a real taxation advantage is available. For many years the level of such tax-free lump sums has been restricted to a maximum in broad terms of one and a half years' pay – comparable to the cash retirement benefit under the Civil Service scheme. Any change towards greater equality of tax treatment of savings must require that steps should be taken to levy tax on lump-sum benefits.

Legislative requirements relating to preservation would continue to necessitate the control of pension schemes by the Occupational Pensions Board and the inclusion of suitable conditions in the documentation for schemes. Schemes contracted out of the state pension scheme would still be subject to more detailed control by the Occupational Pensions Board and would need more complicated provisions in their documentation, but (as at present) these would concern the minimum standards to be achieved and would have no tax implications.

References

Bacon, F. W., Benjamin, B. and Elphinstone, M. D. W. (1954a), 'The growth of pension rights and their impact on the national economy', *Journal of the Institute of Actuaries*, vol. 80, pp. 141–202

Bacon, F. W., Benjamin, B. and Elphinstone, M. D. W. (1954b), 'Opening address', *Transactions of the Faculty of Actuaries*, vol. 22, p. 352

Board of Inland Revenue (1979), *Survey of Personal Incomes*, London: HMSO

Board of Inland Revenue (1983), *Cost of Tax Reliefs for Pension Schemes: Appropriate Statistical Approach*, London: HMSO

The Chancellor (1984), 1984 Budget Statement, *Hansard*

The Chancellor (1986), 1986 Budget Statement *Hansard*

Government Actuary (1981), Occupational Pension Schemes 1979, Sixth Survey by the Government Actuary, London: HMSO

Kaye A. M. (annual), *Tax Planning Ideas for Individuals*, London: Leigh, Carr and Partners

Kipling, M. R. (1985), 'Small self-administered schemes in practice', *Journal of the Institute of Actuaries' Students Society*, vol. 28, p. 53

Langham, F. R. and Sparks, J. D. (1976), 'Tax treatment of pension provisions', *Journal of the Institute of Actuaries*, vol. 103, p. 323

Meade, J. E. (chairman) (1978), *The Structure and Reform of Direct Taxation*, London: Allen & Unwin

Occupational Pensions Board (1982), *Greater Security for the Rights and Expectations of Members of Occupational Pension Schemes*, Cmnd 8649, London: HMSO

PRAG (1985), *Pension Funds and Value Added Tax: Law Practice and Reform*, Chichester, W. Sussex: Pensions Research Accounting Group

PRAG (1987), *Pension Fund Surpluses*, Chichester, W. Sussex: Pensions Research Accounting Group

Wilkie, A. D. (1985), 'Some experiments with pensions accrual', *Journal of the Institute of Actuaries*, vol. 112, p. 61

Wilson Committee (1980), *Report of the Committee to Review the Functioning of Financial Institutions*, Cmnd 7937, London: HMSO

8 The Demographic Outlook

BERNARD BENJAMIN

Introduction

Over the past 150 years there have been profound changes in the sex and age structure of the United Kingdom, as, first, a rise in the size of birth generations made the age structure very young as compared with a stationary population supported by constant births and experiencing constant mortality and, later, a fall in the annual numbers of births produced an ageing of the population structure. This ageing has been accentuated by steady mortality improvement, more so for women than for men. Small contributions to the ageing of the population structure were made by the virtual cessation of any substantial emigration of young men after the world economic depression of 1930 and by the war losses of young men during 1914–1918 and during 1939–1945. All countries of advanced or advancing economic development have suffered these changes and, to the extent that many have in their economic development leapfrogged over the relatively slower industrial revolution of the United Kingdom, their changes in age structure have been more rapid and, in their economic implications, more violent. It is not the purpose of this chapter to make international demographic comparisions, but it is important to remember that any economic problems arising from the growth in the dimensions of elderly dependency are common to all developed countries and will sooner or later confront the developing countries.

Changes in population structure

Table 8.1 shows the structure of the United Kingdom at the population censuses of 1871, 1901 and 1981. The changes are shown more dramatically by the population pyramids of Figure 8.1. It can be seen that in 1871, after many decades of a rising flow of births, the population structure of the United Kingdom was extremely youthful. With the prevailing mortality rates, a stationary population deriving from a constant size of generations of birth would have 26.36 per cent of persons under age 15 and 8.38 per cent over age 65. In fact the respective percentages were 36.12 and 4.87. The actual population pyramid of

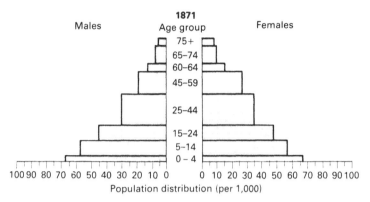

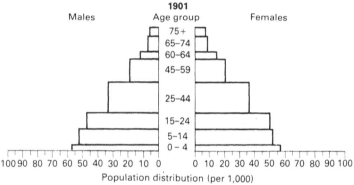

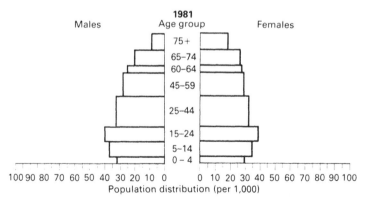

Figure 8.1   *The population distribution of the*
United Kingdom in 1871, 1901, 1981

Source: Table 8.1

Note: The areas are proportional to the population per 1,000 in the age groups; thus, if
the age group is wider, the base of the rectangle is correspondingly narrower.

Table 8.1 *The population of the*
United Kingdom[a] *in 1871, 1901, 1981 ('000s)*

	1871		1901		1981	
	No.	%[b]	No.	%[b]	No.	%[b]
Males						
0–4	1,850	6.74	2,190	5.73	1,766	3.14
5–14	3,124	11.39	4,024	10.52	4,165	7.40
15–24	2,460	8.97	3,636	9.51	4,510	8.02
25–44	3,347	12.20	5,153	13.48	7,419	13.19
45–59	1,560	5.69	2,214	5.79	4,757	8.46
60–64	363	1.32	489	1.28	1,398	2.48
65–74	435	1.58	565	1.48	2,267	4.03
75+	169	0.62	219	0.57	1,062	1.89
Total	13,308	48.51	18,490	48.36	27,344	48.61
Females						
0–4	1,841	6.71	2,190	5.73	1,675	2.98
5–14	3,094	11.28	4,016	10.50	3,954	7.03
15–24	2,611	9.52	3,865	10.11	4,347	7.73
25–44	3,735	13.61	5,647	14.77	7,322	13.01
45–59	1,701	6.20	2,424	6.34	4,875	8.67
60–64	412	1.50	577	1.51	1,583	2.81
65–74	509	1.86	712	1.86	2,948	5.24
75+	221	0.81	312	0.82	2,204	3.92
Total	14,124	51.49	19,743	51.64	28,908	51.39
Grand Total	27,432	100.00	38,233	100.00	56,252	100.00

Notes:
[a] United kingdom includes England, Wales, Scotland and Northern Ireland.
[b] Percentage is percentage of grand total.

Sources: 1871, 1901 – Registrar General, Census figures; 1981 – mid-year as adopted by Government Actuary for projection purposes.

Figure 8.1 for 1871 has a wide base and a rapid thinning down to a narrow top. In 1901, after the birth flow (annual numbers of births) had been declining slowly, the structure had become slightly less youthful; the comparable percentages were 32.48 and 4.73. The change in the shape of the population pyramid is hardly noticeable. But soon after the turn of the century the birth rate fell sharply, partly as a consequence of an equally sharp decline in foetal and infant mortality so that there was less birth wastage to overcome to produce a family of a desired size, and partly as a consequence of the deterioration in economic conditions (interrupted by the war of 1914–18 but culminating in the general strike of 1926 and the world depression of the early 1930s). Since legislation against child labour and the introduction of compulsory primary education in the latter part of the nineteenth century, children had ceased to represent an addition to the economic strength of the family but had, on the contrary, become an economic liability.

Smaller families became the order of the day. It has been stressed that 'in the face of lack of access to contraceptives, the change in public attitude, though not necessarily coherent or articulate, must have been resolute' (Glass, 1976). The base of the population pyramid became rapidly narrower as successive generations became progressively smaller. A bulge moved up the population pyramid and by 1981 had disappeared. Successive generations continued to decline in size, if less rapidly, until 1955 when there was a recovery lasting but ten years. In the 1981 population pyramid this can be seen as a bulge at ages 15–24. After 1965 fertility continued its downward trend, as can be seen in the 1981 pyramid by the narrowing towards the base. The age structure is no longer youthful; it is very close to that of a stationary population. The percentage of the population under 15 in 1981 was 20.55; the percentage of those over 65 was 15.08; these values compare with 20.08 and 16.06 for a stationary population.

Before looking forward to the likely or possible changes in the age structure in the future it may be useful to examine in more detail the factors operating to produce these past changes.

Fertility changes

It has to be stressed that hitherto the most important factor determining the proportion of older people in the population has been not the improvement in the capacity to survive to pension age (though this is by no means negligible) but the changes in the sizes of the generations available *to* survive; that is, changes in fertility.

If we concern ourselves only with changes in this century, we note that the very sharp decline in the annual number of births in the United Kingdom after 1910 meant that successive generations were progressively smaller so that, as the older generations advanced to pension age, they were replaced by smaller numbers. The *proportion* of younger people in the total population decreased and correspondingly the proportion of older people increased. The change in the proportion aged 65 and over between 1911 and 1951 is analysed in Table 8.2 (Benjamin, 1964). It can be seen that until 1951 the total changes in fertility (including the abnormally high fertility prior to 1911) made an overwhelming contribution to the increase in the proportion of the elderly in the population.

The change in the proportion aged 65 and over from 10.9 per cent in

Table 8.2 *Change in the proportion of the elderly in the UK population, 1911–1951*

	%
Aged 65 and over in 1911	5.2
Increases due to	
abnormal age structure in 1911*	+ 2.5
fall in fertility alone since 1911	+ 2.0
fall in mortality alone since 1911	+ 1.2
Aged 65 and over in 1951	10.9

* The change in the proportion that would have occurred had both fertility and mortality remained unchanged.

1951 to 15.1 per cent in 1981 is analysed in Table 8.3. It will be seen that mortality improvement now makes a larger contribution to the growth in the proportion of the elderly but that the predominant contribution still comes from the larger generations of births, especially prior to 1911 but even after that year, which have not been subsequently reproduced.

Table 8.3 *Change in the proportion of the elderly in the UK population, 1951–1981*

	%
Aged 65 and over in 1951	10.9
Increases due to	
earlier high fertility and ageing of youthful age structure	+ 2.7
fall in fertility alone since 1951	+ 0.2
fall in mortality alone since 1951	+ 1.6
immigration	− 0.3
Aged 65 and over in 1981	15.1

There was a minor recovery of fertility in those couples who married just before and during the war of 1939–45 and in the years up to the mid-1960s. Completed family size, either actual or projected from current fertility trends, has been below population replacement level for marriages in the years since about 1970 and there is no prospect of an early recovery or of any arrest to the progressive ageing of the population structure arising from this cause (Benjamin, 1981).

Mortality changes

Meanwhile the ageing of the population structure is being further advanced by mortality improvement. The prospects for mortality improvement were reviewed in 1979 for the purpose of projecting numbers of pensioners (Benjamin and Overton, 1981) and there has not been any significant change to warrant a fresh review.

At that time three mortality projections were made, based on pessimistic, medium and extreme assumptions.

Projection 1 – pessimistic assumptions   For this projection it was assumed that there would be little further improvement in mortality, except at ages below 15 where a somewhat slower rate of improvement than indicated by recent trends was extended into the future. At ages of 15 and above it was assumed that the rate of improvement would quickly taper off to zero. It was not considered that these assumptions would be likely to be realized in the event, but they provided a lower bound to the widening spectrum of uncertainty in the future.

Projection 2 – medium projection   This was based on the assumption that the trend of age-specific mortality rates for the United Kingdom in the past two decades had at all ages been approximately such that each year's rate bore a constant ratio to the rate for the previous year, i.e. that for any particular sex/age group the logarithms of the death rates followed a linear trend with time.

These trends were established:

(a)   by plotting the death rates on logarithmic paper and fitting a straight line to the plotted points by visual inspection and judgement;
(b)   by a least-squares linear fit using an appropriate computer program applied first to the whole series of death rates and subsequently to more recent years only.

On the basis of a comparison of the results of these three fits, which were reasonably close, a judgement was made as to the likely improvement rates that should be applied to the latest available death rates (i.e. those for 1977) to project rates for the year 2017. These improvement rates, shown as percentage reductions from the 1977 levels, are shown in Table 8.4. The improvement rates concurrently assumed by the Government Actuary for national population projections purposes are shown in Table 8.4 as 'GAD 1977'.

The age-specific mortality rates in 2017 emerging from this projection have been put in the form of an abridged life table as in Table 8.5.

Projection 3 – extreme assumptions   Dealing first with males, the

Table 8.4 *Percentage reduction in mortality rates over a forty-year period*

	Males		Females	
Age	GAD 1977	Projection 2 1977	GAD 1977	Projection 2 1977
Infant mortality	25	70	25	70
1–4	25	70	25	70
5–9	25	65	25	65
10–14	25	62	25	65
15–19	0	27	0	43
20–24	12	30	14	32
25–29	17 }	45	25 }	50
30–34	10 }		25 }	
35–39	10 }	40	10 }	42
40–44	0 }		1 }	
45–49	0 }	17	0 }	19
50–54	0 }		0 }	
55–59	6 }	21	3 }	14
60–64	15 }		10 }	
65–69	20 }	26	14 }	26
70–74	17 }		16 }	
75–79	15 }	22	17 }	29
80–84	13 }		18 }	
85–89	13	15	19	20

following extreme assumptions were made about *possible* changes over the next forty years:

- that deaths from congenital malformations and diseases of early infancy would be reduced to one-third of their present numbers, the lives saved being assumed to die over all ages in proportion to the total deaths of the life table as finally modified in relation to the specified causes;
- that, as a result of a drastic reduction in the level of cigarette smoking, some 90 per cent of all deaths from cancer of the lung and bronchus and one-third of all deaths from ischaemic heart disease prior to age 65 (the proportions currently attributable to smoking) would be saved and proportionately redistributed by age in the finally modified life table;
- that, as a result of improved therapy and maintenance, the whole of the remaining deaths from ischaemic heart disease, cerebrovascular lesions and other heart and circulatory diseases would be deferred by ten years;

Table 8.5   *Abridged life tables based on projection 2 as at 2017*

		Males			Females	
Age (x)	l_x	$\mathring{e}_x$	T_x	l_x	$\mathring{e}_x$	T_x
0	10,000	74.4	743,774	10,000	80.4	803,758
5	9,948	69.8	693,904	9,958	75.7	753,863
10	9,942	64.8	644,179	9,954	70.7	704,083
15	9,936	59.8	594,484	9,951	65.8	654,320
20	9,906	55.0	544,879	9,942	60.8	604,587
25	9,874	50.2	495,429	9,928	55.9	554,912
30	9,851	45.3	446,116	9,917	51.0	505,299
35	9,824	40.4	396,928	9,901	46.0	455,754
40	9,782	35.6	347,913	9,872	41.2	406,321
45	9,710	30.8	299,183	9,821	36.4	357,088
50	9,515	26.4	251,120	9,695	31.8	308,298
55	9,190	22.2	204,357	9,500	27.4	260,310
60	8,695	18.4	159,644	9,192	23.2	213,580
65	7,921	14.9	118,104	8,725	19.3	168,787
70	6,881	11.8	81,099	8,151	15.5	126,597
75	5,514	9.1	50,111	7,239	12.2	88,122
80	3,857	6.9	26,683	6,030	9.1	54,949
85 +	2,266	5.0	11,375	4,401	6.6	28,871

l_x = No. attaining exact age x.
$\mathring{e}_x$ = Expectation of life at age x.
I_x = Total no. living at ages x and over.

- that, as a result of environmental improvements including the avoidance of cigarette smoking, all deaths from bronchitis, emphysema and asthma would be prevented and redistributed;
- that all deaths from cancer, other than cancer of the lung, would be avoided by the introduction of new therapy, these deaths being redistributed to other causes;
- that the risk of death by accident would remain unchanged, some environmental improvements being balanced by the appearance of new hazards (excluding nuclear hazards);
- that the small residuum of deaths from tuberculosis and diabetes would remain as at present;
- that all deaths in the unspecified cause group would be deferred for ten years, except those in the first year of life, which were assumed to be prevented.

The total result of this redistribution of deaths is shown in Table 8.6 in life-table form.

Modifications to the relative risks of dying from different diseases

Table 8.6   *Life table according to projection 3*

Age (x)	Males l_x	$\mathring{e}_x$	T_x	Females l_x	$\mathring{e}_x$	T_x
0	10,000	81.3	812,564	10,000	87.1	870,949
5	9,944	76.7	762,704	9,962	82.4	821,044
10	9,935	71.8	713,006	9,955	77.5	791,281
15	9,925	66.8	663,356	9,947	72.5	721,496
20	9,900	62.0	613,793	9,934	67.6	671,793
25	9,870	57.2	564,368	9,924	62.7	622,148
30	9,833	52.4	515,110	9,905	57.8	572,578
35	9,791	49.6	466,050	9,883	52.9	523,105
40	9,728	42.9	417,252	9,845	48.1	473,784
45	9,664	38.2	368,772	9,807	43.3	424,655
50	9,584	33.5	320,652	9,760	38.5	375,737
55	9,486	28.8	272,977	9,710	33.7	327,062
60	9,252	24.4	226,132	9,600	29.0	278,787
65	8,893	20.3	180,769	9,441	24.5	231,184
70	8,365	16.5	137,624	9,194	20.1	184,596
75	7,587	12.9	97,744	8,800	15.9	139,611
80	6,283	10.0	63,069	8,059	12.1	97,463
85	4,673	7.6	35,679	6,881	8.7	60,113
90	2,916	5.7	16,706	5,086	5.9	30,195
95	1,478	3.9	5,721	3,088	3.2	9,760
100	405	2.5	1,013	408	2.5	1,020
105	0	–	0	0	–	0

would normally require the use of multiple decrement methods to allow for the simultaneous operation of competing risks from the various diseases, but in view of the very arbitrary assumptions of projection 3 refined methods were regarded as out of place.

A special word must be said about the mortality of females. The current mortality trend for females is a deteriorating one at middle ages. Women have been copying the smoking habits of men sufficiently long to begin to incur the penalty of rising death rates from lung cancer and ischaemic heart disease. So, for females, things may be going to get worse before they can get better (this has been implicitly taken into account in projection 2). Nevertheless, having drawn attention to this possibility, it was considered acceptable to apply the same projection 3 assumptions as for men. The percentage reductions in mortality rates over forty years implied by projection 3 are shown in Table 8.7 for comparison with Tables 8.4 and 8.6.

The consequences for population structure

In order to illustrate the effect of the possible trends in fertility and mortality, four population projections have been carried out (using the Government Actuary's computer program) as detailed below:

Demographic projection	Assumptions	
	Fertility	*Mortality*
A	TPFR rising fairly quickly to 2.1	Projection 2
B	TPFR rising fairly quickly to 2.1	Projection 3
C	TPFR rising but levelled off at 2.0	Projection 2
D	TPFR rising but levelled off at 2.0	Projection 3

TPFR = total period fertility rate

Of the four projections, projection A represents the smallest increase in the proportion of elderly persons and projection D represents the largest.

Table 8.8 shows the numbers and percentages in various age/sex groups in the actual UK population for 1981 and as projected to 2021 by population projections A and D. Population pyramids for projections A and D are shown in Figure 8.2. It will be seen that, on the basis of projection A, the proportion in the child population (for this purpose 0–14) will fall from its 1981 value of 20.55 per cent to 19.63 per cent and the proportion in the national insurance pension age group (60+ for women and 65+ for men) will increase from 17.89 per cent in 1981 to 20.04 per cent. On projection D, the fall in the child proportion will be greater – to 17.57 per cent; and the rise in the pensioner proportion will be much greater – to 25.44 per cent. It is important to note that on the basis of these projections the rise in pensioner dependency will be partly offset by a fall in child dependency. Looked at from an individual point of view this means that married couples could maintain their level of living with lower net incomes, if, for example, they had to pay higher contributions for prospective pensions.

Changes in dependency

What are the overall effects of changes in population structure since the beginning of the century and those likely in the future on the proportion

Table 8.7 *Percentage reduction in mortality rates
over a forty-year period: projection 3*

Age	Males	Females
0 – 4	72	75
5 – 9	48	43
10 – 14	38	23
15 – 19	41	27
20 – 24	38	51
25 – 29	12	20
30 – 34	19	33
35 – 39	15	29
40 – 44	51	60
45 – 49	67	71
50 – 54	77	80
55 – 59	67	71
60 – 64	68	73
65 – 69	70	73
70 – 74	70	74
75 – 79	62	70
80 – 84	61	69
85 – 89	55	61
90 – 94	47	54
95 – 99	25	– 5
100 – 104	66	66

of the population who represent the dependent groups? For convenience we take these groups as:

● children under age 15
● non-gainfully occupied women
● persons who have attained the current minimum retirement ages (for national insurance purposes) of 6.3.

The balance may be regarded as indicative of the supporting section of the population, though it should be borne in mind that, at the present time and posssibly for some time in the future, more than one-tenth of this balance are themselves dependants as members of the unemployed. We refer to this reservation again later. Changes in the numbers and proportions in these groups are shown in Table 8.9.

It might be argued immediately that:

(a) these rations are not true measures of dependency; and
(b) the ratios are so incomparable in real economic terms that they

Table 8.8 *The population distribution of the United Kingdom at Census 1981 and as projected to 2021 on various assumptions*

Sex	Age	1981		Projection A 2021		Projection B		Projection C		Projection D	
		No.	%	No.	%	No.	%	No.	%	No.	%
Males	0–14	5,931	10.54	6,028	10.10	6,026	9.39	5,723	9.74	5,720	9.04
	15–24	4,510	8.02	3,979	6.67	3,977	6.19	3,829	6.52	3,827	6.05
	25–44	7,419	13.19	7,508	12.58	7,491	11.67	7,490	12.74	7,474	11.81
	45–64	6,155	10.94	7,447	12.47	7,748	12.07	7,446	12.67	7,747	12.24
	65–74	2,267	4.03	2,586	4.33	3,157	4.92	2,586	4.40	3,156	4.99
	75+	1,062	1.89	1,615	2.71	2,990	4.66	1,615	2.75	2,992	4.73
Total		27,344	48.61	29,163	48.86	31,389	48.90	28,689	48.82	30,916	48.86
Females	0–14	5,629	10.01	5,689	9.53	5,687	8.86	5,399	9.19	5,398	8.53
	15–24	4,347	7.73	3,785	6.34	3,784	5.89	3,645	6.20	3,643	5.76
	25–44	7,322	13.01	7,374	12.35	7,365	11.47	7,356	12.52	7,348	11.61
	45–59	4,875	8.67	5,919	9.92	6,025	9.39	5,919	10.07	6,023	9.52
	60–64	1,583	2.81	1,817	3.04	1,926	3.00	1,817	3.09	1,928	3.05
	65–74	2,948	5.24	3,117	5.22	3,521	5.48	3,117	5.30	3,520	5.56
	75+	2,204	3.92	2,829	4.74	4,497	7.01	2,829	4.81	4,498	7.11
Total		28,908	51.39	30,530	51.14	32,805	51.10	30,082	51.18	32,358	51.14
TOTAL		56,252	100.00	59,693	100.00	64,194	100.00	58,771	100.00	63,274	100.00

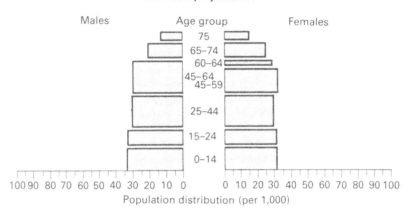

Based on projection A

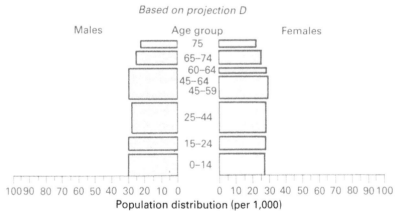

Figure 8.2 *The population distribution of the United Kingdom, projected to 2021*

Source: Government Actuary.

should not be added together to produce the overall index of column 10.

As to (a), it should be emphasized that these ratios are indices and *not* absolute measures. The relative changes over time are important; absolute values are not. As to (b), it is agreed that a straight addition of the indices may not be supportable. On the other hand, if a weighted combination were required what weights should be used? If one considers *all* the goods and services (especially services) consumed by the various groups it becomes very difficult to argue that they are substantially incomparable.

Table 8.9 The economic pressure of the dependent population in the United Kingdom (numbers in '000s)

Demographic projection	Year	Home population all ages	Children under 15	Non-gainfully occupied females 15-59	Pensionable class (males 65+, females 60+)	Remainder	Col. 3	Col. 4	Col. 5	Cols. 3+4+5	Proportion of economically active population to unemployed
					Ratio to remainder of						
	(1)	(2)	(3)	(4)	(5)	(6)	(7)	(8)	(9)	(10)	(11)
	1901	38,237	12,421	7,717	2,386	15,713	0.79	0.49	0.15	1.43	
	1921	44,027	12,304	9,560	3,501	18,662	0.66	0.51	0.19	1.36	0.093[b]
	1931	46,038	11,174	9,819	4,421	20,624	0.54	0.48	0.21	1.23	0.110[b]
	1951	50,225	11,325	9,211	6,827	22,862	0.50	0.40	0.30	1.20	0.009[b]
	1961	52,709	12,336	8,629	7,733	24,011	0.51	0.36	0.32	1.19	0.012[b]
	1971	55,515	13,387	7,325[a]	9,015	25,788	0.52	0.28	0.35	1.15	0.035[b]
	1981	56,252	11,560	8,272[a]	10,064	26,356	0.44	0.31	0.38	1.13	0.114[b]
A (Medium)	1991	56,948	11,140	8,455[a]	10,479	26,874	0.41	0.31	0.39	1.11	
	2001	58,087	12,277	8,538[a]	10,259	27,013	0.45	0.32	0.38	1.15	
	2011	58,639	11,490	8,615[a]	10,902	27,632	0.42	0.31	0.39	1.12	
	2021	59,693	11,717	8,539[a]	11,964	27,473	0.43	0.31	0.44	1.18	
D (Extreme)	1991	57,649	11,140	8,468[a]	11,085	26,956	0.41	0.31	0.41	1.13	
	2001	59,777	12,117	8,566[a]	11,902	27,192	0.45	0.32	0.44	1.21	
	2011	61,252	11,019	8,643[a]	13,719	27,871	0.40	0.31	0.49	1.20	
	2021	63,274	11,118	8,507[a]	16,094	27,555	0.40	0.31	0.58	1.29	

Notes:
[a] Estimated as 50% of age group.
[b] Census figures.

With all its defects a straight addition seems as justifiable as a weighted addition. Again, no *absolute* meaning should be attached to column 10; we are concerned only with relative changes over time.

Several interesting features emerge from Table 8.9. The first is that the total pressure of national dependency (column 10) declined between 1901 and 1981, and only then began to rise. By 1971 the growth in the total pensioner dependency had been matched by the increased employment of women (mainly married women) and the overall index had fallen below the levels of 1931 and 1951. (This is a quite remarkable development in the British economy.) Furthermore, there is a very real offset to the growth of pensioner dependency provided by the reduction in child dependency. It may be argued that child dependency is of a different nature from that of pensioner dependency and that the employed segment of the population will have a different, perhaps more sympathetic, attitude towards it. However that may be, it should be noted that the government has no such reservations and in its zeal to cut back on public expenditure has been quick to grasp at the savings to be made from falling fertility as an offset to the rise in the costs of services for old people. As a result, the total dependency ratio was slightly lower in 1981 than in 1971.

Over the next forty years, on the moderate assumptions of projection A, it appears that child dependency will decline slightly and pensioner dependency will increase by about one-sixth, while the dependency of non-earning women will remain unchanged. This will leave the overall dependency index higher than in 1981, but not greatly so, and only a little higher than in 1971. It is important to note, too, that pensioner dependency does not rise until after 2011. There is therefore still a decade or two in which to plan ahead for the additional economic strain. Even on the extreme assumptions of projection D, though pensioner dependency will be much higher than it has ever been, the overall dependency index will not be much larger than it was in 1951 (when the UK economy was recovering from war and when, unlike now, manpower was in short supply). The rise in pensioner dependency too is not substantial until after the end of the century. Moreover, we have to emphasize that the extreme assumptions that form the basis of projection D really are extreme. The majority of observers regard the outcome as likely to be closer to A than to D. Indeed, there is a danger that persistent high unemployment coupled with economies in the health and social services may produce a higher incidence of poverty than has been seen for several decades. It is probable that these factors may retard or even arrest the decline in mortality so that a pessimistic mortality projection may prove to be justified.

It has to be stressed that the dependency ratios for 1981 and in the future are not comparable with earlier values because technological improvements have greatly reduced the number of workers needed to produce the goods and services required by pensioners – if this were not so we should not be seeing such a serious rise in unemployment. And even if the same number of workers *were* required as formerly, then they are there – some 3–4 million of them – waiting for work. Column 11 of Table 8.9 shows the ratio of the unemployed to the economically active population. This is a part of total dependency that cannot be blamed on demography or pension rights.

Savings in public expenditure

A report by the Central Policy Review Staff (1977) examined the implications for social expenditure of the main changes in population size and structure that prospect over the next fifteen–twenty years. The report does not quantify the savings but these are clearly regarded as a substantial offset against the growth of expenditure on services for the very elderly. The report says that, because of the decline in fertility, there is currently overprovision of maternity services and savings are possible. It argues that there will be fewer children of compulsory school age in the 1980s so that there can be substantial savings on school accommodation. Hospital services for children will be less in demand and the resources can be redeployed to other users. Conversely, demand for higher education facilities will increase for a short time. There will be extra demands on health, personal social services and special housing for the increasing number of the very elderly.

It is significant that the report says much more clearly and firmly than any government – or for that matter any non-government institution – has said before, that demographic changes are less likely to injure the national economy if the likelihood of such changes is properly taken into account in immediate and long-term policy making.

Under the pressure of Population Action Year and the World Population Conference of 1974, the government made a minister in the Lords responsible for population matters. Little has been heard of this since, but the government has been reminded that we do have our own population problems and that they are more easily solved if faced. They have also been reminded that there are benefits as well as costs in the prospective population changes.

It has to be emphasized that, looking at society as a whole, pensioner dependency is only a fraction of total dependency. In 1901 it was little more than one-tenth, in 1931 less than one-fifth, and even in 1981 it was almost exactly one-third. It will be seen that, even if we ignore the present huge reserve of labour, a rise in pensioner dependency could be offset by a comparatively small expansion in the number of married women in paid employment if work were available. Pensioner dependency itself could be significantly lowered by postponement of retiring age if that were socially acceptable in present conditions. The Phillips Committee (1954) considered the latter possibility and came to the conclusion that the 'medical evidence and the numbers of elderly people who do in fact work until ages well beyond the minimum (National Insurance) pension ages of 65 for men and 60 for women indicate that over a wide field these ages do not by any means represent the limit of working life'. They recommended: 'Provision should now be made to raise the ages at which the standard rate of pension can be claimed by one year after an interval of not less than five years and that ages should ultimately be raised in the same way to 68 for men and 63 for women.' But, of course, the Phillips Committee deliberated at a time of full employment. In an era of massively high unemployment the social pressure is not for later but for earlier retirement to create more job opportunities.

In summary, therefore, a decline in the birth rate and some mortality improvement (particularly a reduction in child mortality) have already been encompassed once this century without serious economic strain, and claims that further demographic changes will be economically intolerable do not seem to be founded on past experience, or on the facts about likely changes in population structure.

The ageing population: a burden or a resource

An ageing population would not present an economic or a social problem if the behaviour or attitudes of members of the population were not closely linked with age. Past and future demographic trends suggest that most European countries are almost stationary as regards generation replacement. Many states are moving towards a very low level of mortality and in particular there has been a sharp decline in mortality among the very old (Guilmot, 1978). The discussion of the previous sections applies to many European countries: the total dependency ratio (proportion of people aged 0–14 together with proportion of people aged 60 and over per 100 of the population aged 15–59) will still *decrease* slightly in many countries during the last decades of this century because the increase in the elderly component has not yet outweighed the fall in the child component (see Table 8.10). It could be assumed that this fall in the dependency ratio would make it possible to increase productivity provided that available resources were to be effectively utilized. The situation, however, is very likely to change when the large generations born after the war reach retirement age in the third and fourth decades of the next century (as indicated in previous sections).

The current high unemployment of several Western European countries may cause increased tension between the economically active and the older population groups. The older labour force is criticized for its lack of mobility, rigidity and the outdated nature of its education.

Table 8.10   *Dependency ratios in different regions of Europe. Development 1960–1970 and projections to 2000 (population aged less than 15 and population aged 60 and over per 100 population aged 15–59)*

Region	Year				
	1960	*1970*	*1980*	*1990*	*2000*
Europe	67.3	71.1	64.4	63.4	66.9
Eastern Europe					
(excluding USSR)	68.6	67.4	63.0	66.1	65.0
Northern Europe	68.1	73.7	69.1	64.4	66.2
Southern Europe	65.2	54.8	65.4	65.2	48.8
Western Europe	67.8	74.0	62.1	59.2	66.8
USSR	68.8	68.3	59.7	67.5	70.2

Source: UN *Population Projections: World population and its age–sex composition by country, 1950–2000.* Demographic Estimation and Projection assessed at 1978.

Gerontological research has shown, however, that the process of ageing does not automatically lead to a decline in performance in all physiological functions, and that in several psychological and social tasks older workers, by means of experience and watchfulness, manage better than younger ones (Heikkenen, 1984).

Projections of the participation of persons aged 65 and over in the labour force suggest that in most Western European countries the present proportion of active men in that category, currently about 25 per cent, will fall by about one-half by the year 2000. In many countries, e.g. Finland, the proportion of economically active older persons (65+) is presently about 5 per cent. Opposite trends have also been reported, as, for example, in the USSR, where the level of pensioners' employment has increased over the past decade while attempts have been made to facilitate the working conditions of older people.

There are difficulties in extending the working life even if employment were available. Although mortality has been considerably reduced, it is not easy to interpret this increased longevity in terms of prolonged activity, that is, in terms of the quality of survival. Postponement of death in an elderly person by improved medical care does not imply the arrest of the relentless process of degeneration.

Statistics supplied by the Government Actuary (personal communication) show that the proportion of the insured male population who had been sick for more than three months at mid-1982 rose from 3.3 per cent at ages 45–49 to 4.5 per cent at ages 50–54. The proportion begins to rise rapidly after age 60, and even before age 65 more than one-seventh of insured men are in poor enough shape to have been on sickness benefit for more than three months. If we move to an older age group, i.e. those over the age of 75, we find that currently in the United Kingdom about 2.5 per cent of this elderly population are in hospital at any one time and that they occupy nearly half of all NHS beds. Projected changes in the age distribution within this elderly group suggest that its requirements for geriatric and other hospital care will continue to grow.

On the other hand, surveys of the aged population have indicated that infirmity is more quickly developed and more passively accepted in conditions of stagnation and boredom and is more effectively resisted and prevented by interest and occupation. As long ago as in 1947 the Committee on the Problems of Ageing and the Care of Old People (1947) reported that they had been 'impressed by the views expressed to them of the higher therapeutical value of occupation and employment in delaying the effects of ageing and they feel that it is in the interests of those who are elderly but not old to be able to continue in employment as long as they wish to do so'. Many others have reported in the same vein.

Health service and social needs of the elderly
Table 8.11 presents extracts from the detailed population projections described earlier. The absolute number of persons aged 75 and over is projected to increase by 20 per cent on bases A/C and 32 per cent on bases B/D by 2001, and by 56 per cent and 181 per cent respectively by 2031. Over the same periods the numbers aged 85 and over will have grown more rapidly. When considering the projected cost of pensions fifty years hence, these implied increased costs for health and social support systems must also be borne in mind. Of course, if biomedical advances result in prevention (rather than cure) of the principal current causes of morbidity (as implied for bases B/D) then the share of the Gross Domestic Product spent on the NHS will decrease despite the ageing of the population, thereby freeing resources for social security and other forms of support.

Current housing activities pay insufficient attention to the ageing of the population and the growth of the numbers of elderly living alone and with no family in close proximity. There is a need for a substantial expansion in the provision of specific types of housing with access to family and/or medical and social services support. The required expansion is something that, properly planned and supported by political consensus, might be provided by investment from pension funds assisting the property development associated with geriatric inpatient facilities and other purpose-built accommodation (Lyon, 1983). In the UK, new patterns of living arrangements have been emerging, particularly among elderly unmarried and unrelated individuals. This usually involves a set of flats or small houses forming a retirement community with wardens and other suitable facilities. Many elderly persons want to stay near relatives and friends but find the upkeep of their homes financially beyond their

Table 8.11   *Persons aged 75 and over in the United Kingdom*

Year	Absolute numbers ('000s)		Percentage of all pensioners aged 75 +	
	Projection A/C	Projection B/D	Projection A/C %	Projection B/D %
1981	3266	3266	32.5	32.5
1991	3918	4314	37.4	38.9
2001	4147	5311	40.4	44.6
2011	4101	6152	37.6	44.8
2021	4444	7487	37.1	46.5
2031	5090	9187	37.9	48.9

reach. The possible extension of the experimental contracts like the Reverse Mortgage Annuity Contract (Sheppard, 1980) should be investigated: these contracts permit the elderly to borrow as income a proportion of the value or equity of their home while they live there, the lender recovering the debt at their death either from other assets in the estate or from proceeds of the sale of the home.

However, at present, a large proportion of the elderly not only have inadequate pensions but do not own a home on which to borrow. Indeed, the major difficulty in planning an expansion of purpose-built housing for the elderly (i.e. with geriatric facilities and warden supervision) is that ownership is beyond the means of the majority of the elderly and the need is for rented accommodation. Moreover, what rent they can afford is very limited. It was estimated in 1980 that, in England and Wales, the numbers of householders over pensionable age who received rent rebates, rent allowances and rate rebates were of the order of 700,000. 175,000 and 2,100,000 respectively; that is, 3 million in total. The number eligible but not taking up the rebates was not known (Young, 1980). If one includes also the pensioners who are receiving help with housing costs through supplementary benefits, this total rises to 4 million (Boyson, 1980). This presents a grave burden for local authorities sorely pressed by current national financial retrenchment.

The economic conditions of the elderly
Of males aged 65 and over, 60 per cent live with a wife and 17 per cent live alone. Of females 65 and over, 33 per cent live with a husband only and 45 per cent live alone. The average size of a household headed by a person aged 65 and over is small – 1.65 persons (Central Statistical Office, 1982). Quite apart, therefore, from financial difficulties there is

clearly a problem of relative isolation, underlining what has been said earlier about housing and also having implications for other social services, medical and nursing supervision, ambulances to day clinics, chiropody, home helps and organized entertainment. All these services are manpower intensive and costly and add considerably to the economic problem of planning ahead for the relative growth in the elderly population.

In 1981, the *gross* normal weekly household income of the average household where the head was aged 65 and over was £86.05 (or £52.09 per head) (CSO, 1982). Of this amount 19 per cent came from employment, 11 per cent from savings, 7 per cent from imputed income derived from owner-occupancy, 14 per cent from private pensions and 49 per cent (i.e. almost half) from social security benefit. 'Social security benefit' includes, in addition to basic national insurance pensions or disablement benefits, the supplementary pensions and allowances payable in cases of need. In 1980 there were about 1.7 million retirement pensioners or widow pensioners aged 60 and over who were at any one time receiving regular weekly supplementary pensions (DHSS, 1983). It has been estimated that there were approximately a further 700,000 pensioners who were entitled to a supplementary pension but did not claim it (Boyson, 1980).

In 1981, in households with heads aged 65 and over about 55 per cent of average weekly expenditure (of £71) was taken up by fuel, light and power (9 per cent), housing (22 per cent) and food (24 per cent). Some 10 per cent was allocated to transport, 6 per cent to clothing and footwear, and 5 per cent to durable household goods. About £4.50 (6 per cent) was left for tobacco and alcoholic drink (Department of Employment, 1982).

That a relatively high proportion of the elderly have low incomes and that the elderly form an important proportion of all low income households has long been a matter of recorded and reported fact was accepted by the Royal Commission on the Distribution of Income and Wealth (1978). They referred to the reports of Rowntree in 1951 (Rowntree and Lavers, 1951), Cole and Utting in 1962 (1963), Abel-Smith and Townsend (1965) and the Ministry of Pensions and National Insurance (1966). The Commission reported, on the basis of General Household Survey data of 1975, that about one-third of elderly families received an occupational pension (in addition to the national social security pension) but that in general the amount was small (owing, doubtless, to the fact that the relevant occupational scheme had not been instituted many years before retirement of the household head or that, as in the case of many *ex gratia* non-contributory schemes, the benefit was not related strictly to length of service and earnings). For a retired husband living with his wife the average occupational pension (for those in receipt of such a pension) was only £477 a year.

Conclusion

The present problem, therefore, is more than one of numbers; it is partly one of inadequate coverage and the comparative immaturity of existing occupational pension schemes. This part of the problem should be overtaken before any increase in dependency arising from demographic changes described in earlier sections begins to exert significant pressure. However, even if the lower income status of the majority of elderly people is relieved by more and better occupational pensions schemes (aided by the guaranteed minimum pension requirements of the 1975 Social Security Act), there remains the problem of improving the quality of life of the senior citizen – the backlog of unmet needs in special housing and geriatric services to which reference has already been made. At the same time there remains the likelihood of high unemployment persisting for decades until those older workers (possibly beyond retraining) displaced by advances in technology attain the normal pensionable age. It should at least be a matter for consideration that these two problems could be put together. It is not, of course, possible to argue that the resources now devoted to the dependency of unemployment would be sufficient to pay the unemployed adequate wages for helping to meet the current and future needs of the elderly, but the total resource consumption would be productive and restorative of the work ethic from which the unemployed have unwillingly and sometimes unwittingly been distracted, and it would, even more importantly, be a real contribution to the forward planning of adjustment to the ageing population structure and the resulting economic strains.

Hitherto, we have discussed the elderly as though they constitute a homogeneous and unchanging group of individuals. In relation to their morbidity and mortality prospects this is not the case. Diversity arises from differences and changes in living arrangements (affected by marital status, for example), and selective survival forces among those already old. Whether they are an unchanging population remains to be seen. We have already referred to the health amelioration effects of providing the elderly with activities that are creative and useful whether or not remunerative.

There is certainly much more being done educationally to prepare older workers for impending retirement. It is surely important to both health and well-being that we should provide social roles for the elderly, and help and encourage them to utilize their mental and physical resources to the full not only for their own self-development but (as a consequence) for the benefit of society at large.

What we do not as yet know is whether the current improvement in longevity will be matched by a reduction in sickness or if we are merely keeping sick people alive longer. Currently disability rates in the older working age groups are still as high as ever and have recently actually increased (though high unemployment is probably a factor). It would, however, be reasonable to assume that improvements in life style (for example, reduction in smoking, increased physical exercise, improved nutrition) will result in the reduction of disease prevalence; that medical advances will be preventive as well as curative. If this happens then there will be welcome easing of the pressure on health and social services for the elderly. From this point of view, it would be good forward demographic planning and sound economic investment for the nation to put much more money than at present into preventive medicine and health education.

References

Abel-Smith, B. and Townsend, P. (1965), *The Poor and the Poorest*, London: Bell

Benjamin, B. (1964), 'Demographic aspects of aging', *Journal of the Institute of Actuaries*, vol. 90, pp. 213–53

Benjamin, B. (1981), 'Recent and prospective fertility trends in Great Britain', in D. F. Roberts and R. Chester (eds), *Changing Patterns of Conception and Fertility*, Report of the proceedings of the 19th Eugenics Society Symposium, London: Academic Press

Benjamin, B. and Overton, E. (1981), 'Prospects for mortality decline in England and Wales', *Population Trends*, vol. 23, pp. 22–28

Boyson, Dr Rhodes (1980), Answer to Parliamentary Question, *Hansard*

Central Policy Review Staff (1977), *Population and the Social Services*, London: HMSO

Central Statistical Office (1982), *Social Trends 13*, London: HMSO

Cole, D. and Utting, J. (1962), *The Economic Circumstances of Old People*, London: Codicote Press

Committee on the Problems of Aging and the Care of Old People (1947), *Report*, London: Nuffield Foundation

Department of Employment (1982), *Family Expenditure Survey 1981*, London: HMSO

DHSS (1983), *Social Security Statistics 1981*, London: HMSO

Glass, D. V. (1976), 'Recent and prospective trends in fertility in developed countries', Phil. Trans. 274B.9, London

Guilmot, P. (1978), 'The demographic background', in Council of Europe, *Population Decline in Europe. Implications of a Declining or Stationary Population*, London: Edward Arnold

Heikkenen, E. (1984), 'Effect of the main demographic trends in elderly people', Chapter 8 in R. L. Cliquet and A. Lopez (eds), *Trends in the Demographic Structure of the European Region: Health and Social Implications*, Geneva: WHO

Lyon, C. S. S. (1983), 'Presidential address: The Outlook for Pensioning', *Journal of the Institute of Actuaries*, vol. 110, pp. 1–16

Ministry of Pensions and National Insurance (1966), *The Financial and Other Circumstances of Retirement Pensioners*, London: HMSO

Phillips Committee (1954), *Report of the Committee on Economic and*

Financial Provisions for Old Age, Cmnd 9333, London: HMSO

Rowntree, B. S. and Lavers, G. R. (1951), *Poverty and the Welfare State*, London: Longman

Royal Commission on the Distribution of Income and Wealth (1978), *Report No. 6, Lower Incomes*, London: HMSO

Sheppard, H. (1980), 'Biomedical revolution', in L. M. Delgadillo (ed.) *The Future of Life Expectancy*, Chicago: Society of Actuaries

Townsend, P. and Wedderburn, D. (1965), *The Aged in the Welfare State*, London: Bell

Young, Sir G. (1980), Answer to Parliamentary Question, Hansard

9 Employment Trends

STEVEN HABERMAN

Employment trends: historic

Because of the proximity of the 1939–45 war and the exceptional post-war circumstances it was not possible in the context of the 1954 review of pension funds and the economy (Bacon, Benjamin and Elphinstone, 1954) to consider historic projected employment trends. However, at the present time, over thirty years' data and analyses are available and so it is possible to examine employment trends in the same manner as demographic trends (as in Chapter 8).

A brief review of the last decade might be of value at this point. These last ten years have been characterized by changes in the economic roles of adults. Economic activity rates are used to measure membership of the labour force and it should be noted that the unemployed are considered to be 'members' of the labour force. For males, age-specific economic activity rates have remained steady (in the range 90–99 per cent) with the rates, however, falling at ages 55–64, reflecting a trend towards earlier retirement. Owing to longer periods of formal education, the increased prevalence of single-parent families and of cohabitation and the residual nature of the never-married group, non-married women have experienced a fall in economic activity. Married women show a rise at all ages, reflecting the increasing economic and social importance of the employment of married women, both part time and full time (Department of Employment, 1981). Similarly, female participation in further and higher education has increased. The recent severe economic recession has produced very high levels of unemployment among young adults and removed many married women in marginal employment from the labour market (leading to a fall in activity rates). The economy has been characterized by declining numbers employed in the manufacturing sector. This may be matched by a similar squeeze in the service sector with high wages and improved technology encouraging employers to replace people with machines to raise productivity and profits. This description takes no account of the alternative economies that simultaneously may gain in importance – for example, the 'black economy', voluntary work, housework, household support, do-it-yourself.

Current economic projections suggest the European countries are likely to require much smaller workforces in the generation of material wealth, which will itself derive less from steel construction and ship-building and other central industries and more from light, high-technology industries like electronics. Among the important implications of this trend are a reduced period of life spent at work, shorter working hours, increased leisure and pressure to restrict employment opportunities for women. Greater occupational mobility is likely to be needed, and this may require major retraining programmes and the participation of mature students in higher education on a part-time as well as full-time basis. The unskilled may create special problems as they fall further behind in a society that is becoming increasingly technological and form a residual group in large inner cities (for example, Glasgow or Liverpool). The growth of alternative economies based on housework and skills acquired at home or at leisure could be fostered by the increased availability of labour and, *inter alia*, the increased 'need' created by the numbers of elderly with their special problems and impairments. They may receive greater recognition and incentive schemes could be developed for them. If the economic participation of women is to continue at a high level, if not increase further, then greater flexibility in working conditions will be required to allow married couples increased freedom in deciding upon their respective roles and the timing of their participation in the labour force. Such changes in employment patterns will continue to affect the social structure as societies become more white-collar and less blue-collar dominated, with fewer ties with capital and labour (human) than previously. This again has wide implications for the behaviour and circumstances of adults into the next century, particularly when these are determined by social background and attitudes.

In the light of the above, projections of employment trends are necessarily more subjective than projections of mortality rates. It would be possible to set up a wide range of projections. Our purpose, however, is to illustrate the trends arising from reasonable sets of assumptions, indicating the effect of departures in the values of the principal parameters.

There are a multitude of parameters that should be allowed for in projecting employment patterns and consequently the restricted set of figures produced here can only be illustrative. Among the important trends that should be incorporated are:

1 changes in the school leaving age and the introduction of Youth Opportunities Programme (YOP) and the Youth Training Schemes (YTS);
2 changes in the level of unemployment and demand for employment;
3 changes in the normal retirement age;
4 introduction of flexible retirement schemes;
5 introduction of flexible working schemes, for example, retraining, job-

sharing, regular sabbaticals, part-time working, treatment of early leavers;

6 changes in the importance of married women's employment and its relationship to family-building.

It is not possible to allow for each of these factors because of their speculative nature and the paucity of data available. The effect of some will be allowed for in the long-term projections, for example, (2), (3), (4). The effect of others, for example (1), will be allowed for only in the early part of the projections and then held constant. However, reference will be made to some of these items in the discussion parts of the section on projected trends. It should further be noted that there are likely to be behavioural reactions on the part of the working population to many of the changes and trends mentioned. Such reactions are necessarily unforeseen and only limited allowance can be made in advance for the effect of these responses.

General approach
The general approach will be to use projected employment trends to estimate the average contribution record of members (of either sex) of occupational pension schemes. Pension provision for those who are self-employed is excluded from this study.

The question of timing of years within an individual's contribution history will be ignored in making these estimates. This is justified because of the final salary nature of most current occupational pension schemes. Any approach aimed at looking at timing is baulked by the paucity of relevant, reliable data. However, there are problems with the so-called 'early leavers', which will be discussed in due course in some detail. We shall concentrate (in Chapter 11) on the total number of years that an average person would accumulate from membership of occupational pension schemes.

Estimates will be prepared of the size and structure of the membership of occupational pension schemes and of the annual expenditure on benefits for a year, fifty years from the base date. Thus the projection covers the period 1981–2031.

Sources of data on economic activity
Information on economic activity rates and the composition of the labour force is available from three principal sources, namely the decennial Census and the annual reports of the General Household Survey (GHS), and the Labour Force Surveys.

The regular estimates published by the Department of Employment in their monthly gazette are derived principally from household survey and census data. These estimates allow a full breakdown of numbers by age, sex and marital status. The latest series incorporates the activity analyses from the 1971 Census and the 1975, 1977 and 1979 EC Labour Force Surveys. All labour force figures presented for 1980 and later years are projections from the 1979 base. The survey results are grossed up to the Registrar General's mid-year total population estimates, which extend to 1979, the base year for the population projections. The survey estimates are supplemented by Department of Education and Science information on numbers of full-time students and by information on the non-household or institutional population. Survey estimates are of course subject to sampling and other errors.

It should be noted that there is a difference between being observed as economically active at a given moment and working during a year. Estimates of economic activity numbers and rates prepared both for the Census and by the Department of Employment refer to a point in time. However, it will be assumed that such data may be taken as referring to a period rather than a point of time – such data as are available to test this assumption indicate that the error introduced thereby is of the order of 2–3 per cent (for example, it has been estimated by Joshi and Owen, 1983, that the numbers interviewed in the 1974 General Household Survey and reported as being economically active at interview were 2 per cent in excess of the numbers earning over the equivalent state basic pensionable threshold during the previous year).

Past employment trends: males
The evidence on male activity rates from the four post-war censuses presented in Table 9.1 suggests that there has been little change (in contrast to women) in the chances of men in successive generations being economically active at a given age, at least between ages 20 and 59. If it is assumed that there will continue to be little difference between cohorts, then the length of the average active 'life' from these cross-sectional activity rates may be inferred. If a cohort survived through all of these ages at the rates recorded in the 1951 Census, its average activity rate would be 96.2 per cent. Comparable single figure indices based on the 1961, 1971 and 1981 data are 97.0 per cent, 95.5 per cent and 92.8 per cent. A more detailed presentation of such cross-sectional data for men indicates that between ages 20 and 64 self-employment has maintained a fairly constant proportion at around 9 per cent at each census, and that it is only the chance of being out of employment that has shown much of a trend with the rising levels of unemployment at the time of each census – a trend that seems more likely to continue than to reverse.

More detailed information on the trends since 1971 is provided by the General Household Survey (1983). Table 9.2 shows that since 1973 there has been a decrease in the economic activity rates of men: in 1973, 82 per cent of men were economically active and by 1982 this proportion had fallen to 76 per cent. This decrease was particularly marked among men

Table 9.1 *Economic activity rates for men aged 20–64 and women aged 20–59, Great Britain, 1951, 1961, 1971, 1981 (%)*

Age group	Males				Females			
	1951	*1961*	*1971*	*1981*	*1951*	*1961*	*1971*	*1981*
20–24	94.9	92.7	90.1	89.1	65.4	62.4	60.3	69.3
25–29	97.6	97.9	97.3	96.5	40.3	39.6	43.1	55.3
30–34	98.4	98.7	98.2	97.7	33.5	36.5	45.0	53.5
35–44	98.5	98.2	98.5	97.9	35.1	42.4	57.0	65.5
45–54	97.8	98.6	97.7	97.5	34.4	43.2	60.4	66.0
55–59	95.0	97.2	95.5	94.8	27.6	36.9	50.9	52.1
60–64	86.7	91.0	86.7	66.0	–	–	–	–
20–64 (for males)*	96.2	97.0	95.5	92.8				
20–59 (for females)					38.2	43.4	54.3	61.7

* Unweighted mean of age-specific activity rates.
Sources: 1951 Census of England and Wales, Occupation Tables, Census of Scotland, Vol. 4, London: HMSO, 1956.
1961 Census of Great Britain, Occupation Tables, London: HMSO, 1966.
1971 Census of Great Britain, Economic Activity Tables, Vol. II, London: HMSO, 1975.
1981 Census of Great Britain, Economic Activity Tables, London: HMSO, 1984.

aged 60 and over, reflecting a trend towards earlier retirement, and those aged 16–17. The rate of decline was greatest among men over state retirement age, those aged 65 and over. The GHS shows a clear decrease since 1973 in the activity rate of men aged 60–64, although the figures for this group fluctuated somewhat between 1979 and 1982. Because of the relatively small numbers in the GHS in this age group, some of these fluctuations may be due to sampling error. The figures for the proportion of men aged 60–64 who were working have fluctuated less than the overall activity rates (which include the unemployed) and show a steadier decline, from 80 per cent working in 1973 to only 54 per cent in 1982. These dramatic falls in economic activity in the age groups on both sides of the normal retirement age are confirmed by the recent Department of Employment estimates, which are not reproduced here (Department of Employment, 1981).

The overall fall shown by the GHS since the mid-1970s in the activity rate of young men aged 16–17 is largely explained by the increasing numbers taking part in YOP schemes who, like students, are classified as economically inactive in the GHS. In 1982, the survey found that 10 per cent of 16–17 year old men were on YOP schemes.

Table 9.3 shows that in the period 1973–1982 the proportions of men in all age groups under state retirement age who were unemployed increased. This trend was particularly marked between 1980 and 1981 but

Table 9.2   *Economic activity by sex and age, persons aged 16 and over,
Great Britain, 1973–1982 (%)*

| Age | Percentage economically active[a] | | | | | | |
	1973	1975	1977	1979	1980	1981	1982
Males							
16 – 17	63	55	58	56	53	47	47
18 – 24	91	89	89	91	90	89	89
25 – 34	98	98	98	98	97	97	96
35 – 44	99	98	98	98	97	98	97
45 – 54	98	98	97	96	97	95	94
55 – 59	94	94	93	88	89	90	90
60 – 64	85	84	79	75	67	73	64
65 +	19	16	15	15	12	11	10
16 – 64	94	93	92	92	90	90	89
Total	82	81	80	79	77	77	76
Non-married females[b]							
16 – 17	57	52	48	53	47	40	34
18 – 24	84	82	79	79	82	83	81
25 – 34	82	76	74	76	81	76	78
35 – 44	76	75	78	70	80	75	75
45 – 54	74	77	72	72	74	74	75
55 – 59	69	62	69	61	64	61	64
60 – 64	34	34	27	23	26	23	18
65 +	6	6	5	5	4	4	5
16 – 59	74	72	70	70	72	70	69
Total	45	42	41	42	44	44	43
Married females							
16 – 17	(7)	(3)	(2)	(0)	(4)	(4)	(0)
18 – 24	50	54	55	52	56	57	59
25 – 34	44	52	52	55	56	51	54
35 – 44	64	66	68	70	70	69	68
45 – 54	63	67	68	68	67	69	68
55 – 59	48	49	50	55	52	54	52
60 – 64	25	26	26	25	25	21	22
65 +	8	6	6	6	6	5	5
16 – 59	55	59	60	62	62	61	61
Total	48	51	51	52	52	51	50

Notes:
[a] Full-time students who were working or unemployed in the reference week are classified
as economically inactive.
[b] Single, widowed, divorced, and separated women.
Source: General Household Survey (1983).

Table 9.3 *Percentage unemployed by sex and age,*
Great Britain, 1973–1982 (%)

Age	1973	1975	1977	1979	1980	1981	1982
Males aged 16 and over							
16 – 17	3	7	9	9	10	12	20
18 – 19	4	7	8	8	11	17	20
20 – 24	4	5	7	6	9	16	17
25 – 34	3	3	5	4	6	10	11
35 – 44	3	4	4	3	4	7	8
45 – 54	3	3	3	4	5	6	8
55 – 59	4	4	3	4	5	8	9
60 – 64	6	3	5	4	5	9	11
65 +	1	0	0	0	0	0	0
16 – 64	3	4	5	5	6	10	11
Total	3	3	4	4	5	8	9
Base = $^{100}_{per\ cent}$	11,196	11,455	11,228	10,749	11,116	11,505	9,799
Females aged 16 – 59							
Single	3	5	7	6	8	11	11
Widowed, divorced, separated	3	4	5	5	5	8	9
Married	1	2	2	2	3	4	4
Total	2	2	3	3	4	6	6
Base = $^{100}_{per\ cent}$	8,984	9,146	8,930	8,646	8,821	9,185	7,672

Source: General Household Survey (1983).

it continued between 1981 and 1982; in 1973, 3 per cent of men aged 16–64 were unemployed while 90 per cent were working; by 1982, 11 per cent were unemployed and 78 per cent working. Since the mid-1970s, the proportions unemployed have tended to be higher among those aged 16–24 than among older men. In 1982, among 16–17 year olds (a large proportion of whom were still in full-time education or on a YOP scheme), 20 per cent were unemployed and 27 per cent were in work. These figures compare with 3 per cent unemployed and 59 per cent in work in 1973. The survey data are, of course, collected throughout the year and the proportions economically active, particularly among 16–17 year olds, vary considerably at different times of the year.

Past employment trends: females
The trend towards greater female labour force participation revealed in

Table 9.1 means that successive cohorts of women have an increasing chance and duration of economic activity over their lifetimes (Joshi and Owen, 1981). Therefore, the experience of a cohort cannot be derived by synthesizing across age groups at a point in time as has been suggested for men. The upward trend consists of a decline in the proportion of each generation of women who leave the labour force permanently on marriage as well as an increasing length of time in the labour force by those who remain in it. Cross-sectional data can also be misleading in that the proportion of women who ever participate in employment will be greater than those observed participating at any one time because of movements in and out of work.

Table 9.2 (from the General Household Survey) shows that since 1973 the economic activity rates of non-married women have fluctuated more than those of men, but among non-married women aged 60 and over and particularly among those aged 60–64 the rates have tended to decrease. In 1982, the proportion of those aged 60–64 who were economically active was 18 per cent, compared with 34 per cent in 1973. Similar findings emerge from Department of Employment estimates.

As in the case of young men, there has also been a fall in the activity rate of young women aged 16–17 over the period, and the 1982 survey suggests that the decrease was steeper for young women than for young men. In 1982, 34 per cent of girls aged 16–17 were economically active. The proportion working was similar to that among boys of this age but the proportion unemployed was lower. Girls and boys in this age group were equally likely to be on a YOP scheme but girls were more likely to be in full-time education: 53 per cent of girls aged 16–17 were full-time students compared with 42 per cent of the boys, a difference more marked than in previous years of the survey.

Unlike the activity rates for men and non-married women, those for married women tended to increase during the early 1970s reflecting the continuing post-war trend of increasing participation of married women in the labour force. Since 1978, however, this increase seems to have halted and the GHS (Table 9.2) shows a slight decline in the activity rate of married women, with a fall from 52 per cent in 1980 to 50 per cent in 1982. Among women below state retirement age (those aged 16–59), the fall was smaller, from 62 per cent in 1980 to 61 per cent in 1982 and, given the sample numbers, not statistically significant. Two factors that are thought to have contributed to this sudden reversal of trends are the upturn in the birth rate that occurred in 1977, after over a decade of falling births, and the effect of the current recession on job opportunities.

As in the case of men, the proportion of women who were unemployed rather than working or economically inactive rose between 1973 and 1982. In 1973, 2 per cent of women aged 16–59 were unemployed compared with 6 per cent in 1982, the steepest rise occurring between 1980 and

1981 (Table 9.3). GHS data, not presented here, show that unemployment increased among married and non-married women and among those with and without dependent children. Even so, with the rise in part-time working during the 1970s, the proportions of married women and of women with dependent children who were working were higher in 1982 than they had been in 1973.

Discussion of economic activity rates at distinct time points may obscure the fact that most women at one time or another are in employment. The longer the reference period, the more likely is someone to have worked. Hunt (1968) found from her 1965 survey that among all women (excluding students) 56 per cent were currently active, 80 per cent had worked at some time during the previous ten years and 97 per cent had ever worked at some time. Similarly Martin and Roberts (1984) found from the 1980 Women and Employment Survey that among all women (excluding full-time students) 63 per cent were currently working and 98 per cent had ever worked at some time (although only 25 per cent had always been economically active). Analysis shows that the most common pattern of work history for cohorts old enough to have married before the Second World War seems to have been to give up work at marriage; the younger cohorts are more likely to have worked up to the birth of their first child. Further, the upward secular trend in women's economic activity rates during the 1960s and 1970s can be attributed principally to women spending more time at work over their lifetime.

In summary, therefore, there has been a trend towards higher economic participation of women during times of relative economic prosperity. It is not clear whether these trends will continue or abate in the presence of slower economic growth.

The trend towards higher economic activity of women would be encouraged by greater flexibility in employment conditions. There is evidence from the National Training Survey of 1975 that women have on average a lower occupational 'status' than men, with concentration of women in the 'lowest level jobs' (Stewart and Greenhalgh, 1984). Although more training for women may help to remove these inequalities, training programmes are unlikely to provide a full solution since the inability of many married women to work full time is likely to continue to inhibit their career progress. Consideration should hence be given to programmes for women that combine increased training with the provision of child care, the creation of part-time jobs in higher level occupations, and the recognition of part-time service by employers when considering promotion, to enable married women to move away from low-status, part-time work. However, it is difficult to envisage such developments taking place given the prevailing economic situation.

Table 9.4   *Composition of the labour force by economic activity,*
sex and marital status, economically active persons aged 16 and over,
Great Britain 1979–1982 (%)

Economic activity,[a] sex, and marital status	1979		1980		1981		1982	
Working full time								
Males	54		52		51		49	
Non-married females	10	} 75	10	} 74	9	} 71	10	} 69
Married females	12		11		11		11	
Working part time								
Males	2		2		2		2	
Non-married females	2	} 20	2	} 19	3	} 19	3	} 19
Married females	15		15		14		15	
All working[b]								
Males	56		55		53		52	
Non-married females	12	} 95	12	} 94	12	} 90	12	} 89
Married females	27		27		25		25	
Unemployed								
Males	3		4		6		7	
Non-married females	1	} 5	1	} 6	2	} 10	2	} 11
Married females	1		1		2		2	
All economically active								
Males	59		59		59		59	
Non-married females	13		14		14		14	
Married females	28		28		27		27	
Base = 100 per cent	14,356		14,680		15,073		12,601	

Notes:

[a] Full-time students who are working or unemployed in the reference week are classified as economically inactive.

[b] Including a few persons whose hours of work were not known.

Source: General Household Survey (1983).

Composition of the labour force

Table 9.4 shows how the changes between 1979 and 1982 in the proportions of men and of married women and non-married women working or unemployed affected the composition of the labour force. Whereas, in 1979, full-time workers made up 75 per cent of the labour force, they accounted for only 69 per cent in 1982. The proportion of the labour force accounted for by part-time workers also fell slightly from 20 per cent in 1979 to 19 per cent in the later years. There was a corresponding rise in these years, from 5 per cent to 11 per cent, in the proportion of the labour force who were unemployed.

Further tabulations show, however, that although the proportion of the labour force who were employees decreased over the four-year period, the proportion who were self-employed did not decline. Indeed, among men, the GHS shows a significant increase over the period from 10 per cent to 12 per cent in the proportion of the labour force who were self-employed.

Early retirement
In the prevailing climate of economic recession, early retirement has become and continues to be a substitute for long-term unemployment at the older ages. This has been encouraged by the operation of the Job Release Scheme since January 1977. Early retirement leads to a fall in the productive class and is probably encouraged by a general increase in the benefits available. The general problems of dependency mentioned in Chapter 8 could be exacerbated by such a trend. However, there may be little choice if labour mobility is to be stimulated, especially for the under 25s. Whether arising from voluntary or involuntary causes, early retirement, coupled with increasing longevity, would increase the proportion of an individual's lifetime spent in retirement and hence in receipt of a pension, and reduce the proportion spent working and accumulating assets. Of course there will be fewer workers available to maintain any given level of output or growth.

Despite the undesirability of early retirement, there has been a marked trend for both men and women (non-married) to retire from work earlier and this trend seems likely to continue, aided by the effects of high unemployment.

A survey of people near retirement age conducted in 1977 and reported by Parker (1980) suggests that this earlier retirement is, to a large extent, involuntary; 75 per cent of males who had retired early had an illness or disability and nearly half were receiving means-tested benefits (for example, supplementary or housing benefits). It seems likely that the surge in unemployment during the second half of the 1970s pushed many marginally employable older workers into retirement. Men retiring before age 65 do not receive a state pension at present and so have to live on past savings, other state benefits or an occupational pension. Only a small group will therefore be able to afford to retire early – ill-health retirements are separate in that these persons probably receive a state invalidity pension.

In an analysis of the Family Expenditure Survey 1974–77, Altmann (1981) found that, of the men who had retired early,

- 42 per cent received income from an occupational pension
- 43 per cent received income from private savings

- 58 per cent received income from health-related national insurance benefits
- 43 per cent received income from means-tested benefits.

These groups are not mutually exclusive, but there is little overlap between men in the first two groups and men in the other two (compromising about 74 per cent of the group). The incomes in the first two groups are higher than those in the second two groups, as illustrated by the figures in Table 9.5.

Parker's survey also shows that men without an occupational pension are nearly twice as likely to continue working as those who have one, and men with an occupational pension are more likely to retire a few years before age 65. The projected growth in the proportion of persons of pensionable age with occupational pension entitlement and in the size of their entitlements demonstrated in later chapters would, therefore, tend to reduce labour force participation among men aged 60 and over through a feedback process. The sensitivity of early retirement decisions to the state of the labour market makes long-term projections of these current developments in economic activity of older workers rather speculative.

There has been considerable recent debate about a common pension age for the two sexes, involving the use of some age intermediate between 60 and 65. No discussion on this aspect will be included here, but the interested reader is referred to the Social Services Committee (1981).

Deferred retirement

There is nothing special about the prevailing normal retirement ages of 60 for females and 65 for males. They are at these levels for historical reasons. As we have dicussed above, longevity is likely to improve. It is also likely that the factors responsible for an extension of the life of older persons also contribute to improvements in their health, thereby also increasing their potential productivity and their disposition to remain in the labour force. Problems with ill health and physical or mental breakdown are expected to decrease in importance. It could be argued therefore that some of the extra periods of lifetime, and healthy lifetime, should be added to an individual's productive lifetime rather than wholly to his/her period of retirement.

Of course it would be difficult to institute a rise in the statutory minimum retirement age given the prevailing economic conditions. It would be preferable and easier for late retirement to be encouraged and for flexibility to be the watchword. This could be done, for example, by replacing the normal by a minimum retirement age, which would be more appropriate subject to some qualification to provide for pensions on ill-health retirement and deferred pensions on withdrawal. It is important to have flexibility both within employers and between employers. Such

Table 9.5 *Income of the early retired*

Early retired receiving income from:	Percentage in category receiving less than *k%* of male average earnings for 1974–77	
	k = 50	*k* = 75
Occupational pension	11	20
Private savings	11	39
Health-related national insurance benefits	23	57
Means-tested benefits	45	90

Source: Altmann (1981).

developments will require a change in attitudes by the government and CBI (and employers in general), trade unions, pension trustees, among others. Clearly there would be difficulties with the likely continuation of high levels of unemployment.

Real choice as regards pension age depends not only on the right to some pension but also on the ability to continue working and the adequacy of the pension when work stops. Two important constraints are:

- health,
- the availability of jobs, and there is currently much pressure on the over 60s at work to relinquish their jobs in favour of younger people.

As has been mentioned above, we believe that health will decrease in importance. Many persons over age 60 have the energies and skills to continue to contribute positively to society through paid employment. However, they will not have the opportunity to contribute in this way unless there are fundamental changes in employment patterns, with very many more opportunities for part-time employment (with a major share of these going to older people), or, given changing needs, in the education and training given to those nearing retirement. The encouragement of part-time work after normal retirement age and the increasing opportunities for retraining during one's working life could help to reconcile the problems of the old and the young in times of serious unemployment.

The encouragement of late retirement might be hindered further in current circumstances by pension schemes' emphasis on a 'normal retirement age' and by the Inland Revenue's use of an earnings rule for males aged 65–69 and females aged 60–64. Parker's survey reveals that 83 per cent of such male pensioners and 18 per cent of female pensioners were affected by this rule.

A general consequence of workers continuing to work part time for a substantial period after they leave full-time employment is that they are helping further to pay for their own pension and extending the period in which assets can be accumulated. The estimates of worker to pensioner ratios associated with the optimistic mortality projections described in Chapter 8 may, therefore, be too low because they do not allow for the likelihood that healthier persons may work longer as well as live longer. Furthermore, a policy that reduces the replacement of earnings by pension may induce more older persons to continue working, at least on a part-time basis; the extent of this effect would depend upon what happens to the 'earnings rule'.

There are many methods of fixing the ultimate pension payable. A late retiree could be given the full actuarial value by way of an increased pension, the country having gained from the added years of productive work. If this is too burdensome, deferment could be rewarded with less than the full actuarial credit or the pension appropriate to age 65 could be paid from the actual retirement age. The late retiree engaging in part-time work could be paid a (part-time) salary and a proportion of his pension entitlement immediately, with the rest being deferred and possibly augmented. This would alleviate the problem of a sudden drop in income on ultimate retirement.

To sum up, there are a number of factors that argue for a trend towards deferred retirement, namely; increased health and vigour; surveys indicating the preferences of pensioners to continue working (hindered by the 'earnings rule'); feelings of anomie and uselessness, sometimes accompanying retirement and leading to early death; benefits to national insurance and occupational pension funds if normal retirement age increased marginally; the fact that discrimination on the basis of sex may become illegal.

The effects of a trend towards deferred retirement would be a potential increase in gross national product; a lower dependency ratio; a reduced burden on pension provision; improved socialization of the elderly; a change in the supply of and demand for labour. The balance between the increasing economic activity of women, a trend towards deferred retirement and high levels of adult unemployment would, however, be difficult to resolve.

Employment trends: projected

The general approach of this projection is to estimate the number of years of pensionable service that cohorts of men and women will have accumulated by retirement in the years around 2031.

Assumptions and basis used for the projection

Age range For males, the age range to be considered for membership of an occupational pension scheme is 16–65 (16–60 for females). In the early stages of description, the age range will be restricted to the band from age 20 to normal pension age for two reasons. First, this eliminates those stages of the life cycle at which there have been differences between cohorts in economic activity because of increased educational participation. Secondly, the minimum entry for many occupational pension schemes is close to age 20 (Government Actuary, 1981). An adjustment will be made subsequently for extending the age range down below 20.

Economic activity rates at ages over the normal retirement ages have been asumed to be effectively zero on the grounds that, ultimately, pension levels will be more generous on an individual basis so that the proportion of pensioners earning income from employment or self-employment is negligible.

Part-time employment Since the principal aim of this discussion of employment trends is to suggest some assumptions for projecting the outgo and contributions for occupational pension schemes, it is not proposed to discuss explicitly part-time employment. This would be particularly important for married women. However, the projections allow implicitly for changes in the level of this factor.

Permanent incapacity It is assumed that the proportions of males and females aged between 20 and normal pension age who are permanently inactive is 1 per cent.

The evidence available from the statistics relating to the administration of invalidity benefit (i.e. persons who are receiving more than half a year's sickness benefit) indicates that the average prevalence rate of long-term sickness for males between these ages is 2–3 per cent. For females the figure lies between 1 and 2 per cent. Since we are interested not in the proportion incapacitated at any time but rather for the whole working lifetime, an estimate of 1 per cent does not seem unreasonable.

Unemployment The approach here will be to assume a fixed level of unemployment throughout for both sexes taken as 6 per cent, 9 per cent or 12 per cent. A basic assumption of 6 per cent unemployment has been used by both the Government Actuary (1982), in the First Quinquennial Review of the National Insurance Fund, and Field (1983). The advantage of using a fixed unemployment level is that it enables the upward trend in pension provision, due to the emerging costs of the new state earnings-related pension scheme and of the maturing of occupational pension schemes, to be clearly demonstrated. These unemployment rate assumptions use a level taken to be independent of age. The unemployment rate, however, does vary markedly with attained age for both sexes; for example, in mid-1982 the rate for males in the UK varied between about 9 per cent at ages 35–54 up to about 20 per cent at ages 18–19 (for females the range was between about 3 per cent at ages 45 and over and 15 per cent at ages 18–19). However, the use of age-specific unemployment rates adds complexity to the model without clearly improving the credibility of the results. It has, therefore, been decided to dispense with this added level of detail.

One conseqence of the high current levels of unemployment seems to be growing acceptance by some men aged over 60 and by some married women that they will be unable to find work in present circumstances. They therefore no longer register as unemployed and they disappear from the economically active. This 'discouraged worker effect' has been allowed for in the 1982 calculations of the Government Actuary but is omitted here on the grounds of simplicity and the smallness of the effect in our consideration of occupational pension schemes.

It should be noted that the unemployment rate as conventionally calculated omits married women who pay reduced-rate state pension contributions (they receive neither benefits nor contribution credits when employed) from the numerator and denominator of the rate. These optants now form a closed group and are expected to decline rapidly over the next twenty years, so the propensity for married women to register when unemployed will increase. Similarly, current unemployment rates probably understate the real level of unemployment for married women because of this effect.

There is evidence to suggest that the incidence of unemployment and physical incapacity are positively correlated (Stern, 1983). Further, we would expect that those in occupations that tend to be pensionable have less unemployment (and probably sickness) than the average and that they are more likely to be able to retire early on a pension if they are in serious ill health. These putative correlations have not been incorporated into the projections discussed below.

The projected working lifetime of the average male
Our starting point is the published economic activity rates from the 1971 Census. (At the time of writing, detailed data from the 1981 Census are not available.) If male economic activity rates were to remain fixed over time at the levels measured in the 1971 Census, the average male lifetime between ages 20 and 65 would be distributed as in Table 9.6. This average includes some individuals who are out of employment for a sufficiently long time for them to have lost their jobs or the right to a pension

Table 9.6 *Average male working lifetime,*
ages 20–65 (1971 Census)

	%	Years
Student	1.4	0.6
Retired	1.0	0.5
Other inactive	2.1	1.0
Self-employed	9.3	4.2
Out of employment	4.9	2.2
Employee	81.3	36.6
	100.0	45.0

in respect of this period (either an occupational pension or the state earnings-related pension). Such individuals are made up of two groups: the more or less permanently inactive, and the self-employed.

The allowance to be made for these groups is problematic. Data from the National Insurance Scheme and the 1971 and 1981 Censuses suggest that an overall prevalence rate for long-term invalidity benefit is about 1 per cent.

Self-employment is wholly outside the scope of this report. It appears that only a few careers are wholly in self-employment and so to be excluded from our consideration. There are three broad types of career that include self-employment: professional, managerial, building trades. Measures of self-employment (in particular in relation to building workers who frequently alternate between the employed and self-employed statuses) are complicated by transfers between employment and self-employment. Joshi and Owen (1983) present some data from the DHSS Stagger and Seasonal and Intermittent Workers Enquiry which give some information on male transfers between class 1 and class 2 (state pension contribution status) employment. After one year's follow up, 8 per cent had a complete self-employment record and 2 per cent had a mixed record. After four years, the corresponding figures were 7 per cent and 6 per cent. Extrapolating over a lifetime history is speculative. However, we shall assume that 6 per cent of males are permanently self-employed (an approximation that has also been used by Field, 1983).

Thus 7 per cent of the population are to be excluded. The remaining 93 per cent of the population are assumed to have an average lifetime distributed as in Table 9.7.

Table 9.7   *Average male working lifetime, ages 20–65 excluding self-employed and permanently inactive (1971 Census)*

	%	Years
Student	1.4	0.6
Retired	1.0	0.5
Spells of inactivity	1.2	0.5
Self-employed	3.5	1.6
Off work	5.3	2.4
Employment	87.6	39.4
	100.0	45.0

The unpublished 1978/79 state pension contribution statistics confirm broadly this picture, but neither these data nor the Census provide cross-sectional information by age on the membership of occupational pension schemes.

These calculations may be repeated for different ages at retirement, to give the figures shown in Table 9.8.

Table 9.8   *Average length of working life in full-time employment: different ages at retirement (1971 Census)*

Normal retirement age	Working life in full-time employment	
	%	Years
60	88.9	35.5
65	87.6	39.4
70	85.7	42.9

The increase in retirement age has been incorporated using some simple extrapolation of the age-specific activity rates. These supplementary figures are for illustrative purposes.

The same set of calculations using the projected Department of Employment 1985/86 economic activity rates gives the results shown in Table 9.9. It is assumed again that the level of self-employment is as for the 1971 Census and that 7 per cent of the male population is either permanently inactive or self-employed. Three different levels of unemployment have been used – 6 per cent unemployment, for example, has been taken to be equivalent to males spending on average 6 per cent of their working lifetime unemployed. The extra set of figures shows the result of a decrease in economic activity rates at ages 60–64 to 50 per cent,

Table 9.9 *Average male working lifetime: different ages at retirement and unemployment levels (1985/86 activity rates)*

Normal retirement age	Working lifetime employed Unemployment level					
	6 per cent		9 per cent		12 per cent	
	%	Yrs.	%	Yrs.	%	Yrs.
60	86.0	34.4	82.8	33.1	79.5	31.8
65 with early retirement	80.5	36.2	77.2	34.7	73.9	33.3
65	82.8	37.3	79.5	35.8	76.3	34.3
70	78.1	39.1	74.8	37.4	71.6	35.8

reflecting increases in early retirement, and indicates that a fall of about 1.1 years in the expected lifetime in full employment would result compared to the estimate based on a normal retirement age of 65 and the projected 1985/86 economic activity rates.

Again the figures for early and deferred retirement are for illustrative purposes only. In particular the likely interaction with level of unemployment has been ignored and the calculations performed automatically. The figures for 12 per cent unemployment and a normal retirement age of 70 must clearly be viewed in this light.

The effect of an increase in the level of unemployment by 3 per cent is to reduce the percentage of working lifetime in full-time employment by a similar percentage, namely, 3.2–3.3 per cent.

The projected working lifetime of the average childless woman
The econometric and demographic analyses of Joshi and Owen (1981) note the important relationship between female economic activity rates and the presence of young children. Because of this link we shall deal with childless women and mothers separately.

Given the uncertainties in projecting economic activity rates for women, a range of assumptions will be used. For childless women, the basic employment assumptions are as follows:

Assumption 1 (E1)
An extreme assumption would be that, for the generations retiring around 2030, women will be permanently inactive with the same frequency as men in the absence of any 'child effects'. The duration of women's earning lives will remain shorter than men's because of their greater involvement in looking after young children and elderly relatives. In this

'unisex' environment the main distinction will be not between the sexes but between childless women and mothers. Under such extreme assumptions, the working lifetimes of childless women would resemble those of men, as described earlier.

Assumption 2 (E2)
A less extreme assumption is that observed trends moderate, for example because current low employment levels may indicate a lower level of demand for labour than has hitherto been the case. Under this assumption E2 there is little advance in lifetime experience after the 1941 birth cohort and this means that in a steady state female labour force participation would remain at approximately the same level as that prevailing at the 1981 Census.

Assumption 3 (E3)
To take a more pessimistic point of view, we assume that all cohorts have the same lifetime pattern as those retiring in 1981, that is, the 1921 birth cohort. In a steady state this assumption would imply female employment returning to the levels prevailing during the 1960s.

If the lifetime economic activity rates for childless women became exactly equal to those for men as projected by the Department of Employment for 1985/86, then the average childless women's working history would be as in the first column of Table 9.10. The distributions under the two alternative assumptions in Table 9.10 were obtained by adjusting each category of activity by 0.90 and 0.76, respectively, with the balance of time accruing to the inactive category. These factors refer to the proportion of time spent working for childless women relative to men and correspond to the 1941 and 1921 birth cohorts (Joshi and Owen, 1981). The figures for the proportion of the working lifetime allocated to self-employment have been based on the male figures for the 1971 Census.
The 'increase' in inactive time under the two lower assumptions would be the result of some combination of shorter working lives and the survival (or re-emergence) of the one-earner couple. It would be an extreme and unlikely version of the middle assumption if 14.7 per cent (i.e. 17.1 per cent less 2.4 per cent for students and retired) of childless women remained inactive throughout their adult years. The other extreme – all childless women working at some time – appears more plausible.

The projected working lifetime of the average mother
A number of papers have investigated the work history of women and in particular married women – including Hunt (1968), Sweet (1970), Young (1977), Stewart and Greenhalgh (1984), Martin and Roberts (1984). Of this group, Sweet's work is distinctive in that a quantitative analysis is

Table 9.10   *The working lifetime of the average childless woman, 1985/86 projected basis*

| | E1 | | E2 | | E3 | |
	%	Yrs	%	Yrs	%	Yrs
6% unemployment						
Inactive	7.9	3.2	17.1	6.8	29.9	12.1
Self-Employed	9.3	3.7	8.4	3.3	7.1	2.8
Unemployed	6.0	2.4	5.4	2.2	4.6	1.8
Employee	76.8	30.7	69.1	27.7	58.4	23.3
	100.0	40.0	100.0	40.0	100.0	40.0
9% unemployment						
Inactive	7.9	3.2	17.1	6.8	29.9	12.1
Self-Employed	9.3	3.7	8.4	3.3	7.1	2.8
Unemployed	9.0	3.6	8.1	3.2	6.8	2.7
Employee	73.8	29.5	66.4	26.7	56.2	22.4
	100.0	40.0	100.0	40.0	100.0	40.0
12% unemployment						
Inactive	7.9	3.2	17.1	6.8	29.9	12.1
Self-Employed	9.3	3.7	8.4	3.3	7.1	2.8
Unemployed	12.0	4.8	10.8	4.3	9.1	3.6
Employee	70.8	28.3	63.7	25.6	53.9	21.5
	100.0	40.0	100.0	40.0	100.0	40.0

Assumption spans the E1, E2, E3 columns above.

provided of the employment patterns of American wives in relation to their family composition using 1960 Census material. For Great Britain, the only published, quantitative analysis of the relationship between female employment and fertility comes from Joshi and Owen (1981, 1983) and Joshi, Layard and Owen (1985). The projections here are based on some of their findings. Using the parameters from Joshi and Owen's cross-sectional regressions it is possible to estimate the effect of children on the mother's lifetime economic activity. The following are typical examples of the extent to which the number of years of activity is lowered:

4.3 years for a 1 child family
4.7 years for a 2 children family (with birth-spacing of two years)
6.0 years for a 3 children family (with birth-spacing of two years)

The demographic projections described earlier use two alternative assumptions for the long-term completed family size – 2.1 and 2.0 children per woman. Assuming a level of childlessness of 12 per cent (Britton, 1979) and converting these estimates into children per mother, it is possible to estimate the number of years of economic activity lost because of bringing up children – this comes approximately to 5.3 years. Further, some estimates are being developed for a long-term completed family size of 1.8 children per woman, which has been taken to differ from the above only in that childlessness is at 20 per cent rather than 12 per cent (see models A and F in Britton, 1979).

These estimates may be used to give the distribution of the working lifetime of the average mother. This is as for a childless woman except that each category of activity in Table 9.10 would be reduced. The reduction factor for assumption E1 at 6 per cent unemployment would be about 17 per cent (i.e. 5.3/30.7) and the extra time would be allocated to the 'child effect' category. The distributions for the other two employment assumptions are derived exactly as for childless women with this adjustment made. The reduction factors for 9 per cent and 12 per cent unemployment have been applied similarly. The results are shown in Table 9.11 (corresponding to Table 9.10 for childless women).

The child effect in Table 9.11 refers only to the extra time that mothers spend out of the labour market relative to childless women. It does not necessarily refer to total time spent caring for children except under the unisex assumption (E1). Under Assumptions E2 and E3, much of the extra 'inactive' time would coincide with years that dependent children were present.

We expect that women's earnings-related state pension and occupational pension entitlements will remain significantly below men's so long as they retain the primary responsibility for child care, which we assume will continue to account for substantial reductions in the length of mothers' earning lives. There will probably also continue to be a further disadvantage to mothers from lower earnings while at work; not only are their hours of employment reduced by their domestic responsibilities, but their hourly rates of pay tend to suffer from less than complete employment histories.

Part-time working plays an important role in women's employment. Thus, the proportion of women earning more than (the equivalent of) the lower earnings limit (LEL) for state pension in the 1974 GHS was half as great as that for men. Joshi and Owen (1983) have shown that part-year working plays a fairly minor role in keeping married women's earnings low. Using multiple regression analyses they estimate the effect of the presence of children on the level of earnings. Given the importance of annual earnings in excess of the lower earnings limit (LEL) in determining entitlement to state pensions and in its relationship with contracted-out occupational pension schemes, we shall use Joshi and Owen's results to

Table 9.11 *The working lifetime of the average mother,*
1985/86 projected basis

	E1 %	E1 Yrs	Assumption E2 %	E2 Yrs	E3 %	E3 Yrs
6% unemployment						
Inactive	7.9	3.2	17.1	6.8	29.9	12.1
Self-Employed	7.7	3.1	6.8	2.7	5.5	2.2
Unemployed	5.0	2.0	4.4	1.8	3.6	1.4
Employee	63.5	25.4	55.9	22.4	45.1	18.0
Child effect	15.9	6.3	15.9	6.3	15.9	6.3
	100.0	40.0	100.0	40.0	100.0	40.0
9% unemployment						
Inactive	7.9	3.2	17.1	6.8	29.9	12.0
Self-Employed	7.6	3.0	6.7	2.7	5.4	2.1
Unemployed	7.4	3.0	6.5	2.6	5.2	2.1
Employee	60.5	24.2	53.2	21.3	42.9	17.2
Child effect	16.6	6.6	16.5	6.6	16.6	6.6
	100.0	40.0	100.0	40.0	100.0	40.0
12% unemployment						
Inactive	7.9	3.2	17.1	6.8	29.9	12.0
Self-Employed	7.6	3.0	6.7	2.7	5.3	2.1
Unemployed	9.8	3.9	8.6	3.4	6.9	2.7
Employee	57.5	23.0	50.5	20.2	40.6	16.2
Child effect	17.2	6.9	17.2	6.9	17.2	7.0
	100.0	40.0	100.0	40.0	100.0	40.0

exclude those working periods with earnings below this threshold in the belief that this will ultimately produce a 'better' estimate of the average period of pensionable service. They have estimated that, for various family sizes and compositions, the effect of children on the probability of earning more than this threshold in a year is 1.4 times as great as their effect on labour force participation. Hence, under the assumption of 6 per cent unemployment, mothers will have 8.8 fewer years earning more than Lower Earnings Level (i.e. 8.8 = 6.3 × 1.4 from Table 9.11). The LEL is £38 per week for the financial year April 1986–March 1987.

As for males, the figures in Tables 9.10 and 9.11 include females who are either permanently inactive or self-employed. We shall assume that, as for males, the prevalance of permanent inactivity is 1 per cent. The percentage levels of self-employment are taken, somewhat arbitrarily, as:

Assumption	Childless women	Married women
E1	6	5
E2	5	4
E3	4	3

For the rest of the childless women we use the figures in Table 9.10 and adjust as for males to give the figures in Table 9.12. The character of employment assumption (E1, E2, E3) is seen to be more significant than the prevalence of unemployment.

For mothers the same procedure is followed except that the child effects from Table 9.11 require adjustment. The results are shown in Table 9.13. The changes in the figures in Tables 9.12 and 9.13 are of the order of 3 per cent when the level of unemployment changes by 3 per cent.

The proportions in Tables 9.12 and 9.13 are of a similar order of magnitude to those reported for currently working women aged 45–54 in the 1975 National Training Survey (Stewart and Greenhalgh, 1984).

The estimates presented earlier for men and in Tables 9.10–9.13 for women all refer to an average person. In reality of course there will be a distribution of individuals spread around these averages (assuming they are reasonably unbiased estimates). Thus, an average of 0.6 years spent as a student after age 20 will clearly not involve all persons in spending 0.6 years – rather it might be reasonable to suggest that about 30 per cent of individuals spend an average two years in that category. To give some idea of the amount of variation underlying these central estimates, we shall consider the proportion of males with incomplete histories between ages 20 and 65. We estimate, somewhat arbitrarily, that:

30 per cent are students
20 per cent experience inactivity or early retirement
 8 per cent transfer between employment and self-employment
30 per cent experience periods of sickness and/or unemployment.

If these groups are mutually independent then the proportion of males with incomplete records is 64 per cent.

A general caveat should be attached to the use of Joshi and Owen's results that describe the impact of extra birth averaged over all families. They give an idea of the average effect per child in a family of average size, but should not be interpreted as showing the effect of an only child or the effect per child in a very large family.

The specification and analysis of Joshi and Owen that has been used in the foregoing sections depends on the relationship between female economic activity rates and fertility. Joshi and Owen (1981) have shown

Table 9.12 *Percentage of career in employment for the average childless woman, 1985/86 projected basis*

Unemployment	Assumption		
	E1	E2	E3
	%	%	%
6%	82.8	73.5	61.5
9%	79.5	70.6	59.2
12%	76.3	67.8	56.7

Table 9.13 *Percentage of career in employment (with adequate earnings) for the average mother 1985/86 projected basis*

Unemployment	Assumption		
	E1	E2	E3
	%	%	%
6%	61.4	52.7	40.7
9%	57.9	49.6	38.2
12%	54.4	46.4	35.5

that, once child-bearing is allowed for, marriage (in particular marital status) does not appear as an important factor for the explanation or projection of economic activity. Any independent effects of marital status are thought to be too minor (or too complex) to detect in the data that are available.

Conclusion

Assumptions have been made regarding the levels of economic activity, part-time working, permanent incapacity and unemployment, leading to estimates of the structure of the working lifetime of the average man or woman retiring in 2031 (50 years from the base date of 1981). For women the approach has necessarily to be cohort-based because of their increasing levels of labour force participation over the last thirty years. Because of the critical link between female economic activity and the presence of young children, childless women and mothers are dealt with separately and then the results are combined. The final results appear in Tables 9.9 and 9.12.

References

Altmann, R. M. (1981), 'Incomes of the early retired', SSRC Programme: Taxation, Incentives and the Distribution of Income, Discussion Paper No. 28, University College, London

Bacon, F. W., Benjamin, B. and Elphinstone, M. D. W. (1954), 'The growth of pension rights and their impact on the national economy', *Journal of the Institute of Actuaries*, vol. 80, pp. 141–202 (with discussion)

Britton, M. (1979), 'Birth intervals', *Population Trends*, vol. 18, pp. 8–16

Department of Employment (1981), 'Labour force outlook to 1986' *Department of Employment Gazette*, vol. 89, pp. 167–173, London: HMSO

Field, J. L. (1983), 'Projections of the costs of occupational and state pensions', *Journal of the Institute of Actuaries*, vol. 110, pp. 243–270

General Household Survey (1983), *OPCS Monitor* GHS 83/2, London: HMSO

Government Actuary (1981), *Occupational Pension Schemes 1979*, Sixth Survey by the Government Actuary, London: HMSO

Government Actuary (1982), *National Insurance Fund Long Term Financial Estimates*, Report by the Government Actuary on the First Quinquennial Review under section 137 of the Social Security Act 1975, London: HMSO

Hunt, A. (1968), *A Survey of Women's Employment*, London: HMSO

Joshi, H. E. and Owen, S. J. (1981), 'Demographic predictors of women's work participation in post-war Britain', Centre for Population Studies Working Paper No. 81–3, London School of Hygiene and Tropical Medicine

Joshi, H. E. and Owen, S. J. (1983), 'How many pensionable years? The lifetime earnings history of men and women', Government Economic Service Working Paper No. 65, Economic Advisers' Office, Department of Health and Social Security

Joshi, H. E., Layard, R. and Owen, S. J. (1985), 'Why are more women working in Britain', *Journal of Labour Economics*, vol. 3 (supp.), pp. 147–176

Martin, J. and Roberts, C. (1984), *Women and Employment: A Lifetime Perspective*, Department of Employment/Office of Population Censuses and Surveys, London: HMSO

Parker, S. (1980), *Older Workers and Retirement*, London: HMSO

Social Services Committee (1981) *Minutes of Evidence on Age of Retirement to Social Services Committee, given on 21 December 1981*, Session 81/82, London: HMSO

Stern, J. (1983), 'The relationship between unemployment, morbidity and mortality in Britain', *Population Studies*, vol. 37, pp. 61–74

Stewart, M. B. and Greenhalgh, C. A. (1984), 'Work history patterns and the occupational attainment of women', *Economic Journal*, vol. 94, pp. 493–519

Sweet, J. A. (1970), 'Family composition and the labour force activity of American wives,' *Demography*, vol. 7, pp. 195–209

Young, C. (1977), *The Family Life Cycle*, Canberra: Australian National University

10   Future Dependency

STEVEN HABERMAN

Dependency: total and pensioners

For both state pensions (pay-as-you-go) and occupational pensions
(principally funded) the average benefits that can be paid to each
pensioner relative to the level of earnings depend upon the demographic
structure of the population and the level of contributions. If a certain
degree of replacement of earnings by retirement pension is to be
maintained, then changes in the ratio of workers to those retired must be
offset by changes in the contribution rate. Assuming this degree of
replacement is held constant, we shall investigate the broad interaction
between demographic changes and level of contributions by using the
results of the projections described in Chapters 8 and 9.

Table 10.1 shows the historic and projected trend in the number of
economically active persons per pensioner from 1901 up to 2031. The
figures indicate the relationship between the numbers of pensioners (i.e.
men aged 65 and over and females aged 60 and over) and the economically
active population. As in Chapter 8, for years after 1971 the number of
non-gainfully occupied women has been estimated in a rather crude way
as 50 per cent of the 15–59 age group and no allowance has been made
for men being non-gainfully employed. Using the 1985/86 Department of
Employment economic activity rate projections, an attempt can be made
to project the numerator of this rate more accurately. The figures for 2031
in terms of number of economically active persons per pensioner then
become:

Demographic projection	A 2.05
	B 1.49
	C 2.01
	D 1.45

that is, about 0.03 to 0.05 higher than in Table 10.1. Projected
proportions married from the 1979 GAD UK population projections by
marital condition were used for this purpose (OPCS, 1981).

More detailed versions of these projections (not included here) would
show that under bases A and C the number of economically active persons

Table 10.1 *Economic pressure of dependants in the
UK population, 1901–2031*

Year	Demographic projection[a]	No. of economically active persons per pensioner[b]
1901		6.59
1921		5.33
1931		4.67
1951		3.35
1961		3.11
1971		2.86
1981		2.62
2021	A	2.30
	B	1.73
	C	2.28
	D	1.71
	GAD 1981	2.27
2031	A	2.00
	B	1.45
	C	1.96
	D	1.42

Notes:
[a] A: TPFR = 2.1, medium mortality
  B: TPFR = 2.1, low mortality
  C: TPFR = 2.0, medium mortality
  D: TPFR = 2.0, low mortality
[b] Economically active consists of all males aged 15–64 and 50% of females aged 15–59 as an approximation for years after 1971.

per pensioner rises a little between about 1981 and 2001 and then falls rapidly to well below its current level. This occurs because the old come from the fairly small generations born before, during and after the Second World War, while those of working ages include the larger generations born between about 1955 and 1965. The numbers leaving school and entering the workforce would come from the smaller generations born since then; as the larger, earlier generations pass normal retirement age, the ratio falls dramatically.

Table 10.2 presents the dependency position for 2031 in a different way but similar to that discussed in Chapter 8. Dependency is recognized as having four components: children, non-gainfully occupied males aged 15–64, non-gainfully occupied females aged 15–59, and pensioners. Assuming the 1985/86 projected economic activity rates are held fixed, the calculations give the results in Table 10.2. The ratios are the inverse in format of those described in Table 10.1, that is, the number of dependent persons per economically active. For pensioners only these are:

Demographic projection	A	0.49
	B	0.67
	C	0.50
	D	0.69

The complexity of the projections can be taken one step further. The assumptions E1, E2 and E3 for female economic activity described in Chapter 9 can be used to project the dependency ratios. Assuming that 12 per cent of women are childless (for consistency with the projections of Chapter 9), the figures for 2031 in terms of number of economically active persons per pensioner are shown in Table 10.3. The overall picture presented by these estimates is as follows for 2031:

medium mortality (projections A and C): 1.9–2.2 active persons per pensioner
very low mortality (projections B and D): 1.4–1.6 active persons per pensioner relative to a current level of 2.6.

If the level of unemployment does not change, the ratio of workers to pensioners increases up to the turn of the century (not shown in Table 10.1). All four demographic bases then show a fall in this ratio during the first three decades of the next century. Comparing the 2031 and 1981 figures from Table 10.1 indicates that, for a constant level of earnings replacement, the total contribution rate (employer plus employee) would have to be increased in the following proportions:

Demographic projection	*1981–2031*	*1981–2021*
A	+31%	+14%
B	+81%	+51%
C	+34%	+15%
D	+85%	+53%

The figures for the period 1981–2021 indicate the steepness of the rise required in the third decade of the next century. It should be remembered that bases A and C are more credible than the other pair, which require extreme falls in the level of mortality rates. These figures may be compared with the projections provided by the Government Actuary

Table 10.2 *Projected economic burden of the dependent population of the UK, 2031*

		Nos. in thousands					Ratio to remainder of			
	Home population all ages	Non-gainfully occupied			Pensionable class	Remainder				
		Children under 15	females 15–59	males 15–64						
Demographic projection	(1)	(2)	(3)	(4)	(5)	(6)	(2)	(3)+(4)	(5)	(2)+(3)+ (4)+(5)
A	60,719	12,190	5,655	1,847	13,436	27,591	0.44	0.27	0.49	1.20
B	66,419	12,183	5,683	1,768	18,804	27,981	0.44	0.27	0.67	1.38
C	59,203	11,368	5,528	1,805	13,436	27,066	0.42	0.27	0.50	1.19
D	64,903	11,361	5,555	1,870	18,804	27,313	0.42	0.27	0.69	1.38

Table 10.3 *Number of economically active persons per pensioner in 2031: different demographic and employment assumptions*

Demographic projection	*E1*	Assumptions *E2*	*E3*
A	2.20	2.09	1.93
B	1.59	1.51	1.40
C	2.16	2.05	1.89
D	1.56	1.48	1.37

(1982) in the Quinquennial Review of the state scheme. On the basis of long-term annual increases of earnings of 8 per cent and of prices of 6 per cent, these estimates revealed a rise in the level of class 1 national insurance contributions from 1985/86 to 2025/26 of about 42 per cent. The demographic basis used is similar to basis A but the relative rise is higher because of the introduction of the state earnings-related pension scheme, which increases necessarily the average level of replacement of earnings by pension.

Whether these higher contribution rates will meet resistance from the working population will depend on the speed of increase. The actual increase in contribution rates will be higher than that suggested by the calculations of the previous paragraph because of the maturing of the state earnings-related pension scheme (and of the bulk of occupational pension schemes) and possible shifts in the age distribution of pensioners. The relationship to the economy has been discussed in Chapter 5. With moderate economic growth these forecast increases may not be excessive but in a sluggish economy the burden of contributions may be less tolerable in its effect on real disposable incomes.

The demographic problems of an ageing population are of course not unique to the UK. Comparable projections for other industrial countries show that the proportion of pensioners in the population is expected to change little before 2000 in most countries, with the exception of Japan where a 50 per cent rise is predicted. In all these countries, the proportion is anticipated to rise between 2000 and about 2030, with the greatest rise being predicted for North America (Social Services Committee, 1981).

The calculations of total dependency assume that the burdens from children, non-employed adults and pensioners are comparable. Non-gainfully employed women are clearly less of a burden on the economy as they care for the elderly and young children. Without this support, the burden might be greater. Equal weighting has been given to children and to the elderly although the former probably consume less goods and services, in terms of housing, food, clothing and heating (although children need more resources in terms of education and training). For example, in projections of 'total personal disposable income', economists at the Department of Health and Social Security have used a weighting of 1/2 for children aged under 16 (DHSS, 1984). These arguments are perfectly valid, but the purpose of the calculations is illustrative only and it is necessary to align the definitions with those used by economic statisticians, for consistency, in deciding who is to be regarded as contributing to the economy.

Dependency of the elderly

Dependency related to care for the elderly is quantified in Table 10.4, where a comparison is made between persons aged over 75 and women aged 50–59 – that is, the group about 25 years younger (previous generation) and most likely to be caring for the elderly. The risk of having elderly dependants as measured by this crude index had been steady at about 0.36 during the first third of this century and is projected to rise dramatically from its current level of just below 1.0. Under the medium mortality projections (A and C), the index rises to 1.30 in 1991 then falls to 1.06 in 2021 and rises again to 1.56 in 2031. Under the extreme low mortality projections (B and D), the index increases monotonically from 1.42 in 1991 to 1.75 in 2021 and then accelerates up to *2.76* in 2031. All of these projected values would be historically high.

As the index increases over time, adults approaching age 60 would be under increased strain and hence less keen to retire if they themselves have aged parents to support. Those projections that are based on increasing economic activity for married women may involve such women in being less able (or less willing because of career commitments) directly to help their aged relatives, who consequently have to turn to community services for support. In the UK, however, the Home Responsibility Protection system does give carers state basic pension 'credits' for years spent supporting an aged infirmed person, which would mitigate the above effect to some extent (Haberman, 1985).

Dependency of the unemployed

Unemployment can clearly affect the worker to pensioner ratio discussed above (and the implied level of contributions required to maintain the income replacement ratio). The ratio of the employed labour force to the pensioner population is projected to improve until the end of the century, although this might be offset by a worsening of the level of unemployment. However, the demographic changes projected to occur after 2000, and in particular after 2020, are likely to dwarf the effects of any plausible variation in the unemployment rate.

Table 10.4 *Ratios of old people to women a generation younger: UK*

Year		No. in thousands Women aged 50–59 (1)	Persons aged over 75 (2)	Ratio (2)/(1)
1901		1,473	531	0.36
1911		1,751	623	0.36
1931		2,673	957	0.36
1971		3,438	2,609	0.76
1981		3,327	3,266	0.98
1991	A/C	3,017	3,918	1.30
	B/D	3,042	4,314	1.42
2001	A/C	3,633	4,148	1.14
	B/D	3,689	5,311	1.44
2011	A/C	3,685	4,101	1.11
	B/D	3,760	6,152	1.64
2021	A/C	4,182	4,444	1.06
	B/D	4,283	7,487	1.75
2031	A/C	3,253	5,089	1.56
	B/D	3,331	9,187	2.76

Conclusion

There are dangers in following a strict, arithmetic analysis of dependency ratios. In particular these relate to the level of unemployment and the demand for labour. The future and past are not directly comparable because of the technological improvements that have greatly reduced the number of workers needed to produce the goods required by the dependent sections of the population. Further, it is possible that, in the future, there would be an increased demand for labour to provide those *services* (rather than goods) that the dependants, for example, the elderly, would require.

References

Department of Health and Social Security (1984), *Population, Pension Costs and Pensioners' Incomes*, Background Paper for the Inquiry into Provision for Retirement, London: HMSO

Government Actuary (1982), *National Insurance Fund Long Term Financial Estimates*, Report by the Government Actuary on the First Quinquennial Review under section 137 of the Social Security Act 1975, London: HMSO

Haberman, S. (1985), 'Home responsibility protection and married women's pension rights', *Insurance: Mathematics and Economics*, vol. 4, pp. 207–224

OPCS (1981), *Population Projections 1979–2019*, Series PP2 No. 11, London: HMSO

Social Services Committee (1981), *Minutes of Evidence on Age of Retirement to Social Services Committee, given on 21 December 1981*, Session 81/82, London: HMSO

11 Future Pension Expenditure

STEVEN HABERMAN

Introduction

The purpose of this chapter is to consider future pension expenditure in relation to the size of the national economy, using a range of economic, demographic and actuarial assumptions. The first section describes a simple model for the estimation of the aggregate loss of pension rights on the transfer of jobs, that is, for 'early leavers'. The second section then goes on to use this simple model and the results of Chapters 8–10 to project pension expenditure.

Estimation of loss of pension rights on transfer of jobs

Job mobility: sources of data
In order to estimate the effect of job mobility on pension rights, we have examined the possible sources of data relating to occupational transfers.

The survey carried out by Parker (1980) shows that 22 per cent of occupational pensioners report having had only one main employer. However, no information is provided on the ages at which any job transfers occur or on how respondents interpreted the phrase 'one main employer'. For those retiring at normal retirement age (of both sexes) the average number of employers is reported as five, but no further information about the distribution is provided. However, some information is available for 399 males aged 55–64 and 199 females aged 50–59 on their distribution by number of employers – these distributions have been smoothed and are used in a subsequent paragraph.

McKormick and Hughes (1984) use data from the General Household Survey (GHS) for 1974 to fit regression models to responses to questions on job mobility. The results indicate wide variations in the rate of turnover according to an individual's characteristics but are not of direct use here.

The annual GHS does provide tabulations regularly on (a) the number of respondents who changed employer in the twelve months before interview, and (b) the average number of changes per working person, subdivided by age and sex. Values for (b) are given in Table 11.1 (for all adult ages). The trend in the percentage of workers who changed their

Table 11.1 *Changes of employer per working person
in the 12 months before interview*

Year	Percentage of workers who made 1 or more changes of employer	Av. no. of changes per working person	Approx. unemployment rate
1972	13	0.18	3.7
1973	15	0.21	2.6
1974	14	0.21	2.6
1975	13	0.16	4.1
1976	10	0.12	5.6
1979	12	0.15	5.6
1980	10	0.13	7.3
1981	7	0.08	10.5

Source: General Household Surveys, 1972–76, 1979–81, OPCS, London: HMSO, 1975–78, 1981–83.

employers in the twelve months before interview is similar to the figures shown in Table 11.1, varying between 15 per cent in 1973 and 7 per cent in 1981. These results suggest that the general economic situation during the 1970s as reflected in unemployment rates has also been reflected in the level of job mobility. At times of rising unemployment people seem to have been somewhat less likely to change job than at times of falling unemployment. The unemployment figures in Table 11.1 are Department of Employment estimates of the annual average percentage of all economically active persons who were registered as unemployed. GHS data on job mobility are not available for 1977 and 1978 when the unemployment rate stabilized at 6 per cent. The increases in unemployment between 1979 and 1981 were accompanied by a fall in the proportion of workers who changed employers in the twelve months prior to interview from 12 per cent to 7 per cent. The fall in mobility occurred among both sexes and in most age groups. The figures for full-time workers show a decline both in the proportion who changed employer once in the year and in the proportion who changed more than once. It would appear therefore that at times of 'high' unemployment about 7 per cent of workers change employers in any year and at times of 'low' unemployment about 15 per cent of workers change employers. Given

Table 11.2   *Distribution of employees by length of service
with current employer*

Length of service (yrs)	All males in full-time employment aged 60–64*	All females in full-time employment aged 50–59
less than 5	16.8	24.8
5 – 10	19.2	28.8
10 – 15	13.9	20.4
15 – 20	10.4	10.4
20 – 30	17.7	10.1
30 – 40	12.0	4.7
40 and over	10.0	0.8
	100.0%	100.0%

* age as at 1.1.79.
Source: Department of Employment (1980), Table 145.

that careers extend over 45 years (for males), this would suggest a range of three to seven job changes on average per career – a crude estimate that is not inconsistent with the figure given by Parker (1980).

Data on the length of time an employee has been with his current employer are gathered at irregular intervals by a special question on the New Earnings Surveys. To date the 1968, 1975, 1976 and 1979 surveys have included such a question. The sampling process is thought to under-represent persons with tenure of under one year – for our crude purposes such details will be ignored. Table 11.2 is taken from the 1979 Survey. The distributions shown are markedly different for the two sexes. These data and in particular the trends between 1968 and 1979 have been subjected to a thorough study by Main (1982).

Stewart and Greenhalgh (1984) use data from the 1975 National Training Survey to describe the work history patterns of women in the UK by current age and marital status. Attention is devoted not to job transfers but to transfers in and out of employment. The detailed figures are of doubtful applicability because they relate to a time of low unemployment.

These sources of data do not relate directly to members of occupational pension schemes, who do not form a random sample of all employees when job mobility is examined because we would anticipate that such persons would have lower mobility (*ceteris paribus*) because of their awareness of the possibility of loss of value of pension rights on transfer. Further, not all the periods of employment mentioned above would necessarily be pensionable. Thus, some industries (for example construction) are characterized by rapid labour turnover and an absence of occupational pension provision.

One data source that does refer to occupational pension scheme members is quoted by the Occupational Pensions Board (OPB). The OPB report on security mentions a survey carried out by a 'leading life office' with a large portfolio of pension schemes (OPB, 1982). A survey of over 39,000 members retiring on pension from over 1,800 schemes during the eleven years up to 30 April 1982 provided some data on the periods of service with the *last* employer. Thus 25 per cent had over 30 years with the last employer, 21 per cent had 21–30 years, 29 per cent had 11–20 years, 18 per cent had 6–10 years and 7 per cent had under 5 years. Of course, these data tell us nothing about time spent with previous employers nor do these data indicate pensionable service with the last employer.

Further data on withdrawal rates have been provided by this 'leading life office'. These withdrawal rates show marked secular trends as well as a strong variation with attained age (falling from nearly 0.20 in the early twenties to about 0.07 in the late fifties).

The overall impression is therefore of some limited data being available that are not directly suitable to the task in hand.

Early leavers

The information available on early leavers comes principally from the GAD Survey 1979 (Government Actuary, 1981), Parker's survey (Parker, 1980), the 1982 National Association of Pension Funds Survey (NAPF, 1982) and a postal questionnaire launched by the OPB into scheme practice in 1978 (OPB, 1981). The statistics show that the provision for early leavers was, in general, not generous, in particular in the private sector. But these statistics (not quoted here) relate to a transitional period when early leavers still retained the option to take refunds for their entire service, so they have limited relevance to the post-1980 situation. Further, as the guaranteed minimum pensions (GMPs), provided by the contracted-out pension schemes, come to be related to longer periods of service, the problem will be eased as GMPs are subject to automatic revaluation.

The information on the prevalence of early leavers is also limited. We have quoted earlier three estimates of the proportion of employees who remain with one employer throughout their career; according to Parker, this is 22 per cent, setting aside any doubts about the reliability of these figures; according to the New Earnings Survey 1979 this is 22 per cent for males and 7 per cent for females; according to the life office survey quoted by the OPB, 25 per cent of pensioners worked for their last employer for more than thirty years (which is effectively equivalent to having one employer for the purposes of computing pension rights). These three estimates are broadly consistent for males.

The OPB comments on the results of this life office survey that, 'in the absence of significant pension rights from earlier employments, over *half* of those in the schemes concerned could not have had pensions amounting to more than *half* of their final salaries, however generous the pension scheme formulae.'

Models for transfers between jobs

The main use of the projection of employment levels is to estimate the effective pensionable service built up at retirement by cohorts of employees retiring in fifty years' time. Following Field (1983) we shall use the abbreviation EPS for effective pensionable service.

For contracted-out schemes the EPS is the period of service that when multiplied by the pension fraction and the final pensionable salary, gives the actual pension paid (at 65 for a male or 60 for a female) from all schemes of which he or she has been a member. For a person who has only *one* pensionable job and remains in it until retirement, the EPS is the actual length of his scheme membership. But, for early leavers, it is reduced to take into account the fact that part of his pension will probably not be based on his salary at retirement but on his salary at withdrawal, with perhaps some allowance, at least on any GMP, for inflation.

The purpose of this section is to estimate the reduction factors to apply for early leavers. In the absence of any specific data on individual career histories, we shall attempt to estimate a likely range of values for the reduction factor that may then be applied to the average employment periods estimated in an earlier section. Pension schemes vary widely in their treatment of early leavers, so the approach is very simplistic.

The OPB (1981) has recommended that all final salary schemes should aim at increasing preserved benefits in line with the percentages specified by the Secretary of State according to section 21 of the 1975 Pensions Act, that is, broadly in line with the movement of national average earnings. In the long term the statutory minimum increase should be the total of,

(a) on any GMP included in the preserved benefits, the increase the scheme is required to give in accordance with the contracting-out legislation; and,

(b) on other benefits subject to the preservation requirements, the lower of the increase calculated on the basis of section 21 and 5 per cent p.a. for the period between the member's date of withdrawal and normal pension age.

It is assumed here that when a member leaves a pension scheme he or she will be awarded a preserved pension payable from the normal retirement age. Increases in these preserved benefits will be calculated on the basis that any GMP will be increased in line with average earnings, and that the remainder of the pension will be increased in line with prices in the public sector and not increased at all in the private sector (except for the increase implicit in the use of average pensionable weekly earnings). A separate set of calculations will indicate the effect of increasing the remainder of pension in the private sector at a rate equal to half the level of price inflation. These assumptions are reasonable in the light of the findings of the 1983 Government Actuary's Survey mentioned in Chapter 2 (Government Actuary, 1986). It will be assumed throughout that 'franking' in respect of deferred pensions and their preserved GMP components has ceased. This was recommended by the 1981 report of the OPB, and the Health and Social Security Act 1984 included powers to enable the DHSS to lay regulations that will prevent 'franking'. To estimate the reduction factors described above we shall consider initially some sample calculations based on the following formulae.

Consider a male employee leaving service at age x after n years' service with salary S. Suppose the date is several years into the future, past the time when deferred pensions might have been improved. We consider a 1/60 final salary scheme with normal retirement age of 65. The preserved pension (PP) is

$$PP = \frac{nS}{60}.$$

We shall assume that GMP is to be revalued from x to 65 at rate e per annum and that the excess of the PP over the GMP is to be revalued at rate p per annum. Then the increase in PP is I, where

$$I = (\frac{nS}{60} - GMP) [(1+p)^{65-x} - 1] + GMP [(1+e)^{65-x} - 1].$$

Total pension at retirement is $PP+I$

$$= \frac{nS}{60} (1+p)^{65-x} + GMP [(1+e)^{65-x} - (1+p)^{65-x}].$$

on simplification.

Consider three male members of an occupational pension scheme with the following career histories:

X: enters pensionable employment at 25, has one employer, retires at 65
Y: enters pensionable employment at 25, transfers at 45, has two employers, retires at 65

Z : enters pensionable employment at 25, transfers at 35, 45 and 55, has four employers, retires at 65.

We assume that all periods of employment between ages 25 and 65 are pensionable in schemes providing an age retirement pension at 65 of 1/60 of final salary for each year of service. We assume that earnings increase over a career at a uniform rate, e, per annum and that e allows for general inflation, with increases for promotion within a career ignored. If the pension schemes concerned all provide deferred pensions without revaluation, and if we ignore for the moment the effects of revaluing the GMP element in pensions from contracted-out schemes, the relative sizes of the pensions in retirement for X, Y and Z are shown in Table 11.3. It will be seen that at an annual rate of earnings growth of 7.5 per cent someone with one job change at age 45 (Y) achieves just over 60 per cent of the stayer's (X) pension. A person with three job changes at ten-year intervals (Z) achieves under 50 per cent.

It has been assumed that X, Y and Z experience the same rate of earnings growth, although in real life, of course, career progression cannot be ignored and job changes are likely to disrupt the rate of personal earnings development both up and down.

These sample calculations can be taken further to incorporate the effect of GMP revaluation. As indicated above, we shall be assuming that in the public sector the rate of increase in the excess of deferred pension over GMP will be equivalent to the rate of increase in prices (p) but in the private sector the rate of increase will be zero or 0.5p.

We shall take the private sector first. The figures in Table 11.3 need to be increased to allow for the revaluation of GMP. GMP is calculated on the basis of lifetime average earnings between the state pension lower earnings limit and upper earnings limit (LEL and UEL respectively) with an accrual rate such that, for males, after 49 years, the pension is 25 per cent of average lifetime earnings restricted to this range. (The lifetime earnings in this calculation are uprated to allow for earnings inflation over the period up to the tax year before retirement.) Currently, LEL and UEL are about 20 per cent and 140 per cent of the average earnings for male full-time manual workers and we shall assume that this relationship holds throughout. Further, we shall assume that the calculations are based on a date sufficiently far into the future for problems with a differential accrual rate and with maturity of the state scheme to be irrelevant. In order to give some idea of the effect of GMP on our calculations we shall use a sample of 3 × 4 = 12 individuals rather than three.

XA : will be as for X but with a salary level throughout his career equal to the average earnings of a male full-time manual worker

XB : will be as for X but with a salary level throughout his career equal to 1.4 times this average earnings (i.e. at the upper earnings limit)

Table 11.3 *The effect of rate of earnings growth on the pension rights of early leavers in final salary schemes*

Annual rate of earnings growth (e) %	Relative size of pension at retirement		
	X	Y	Z
1	100	91	87
2.5	100	81	72
5	100	69	56
7.5	100	62	46
10	100	57	40

XC : will be as for X but with a salary level throughout his career equal to 2.0 times this average earnings

XD : will be as for X but with a salary level throughout his career equal to 3.0 times this average earnings

YA . . . ZD will be similarly defined.

The results of the calculations are shown in Table 11.4. As above, we are assuming that transfers occur only between equivalent schemes. The results in Table 11.4 indicate, for example, that at an annual rate of earnings growth of 7.5 per cent Y and Z achieve 51–68 per cent of the stayer's pension depending on the pattern of transfer and level of salary.

Table 11.5 repeats these calculations for public sector contracted-out schemes with the rate of increases in prices as shown. The first line reproduces figures from Table 11.4. Therefore, p has been chosen to correspond to a level of real earnings growth of 2 per cent per annum. Again choosing an annual rate of earnings growth of 7.5 per cent (and an annual rate of prices growth of 5.5 per cent), the results indicate that Y and Z achieve 79–87 per cent of the stayer's pension depending on the pattern of transfer and level of salary.

If the schemes had been based on a different pension fraction, then the *relative* amounts to be added on in Tables 11.4 and 11.5 for the GMP increases would have been larger. Thus, for a 1/80 scheme these adjustments would have been larger by a factor of 4/3.

Further simple models based (a) on the withdrawal rates provided by the 'leading life office' with a large portfolio of pension schemes referred to earlier, and (b) on sample career histories confirm that the results quoted above are reasonable.

Transfers in and out of employment
Of the data described earlier, the results of Stewart and Greenhalgh (1984)

Table 11.4 The effect of rate of earnings growth on the pension rights of early leavers in final salary schemes: private sector contracted out

Annual rate of earnings growth (e) %	Relative size of pension at retirement											
	XA	YA	ZA	XB	YB	ZB	XC	YC	ZC	XD	YD	ZD
1	100	94	92	100	94	92	100	93	91	100	93	89
2.5	100	86	81	100	86	82	100	85	79	100	83	77
5	100	75	68	100	75	69	100	74	65	100	72	61
7.5	100	67	59	100	68	60	100	66	55	100	65	51
10	100	62	52	100	67	53	100	61	49	100	59	46

Table 11.5 *The effect of rate of earnings and prices growth on the pension rights of early leavers in final salary schemes: public sector contracted out*

Annual rate of earnings growth (e) %	Annual rate of prices growth (p) %	Relative size of pension at retirement											
		XA	YA	ZA	XB	YB	ZB	XC	YC	ZC	XD	YD	ZD
1	0	100	94	92	100	94	92	100	93	91	100	93	89
2.5	0.5	100	88	84	100	89	84	100	87	82	100	86	80
5	3	100	87	83	100	87	83	100	86	81	100	86	79
7.5	5.5	100	86	81	100	87	82	100	86	80	100	85	79
10	8	100	86	81	100	86	81	100	85	80	100	85	78

Table 11.6 *The effect of transfers out of employment on the pension rights of female pensioners in final salary schemes*

	Annual rate of earnings growth (e) %	Relative size of pension*	
		Single females	Married females
Public sector	$e - p = 2$	95	83
Private sector	$e = 2.5$	95	80
	5	92	70
	7.5	91	64
	10	90	62

* size of pension relative to case where all periods of non-employment precede all periods of employment.

Source: Based on data of Stewart and Greenhalgh (1984).

help to quantify the effects of transfers in and out of employment on pension received (rather than transfers between jobs). This is of particular importance for women. Setting aside any questions of applicability at a time of high unemployment, the tabulations described were extended crudely so that they referred to single and married women at retirement. The women were assumed to be members of a 1/60 final salary scheme when in employment. Corresponding assumptions to the previous section were made. The results are shown in Table 11.6. These figures give the relationship between the pension payable at retirement given transfers in and out of employment and that which would have been payable had *all* the periods of non-employment preceded the periods of employment. To avoid undue complications, the effects of GMP have been omitted here.

Table 11.6 shows that for females in the public sector, assuming real annual earnings growth of 2 per cent, deductions of about 5 per cent and 17 per cent for single and married females respectively should be made from the pension that would otherwise be payable to allow for the timing of transfers in and out of employment. The corresponding figures in the private sector, assuming annual earnings growth of 7.5 per cent, would be 9 per cent and 36 per cent respectively.

Further calculations give the following figures for the basis to be used later in the main projections:

		Single females	Married females
$e = 8, p = 6$	Public sector	0.95	0.83
	Private sector	0.91	0.64

Calculations were also performed on the basis that the private sector provided protection for deferred pensions at the rate of half the level of price increases.

It should be remembered that these factors have been derived in a rather artificial manner from historic data. They will be used in projections of pension rights for females under employment assumption E3 (see Chapter 9), which essentially involves a continuation of past economic activity rates. Corresponding factors have been calculated for assumptions E1 and E2, which involve different levels of improvement in the position of females relative to males. These factors have been based on proportionate adjustments and increasing the figures for single females by an arbitrary 0.03 and 0.01 respectively (for males the factor has been assumed to be unity). The relevant factors are then:

		Assumption E1		*Assumption E2*	
		Single females	*Married females*	*Single females*	*Married females*
	Public sector	0.98	0.86	0.96	0.84
$e=8, p=6$					
	Private sector	0.94	0.82	0.92	0.73

Results

Given the investigations described above we now propose a set of reduction factors to apply to career histories to allow for the loss of pension rights consequent on job transfers.

The data quoted in Table 11.2 suggest that about 20 per cent of males have more than thirty years with their last employer and, together with results of Stewart and Greenhalgh (1984), suggest that, if we had to allocate pensioners simply into categories that correspond to the career patterns of persons X, Y or Z then the following might be appropriate:

	X	*Y*	*Z*	*Total*
Males	20%	40%	40%	100%
Females	0	30%	70%	100%

However, we have noted in Chapter 9 that the future trend in female employment rates is highly speculative and that three illustrative assumptions would be of value. Assumption E1 corrresponds to males and females having a similar level of economic activity. Assumption E3 corresponds to a continuation of the experience in the recent past. Assumption E2 is broadly intermediate. It is therefore suggested that the patterns to be used for females should be roughly as follows:

		X	*Y*	*Z*	*Total*
Females	E1	20%	40%	40%	100%
	E2	10%	35%	55%	100%
	E3	0	30%	70%	100%

Table 11.7 The effect of rate of earnings growth on pension of early leavers in final salary schemes

				Relative size of pension at retirement					
	Annual rate of earnings growth (e)		Females: Assumption E1		Females: Assumption E2		Females: Assumption E3		
Sector	%	Males	Single	Married	Single	Married	Single	Married	
Private contracted out, no protection*	2.5	87	86	75	81	69	78	66	
	5	77	74	64	68	54	64	49	
	7.5	70	67	58	60	46	55	38	
	10	66	62	52	55	41	50	34	
Public, contracted out, full protection	2.5	89	88	77	83	72	81	71	
	5	88	87	76	82	72	79	69	
	7.5	87	86	75	82	72	79	69	
	10	87	86	75	81	71	78	68	

* refers to the level of increase for that part of the preserved pension in excess of GMP, between dates of withdrawal and normal retirement.

Table 11.8 *The effect of rate of earnings and prices growth on pension of early leavers in final salary schemes*

| Basis | Sector | Males | Relative size of pension at retirement | | | | | |
| | | | Females: Assumption E1 | | Females: Assumption E2 | | Females: Assumption E3 | |
			Single	Married	Single	Married	Single	Married
Earnings growth 8%	Private contracted out, no protection	69	65	56	59	47	54	38
Prices growth 6%	Private, contracted out, half protection	75	71	62	68	54	62	47
	Public contracted out, full protection	87	82	72	80	70	78	68
Earnings growth 8%	Private, contracted out, no protection	69	65	56	59	47	54	38
Prices growth 8%	Private, contracted out, half protection	78	75	66	71	58	66	52
	Public, contracted out, full protection	100	100	100	100	100	100	100

with assumption E2's pattern being intermediate. Such assumptions are to some extent arbitrary, but it is hoped that they give some indication of the order of magnitude of the results.

With these weighting factors and the results from Tables 11.4–11.6 we estimate that the relative size of pension will be given by the figures in Table 11.7. For the private sector it is assumed that, as above, there is no increase to that part of the preserved pension in excess of the GMP. On average, persons in occupational pension schemes have higher earnings levels than the rest of the population. To make some allowance for this, the figures in Table 11.7 are based on the averages of assumptions B and C, corresponding to persons on 1.4 and 2.0 times national average earnings for male manual workers respectively. In Table 11.8 these calculations are repeated allowing for earnings/price inflation bases of 8/6 and 8/8 and allowing the private sector to provide protection at half the rate of price growth for the excess of the preserved pension over GMP.

For females these estimates (in Tables 11.7 and 11.8) are slight underestimates because of the salary differential in favour of males and the fixing of both the lower and upper earnings limit relative to the average earnings of an adult male manual worker. Strictly the estimates should have not been based on the average of the indices for B and C but should have placed more weight on those for B. This has not been done for reasons of simplicity.

The approach to the indexing of deferred pensions in the private sector has been somewhat cavalier in the sense that some of the early leavers are in fact ill-health retirements, optional age retirements or normal age retirements at, say, age 60. Thus the assumption of no indexing ignores the presence of these groups.

We shall use the figures in Table 11.8 as follows: for childless women the results for single women will be used as a surrogate; for mothers the results for married women will be used as a surrogate. This approximate approach is not thought to introduce any serious distortion into the calculations.

Projection of pension expenditure
The projection is for fifty years from 1981 to 2031.

Assumptions

Demographic Four demographic projections have been set up and described in Chapter 8 (pp. 142–8). Briefly the details are as follows:

	Long-term cohort fertility level	*Mortality level*
A	2.1 children per woman	Medium
B	2.1 children per woman	Optimistic
C	2.0 children per woman	Medium
D	2.0 children per woman	Optimistic

Employment histories For males, employment histories have been projected on the basis of a normal retirement age of 65.

For females, three sets of assumptions have been used for projecting career histories and for estimating the loss of pension rights because of job mobility (described in Chapter 9, p. 181–2). These assumptions have been called E1, E2 and E3.

Unemployment Three levels of unemployment have been used: 6 per cent, 9 per cent and 12 per cent, called U1, U2 and U3 respectively.

Preservation The assumptions for the public and private sector have been described earlier. Two bases are provided for the private sector, which provide either zero (W1) or limited protection for preserved pensions in excess of the GMP (equal to half the rate of price inflation: W2).

Economic The economic assumptions used have been deliberately set up to correspond to those used by J. Field (1983) and to some of the alternatives offered by the Government Actuary (1982) in the Quinquennial Review. Two variants have been taken – prices rising at 6 per cent (V1) and 8 per cent (V2) per annum while average earnings increase at 8 per cent per annum. These bases are meant to be illustrative of the relationship between prices and earnings if there were respectively strong, or very little, economic growth.

Labour force composition The labour force is assumed to continue to be made up of two sectors – public and private – with employees divided between these sectors in the ratios prevailing in 1979 at the time of the Government Actuary's survey. That is, for males the split is 0.29/0.71 respectively and for females the split is 0.34/0.66. We shall assume that an individual remains in a particular sector throughout his working lifetime in order to simplify the model and underlying computations. There are few actual data available to test this assumption. Field's model of 'hypothetical' careers indicates that about one-quarter of men and about one-fifth of women have pensionable service from both sectors (see Appendix Tables 2 and 4 of Field, 1983).

Membership of occupational pension schemes The seventh Government Actuary's survey (1986) indicates the following levels of scheme membership among employees:

	Males	Females
Private sector	50%	25%
Public sector	90%	55%

For the long-term projection it will be assumed that for males in the public sector the level of membership will remain at 90 per cent. For the private sector, a considerable increase will be assumed from 50 per cent to 60 per cent (assumption M1), reversing the decline of the early 1970s, and some indication of the effect of a rise to 70 per cent will be given (assumption M2).

For females the coverage is assumed to increase as 'equal access' takes effect. Three levels have been chosen to correspond to the rationale underlying the three career history estimates for females. Under assumption E1, the coverage is assumed to increase to a level equal to 70 per cent of that for men (corresponding to the approximate relationship between male and female career histories estimated in Chapter 9). The level of 70 per cent has been rounded down arbitrarily from (the more exact) 77 per cent to allow for a continuing tendency (albeit less strong) for women's employment to be in non-pensionable jobs.

For assumptions E2 and E3 interpolation has been used to give the following details:

	Females Assumptions		
	E1	E2	E3
Private sector	42%	37%	31%
Public sector	63%	60%	57%

A similar set of figures may be derived correspnding to the figures of 70 per cent coverage for private sector males. For simplicity, no correlation between prevailing level of unemployment and the trend in scheme membership has been assumed.

The level of contracting out among members will be held fixed at 100 per cent in the public sector and 80 per cent in the private sector.

Benefits on death to dependants of members The payment of widows' pension is assumed to have become universal by the ultimate year in the projections and to be payable at the rate of half of the deceased's entitlement (but see below). It is assumed that all widows' pensions cease on remarriage. To do otherwise, given the limited nature of this work, would be too complex. Further it will be assumed that, for widows' pensions payable on death after retirement, all members are covered in respect of marriages contracted after retirement. Similar assumptions are made in respect of widowers' pensions as part of the benefits for female members (according to recent statements from the Equal Opportunities Commission, the provision of widowers' benefits is being introduced at a rapid speed).

Pensions payable to the surviving spouse on death in service are assumed to depend on the member's service up to and salary at the date of death. Examination of some service tables and calculation of the distribution by age at death of the ultimate projected numbers of deaths in service of scheme members enable reasonable estimates to be made of the average ages at death of married members dying in service. Husbands are assumed to be on average three years older than their wives. Salary at date of death is estimated relative to the average salary at normal retirement age. Years of service at date of death are obtained by adjusting the average career histories discussed in Chapter 9 (for the periods up to normal retirement age, pp. 178–87) by factors less than proportionate by an arbitrary amount to allow for the non-uniform distribution of employment across a cohort's working lifetime. Job mobility thus tends to be concentrated at the younger ages, especially for females with time spent out of the labour force caring for young children (the 'child effect' discussed in Chapter 9, p. 183–4).

In this approximate procedure there will be double counting in that widows, for example, may be receiving two pensions – one in their own right and one because of their husband's membership.

From the population projections, approximate numbers of new widows and widowers are estimated per annum, so that it is possible to estimate approximately the distribution of numbers of widows (in the ultimate state) by age at widowhood (and widowers). Pension benefits to the survivor on death after retirement are taken to be half of those in payment to the spouse. For death in service, further adjustment factors are used for the benefits to the surviving widow and widower to reflect approximately the effective pensionable service at the date of death. Allowance is made (albeit somewhat arbitrary) for the lower mortality of the married and employed sections of the population.

Given the information reported in Chapter 2 (pp. 23–4), we shall assume that the death-in-service lump-sum benefit is on average twice the salary at death and that such a benefit is provided by 85 per cent of schemes. From the population projections, estimates can be made of the annual numbers of deaths, with allowance made for the lower mortality of married persons and of persons in employment relative to the average.

Contracted out   There is a dearth of information concerning benefits for those not contracted out. Following Field, a simplification is adopted by assuming that, in schemes that are not contracted out, the benefits for each £1 of final average earnings and each year of membership are on average only half those in contracted-out schemes. This has been effected by halving the period of membership when calculating the effective service (assumption O1). To give some idea of the sensitivity of the results to this assumption, the calculations have been repeated using a factor of three-quarters rather than one-half (assumption O2).

Mortality differentials   No allowance is made for the greater longevity expected for individuals receiving larger pensions than the average, although mortality differentials by marital status and economic activity have been included.

Pension fraction   For most contracted-out schemes in the private sector, the pension fraction is 1/60. However, at least one-quarter of the benefit is normally taken as a lump sum and so effectively the fraction is 1/80 for actual pension and 3/80 for lump sum. Sometimes a higher proportion of the benefit may be taken as a lump sum, for example, if actual service is less than forty years. In the public sector, the fractions 1/80 and 3/80 are standard. About 25 per cent of contracted-out schemes in the private sector however provide a pension using a fraction of 1/80 only before any deduction for commutation (the minimum allowed for contracted-out schemes). This suggests an average fraction of 1/88 for the private sector after commutation.

Allowing for the relative contributions of private and public sector employment to the effective pensionable service estimates tabulated below, the suggested pension fractions to be used overall are 1/85 for males and 1/84 for females.

For calculating GMPs, the pension fractions are fixed at 1/196 for males and 1/176 for females.

For estimating expenditure on lump-sum retirement benefits, a continuation of the current prevalence of such benefits is assumed (see Chapter 2, p. 22).

Effective pensionable salary at retirement   The effective pensionable salary to be used in the pension formula requires estimation. This average salary will differ from the average gross earnings of all men and women in employment for various reasons: overtime, bonuses and so on are not always pensionable (especially in the private sector); final salaries just before retirement on which pensions are normally based are often greater than average salaries, especially for managers, supervisors and the professions; few pensions are based on part-time earnings; allowance for the loss of value of deferred pensions has been incorporated already.

In the public sector, the pensionable salary is often the actual salary paid in the pre-retirement year less a minor deduction for state flat-rate pension benefits. In the private sector, deductions may be made (as above) and the earnings used may be averaged over a longer past period, which may cause a notable reduction in times of high inflation (for example, nearly 30 per cent with an 8 per cent per annum rate of nominal salary increase). For most occupations, earnings over an individual's lifetime tend to peak at mid-career and so the earnings level near to normal retirement tends to be below this peak and near to the career average. However, for some occupations the differential may be significant, for example, 10–15 per cent.

To estimate effective pensionable salary for this projection, data from the 1981 New Earnings Survey (Department of Employment, 1982) have been used, which indicate that for full-time adult employees average weekly salaries are as follows: males − £140.5; females − £95.3 (i.e. about £7,330 and £4,970 per annum respectively). In a stable economic environment where all earnings follow the pattern by age exhibited by the results of this particular survey, these figures will be equal to career averages for cohorts rather than merely cross-sectional averages. It is a necessary assumption here, in the absence of cohort data, that these cross-sectional averages may be used in this way.

These averages were adjusted to produce estimates of effective pensionable salary (to the nearest £1) of £142 for males and £96 for females. These compare with the estimates used by Field (1983) for the public sector of £135 and £97 respectively and the estimated average weekly earnings in 1981/82 of £149 and £96 obtained for the contracted out from the analyses of contribution income in the Quinquennial Review (Government Actuary, 1982).

All financial estimates are based on these 1981 estimates and so are expressed in terms of 1981 earnings levels. No allowance is made for final salary being modified to take account of national insurance benefits (i.e. integration). Integration is common in the public sector but is usually of a small magnitude. About one-half of private sector scheme members are subjected to integration. To this extent the estimates here will overstate the size of the pension.

Pensions in payment Allowance has been made for the fact that the state scheme now bears the cost of increasing the part of the occupational pension in contracted-out schemes represented by the GMP in line with the increase in the cost of living after award. As far as the occupational pension scheme is concerned, the GMP is fixed after award. The remainder of the occupational pension is here assumed to increase in line with prices for public sector pensions, but only at two-thirds of this rate for private sector pensions. This implies that the real value of this part of a private sector scheme pension will effectively fall after award.

Guaranteed minimum pensions (GMP) Experimental calculations with earnings distributions from the New Earnings Surveys in recent years and the relevant LELs and UELs suggest that, for males, average reckonable earnings (which contribute to GMP) over a lifetime are 75 per cent of average earnings for all full-time male employees. For females, average reckonable earnings are 70 per cent of average earnings for all full-time employees. These estimates recognize that the LEL and UEL are normally fixed with respect to the average earnings of full-time adult *male* manual workers. Similarly, using the LEL and UEL figures for 1981 of £27 and £200 respectively, average reckonable earnings were calculated and compared with estimates of the average pensionable earnings. The ratios are approximately 72 per cent for males and 68 per cent for females. This suggests using slightly lower figures than the above – those chosen, somewhat arbitrarily, are 74 per cent and 69 per cent.

From our earlier results, we therefore estimate the average reckonable earnings for the contracted out for GMP purposes to be £105 and £66 for males and females respectively – corresponding to figures of £105 and £67 estimated by Field (for the private sector) and £96 and £60 (for the public sector).

Summary Table 11.9 summarizes those aspects of the basis where a range of assumptions have been used and indicates the shorthand notation that is used for identifying them.

Table 11.9 *Projections of pension expenditure: range of assumptions*

Nature of Assumptions	Notation			
Demographic	A	B	C	D
Female employment	E1	E2	E3	
Unemployment	U1	U2	U3	
Private sector preservation	W1	W2		
Economic	V1	V2		
Scheme membership	M1	M2		
Non contracting-out benefits	01	02		

The costs presented in the rest of this chapter must be regarded as purely illustrative, representing a set of plausible outcomes out of an infinite variety of possibilities for the ultimate pension expenditure around 2031. Some of these suggestions appear quite unlikely but nevertheless could materialize. Significant assumptions are made about many parameters, including the projected levels of earnings and price growth, mortality, fertility, unemployment, scheme membership and employment trends for females. It should be noted that, underlying all the projections reported here, is the implicit assumption that the provisions and practices of occupational pension schemes and the state system and the conditions of contracting out remain unaltered. It should further be noted that the projections apply to a specific year (2031) rather than to the ultimate state, that is, when the occupational pension schemes have all reached maturity.

Results

Numbers of members and dependants Table 11.10 shows the historic numbers of male employed members of occupational pension schemes together with the projected numbers. The estimated numbers for 1985/86 are in line with the estimates for 1979 from the Government Actuary's survey. The projected results for 2021 and 2031 indicate the sensitivity to changes in the unemployment and scheme membership assumptions. Increasing the unemployment level by 3 per cent reduces the number of members by about 0.4 million. A change in the ultimate level of membership in the private sector (from 60 to 70 per cent) increases the number of members by about 1.0 million.

Table 11.11 similarly deals with female employed members. The range

Table 11.10 *Male employees in occupational pension schemes*
(historic and projected)

Year	Assumption	Numbers (millions)	
1936		2.1	
1953		4.9	
1956		6.4	
1963		9.4	
1967		9.9	
1971		8.7	
1975		8.6	
1979		8.5	
1985/86	U1	8.9	
	U2	8.5	
	U3	8.2	
		M1	M2
2021	U1	11.4 – 11.6	12.5 – 12.7
	U2	11.0 – 11.2	12.0 – 12.3
	U3	10.5 – 10.8	11.5 – 11.7
2031	U1	11.2 – 11.5	12.2 – 12.6
	U2	10.7 – 11.1	11.7 – 12.1
	U3	10.3 – 10.6	11.2 – 11.6

Table 11.11   *Female employees in occupational pension schemes (historic and projected)*

Year	Assumption	Numbers (millions)					
1936		0.5					
1953		1.3					
1956		1.3					
1963		1.7					
1967		2.3					
1971		2.4					
1975		2.8					
1979		3.3					
		E1		E2		E3	
1985/86	U1	3.7		3.2		2.5	
	U2	3.5		3.0		2.4	
	U3	3.3		2.8		2.2	
		E1		E2		E3	
2031		M1	M2	M1	M2	M1	M2
	U1	5.0−5.1	5.4−5.6	4.0−4.1	4.2−4.3	2.8−2.9	2.9
	U2	4.7−4.8	5.1−5.3	3.7−3.8	3.9−4.0	2.6−2.7	2.7−2.8
	U3	4.4−4.5	4.8−5.0	3.5−3.6	3.7−3.8	2.4−2.5	2.5−2.6

of figures in each cell indicates the effects of changes in the demographic assumptions. Increasing the unemployment level by 3 per cent reduces the numbers by about 0.3 million. A change in the employment pattern assumptions (E1, E2) leads to a change in numbers of about 1.1 million. The effect of a change in the private sector level of membership depends on the employment assumption, varying between 0.1 and 0.4 millions.

The corresponding results for pensioners are shown in Tables 11.12 and 11.13. Here the demographic assumptions are very significant in respect of mortality. For example, in Table 11.12 the differences in the number of pensioners estimated for A/C compared with B/D lie between 1.8 and 2.7 millions.

Corresponding to the discussion of dependency in Chapter 9, we present in Table 11.14 the trend in numbers of occupational pension scheme employed members per pensioners (including surviving spouses). The ratio fell between 1936 and 1979 from in excess of 10 to just over 3. This fall is projected to continue down to either 2.3 (on the medium mortality assumption) or 1.6 (on the optimistic mortality assumption). The other assumptions have only a marginal effect on this ratio. The ratio would be expected to fall further to the levels indicated in Chapter 9 for the total UK population if the time horizon were extended beyond 2031.

Table 11.12 *Pensioner members of occupational pension schemes (historic and projected): former employees*

Year	Assumption		Numbers (millions)		
1936			0.2		
1953			0.8		
1956			1.0		
1963			1.5		
1967			1.9		
1971			2.4		
1975			2.8		
1979			3.0		
		E1	E2	E3	
1985/86	U1	3.1	2.9	2.5	
	U2	3.0	2.8	2.4	
	U3	2.9	2.8	2.4	

		E1		E2		E3	
2031		M1	M2	M1	M2	M1	M2
	U1 A/C	5.6	6.1	5.0	5.4	4.4	4.7
	B/D	8.0	8.8	7.3	7.9	6.5	6.9
	U2 A/C	5.3−5.4	5.9−6.0	4.8−4.9	5.2−5.3	4.2−4.3	4.6−4.7
	B/D	7.6−7.8	8.4−8.6	7.0−7.2	7.5−7.7	6.2−6.4	6.6−6.8
	U3 A/C	5.1−5.3	5.5−5.8	4.6−4.8	4.9−5.2	4.0−4.2	4.3−4.6
	B/D	7.2−7.6	7.9−8.3	6.6−7.0	7.1−7.5	5.8−6.2	6.3−6.7

Effective pensionable service In Tables 11.15 and 11.16 the estimates are presented of the effective pensionable service (EPS) for persons retiring around 2031. The figures are in years and are expressed per head of the population, that is, the denominator includes both non-members and non-employees. The figures for females have been developed assuming that 12 per cent of birth cohorts are childless (no data are presented here to show the effect of a lower completed family size, although this could be achieved by altering the weights attaching to childless women and mothers, which are discussed in Chapter 9).

The figures for effective pensionable service are higher on the 8/8 basis than on the 8/6 basis. This is because, when the increase in prices keeps up with the increase in average earnings, the benefits for early leavers do not fall so much behind the final salary-based benefits of those members who continue in service (and shown by the higher level of figures for the 8/8 basis in Table 11.8).

For males the estimates vary between 15.7 and 20.4 years on the 8/6 basis and between 16.7 and 22.0 on the 8/8 basis. On the V1 basis,

Table 11.13   *Pensioner members of occupational pension schemes (historic and projected): widows, widowers, former dependants*

Year	Assumption		Numbers (millions)	
1953			0.1	
1956			0.1	
1963			0.3	
1967			0.4	
1971			0.5	
1975			0.6	
1979			0.7	
			M1	M2
2031	U1	A/C	1.6	1.8
		B/D	2.6	2.8
	U2	A/C	1.6	1.7
		B/D	2.4	2.6
	U3	A/C	1.5	1.6
		B/D	2.3	2.5

the differences attributable to the other assumptions are approximately as follows:

3% change in unemployment	0.8 yrs	(U)
benefits for contracted out	0.6 yrs	(O)
level of scheme membership	1.7 yrs	(M)
private sector preservation	1.0 yrs	(W)

For females the estimates vary widely with the employment assumption. Further details of the sensitivity of the results are given in Table 11.17. The results in Tables 11.15–11.17 indicate that, for males, the assumptions regarding the level of occupational scheme membership and level of preservation in the private sector are significant. For females, the assumption regarding employment is of overriding importance – thus, a change in this assumption can lead to a change in EPS of 1.8–2.7 years. This means that the financial estimates of pension outgo for females will be sensitive to this particular aspect of the basis.

Before attempting a comparison of these estimates of effective pensionable service with other published estimates, the different assumptions regarding benefits for early leavers should be noted. We have assumed that any GMP will be increased in line with average earnings and that the remainder of the pension will be increased in line with prices in the public sector. In the private sector, two alternatives are offered for the protection of this remainder: (a) zero protection or (b) increases in line

Table 11.14 *Ratios of employed members of occupational pension schemes to pensioners (approx.) (historic and projected)*

Year	Assumption		Ratio
1936			13.0
1953			6.9
1956			7.3
1963			6.2
1967			5.3
1971			3.7
1975			3.4
1979			3.2
1985/86	U1		3.2 – 3.5
	U2		3.2 – 3.4
	U3		3.1 – 3.3
2031	U1	A/C	2.3
		B/D	1.6
	U2	A/C	2.2
		B/D	1.6
	U3	A/C	2.2
		B/D	1.5

with half the level of price inflation. Field's assumptions are more complex but broadly agree with the above.

Field's calculations give the following results for a period when a mature position is reached:

Basis	Males	Females
8/6	15.9 yrs	5.9 yrs
8/8	17.2 yrs	6.6 yrs

The corresponding figures from Tables 11.15 and 11.16 for 6 per cent unemployment (U1), not contracted-out benefits taken as 50 per cent of contracted-out (O1), 60 per cent private sector membership (M1), and frozen early leaver deferred pensions in the private sector (W1) are as follows:

Basis	Males	Females
8/6	17.1 yrs	3.5–7.5 yrs
8/8	18.2 yrs	4.5–8.8 yrs

This set of assumptions corresponds closely to those used by Field,

Table 11.15   *Effective pensionable service estimates for males:*
2031 (years per person)

		01			02		
		U1	U2	U3	U1	U2	U3
Basis V1 (8/6)							
M1	W1	17.1	16.5	15.7	17.7	17.0	16.3
M1	W2	18.0	17.3	16.6	18.6	17.8	17.1
M2	W1	18.7	18.0	17.2	19.4	18.6	17.7
M2	W2	19.7	18.9	18.1	20.4	19.6	18.7
Basis V2 (8/8)							
M1	W1	18.2	17.5	16.7	18.8	18.1	17.4
M1	W2	19.5	18.7	18.0	20.2	19.4	18.6
M2	W1	19.8	19.1	18.4	20.6	19.7	18.9
M2	W2	21.3	20.5	19.6	22.0	21.2	20.3

so a direct comparison of results is possible. The range above for females corresponds to the extreme employment assumptions used (E1 and E3). Field's estimates for males are lower by 1 year, and for females lie in the middle of the range indicated, which is not unexpected since his assumptions on female employment rely on a continuation of current conditions and correspond fairly closely to assumption E2.

The Wilson Committee estimates prepared by the Government Actuary (1980) concentrate on a period starting at 2000 before a mature position is reached and assume that, for men, two-thirds of those then retiring will have a pension and that it will be based on an average effective service of 26 years, equivalent to 17.3 years as an overall average. The Wilson Committee estimates were based on a less extensive analysis of the data available, but are broadly in line with those derived here under a series of bases for males. The economic assumptions involved earnings growth of about 7.5 per cent per annum and prices growth of 6 per cent per annum. For women, the Wilson Committee used a factor of 0.20 relative to men to estimate the average effective service per women in the population, that is, 3.5 years, which is rather low compared to the above estimates. This rather crude approach did not allow for the types of trends in women's employment that have been described in detail in Chapter 9. Hence, overall, the results in Tables 11.15 and 11.16 are in line with earlier estimates for males. For females the range indicated does encompass the estimates provided by Field (1983) but not the earlier ones from the Government Actuary (1980).

Table 11.16 *Effective pensionable service estimates for females:*
2031 (years per person)

			01			02		
			U1	U2	U3	U1	U2	U3
Basis VI (8/6)								
M1	W1	E1	7.5	7.1	6.7	7.8	7.3	6.9
M1	W1	E2	5.5	5.2	4.9	5.6	5.3	5.0
M1	W1	E3	3.5	3.3	3.1	3.6	3.5	3.3
M1	W2	E1	7.9	7.5	7.1	8.2	7.7	7.3
M1	W2	E2	5.8	5.5	5.2	6.0	5.7	5.4
M1	W2	E3	3.8	3.6	3.4	4.0	3.7	3.5
M2	W1	E1	8.2	7.7	7.3	8.4	7.9	7.5
M2	W1	E2	5.7	5.4	5.1	5.9	5.6	5.2
M2	W1	E3	3.6	3.4	3.2	3.8	3.5	3.3
M2	W2	E1	8.6	8.1	7.6	8.8	8.4	7.9
M2	W2	E2	6.2	5.8	5.5	6.4	6.0	5.7
M2	W2	E3	4.0	3.8	3.5	4.1	3.9	3.6
Basis VI (8/6)								
M1	W1	E1	8.8	8.4	7.9	9.1	8.6	8.2
M1	W1	E2	6.7	6.3	5.9	6.9	6.5	6.1
M1	W1	E3	4.5	4.2	3.9	4.6	4.4	4.1
M1	W2	E1	9.6	9.0	8.5	9.8	9.3	8.7
M1	W2	E2	7.2	6.8	6.4	7.4	7.0	6.6
M1	W2	E3	5.0	4.7	4.4	5.2	4.9	4.6
M2	W1	E1	9.3	8.8	8.3	9.8	9.2	8.7
M2	W1	E2	7.0	6.6	6.2	7.1	6.7	6.3
M2	W1	E3	4.6	4.3	4.0	4.8	4.5	4.2
M2	W2	E1	10.3	9.7	9.2	10.5	10.0	9.5
M2	W2	E2	7.5	7.1	6.6	7.8	7.3	6.9
M2	W2	E3	5.2	4.9	4.6	5.3	5.0	4.7

Years contracted out In order to estimate the level of GMPs, some idea
of the distribution of earnings for individuals over their earnings lifetime
is required – in particular, the relationship between earnings and the
lower and upper earnings limits (LEL and UEL, respectively). In the
absence of such data, experimental calculations have been carried out,
which were described earlier.

The number of contracted out years is required in order to estimate
GMP and this has been carried out along the lines of the model used for
effective pensionable service described in the previous section. The details
are not given here. Field has estimated the average number of contracted-

Table 11.17 *Effectice pensionable service and change in basis*

| Males | Approximate sensitivities (years) | | | | | |
	V1	V2				
3% change in unemployment	0.8	0.8				
benefits for contracted-out	0.6	0.7				
level of scheme membership	1.7	1.7				
private sector preservation	1.0	1.4				

| Females | E1 | | E2 | | E3 | |
	V1	V2	V1	V2	V1	V2
3% change in unemployment	0.4	0.5	0.3	0.4	0.3	0.3
benefits for contracted-out	0.2	0.3	0.2	0.2	0.1	0.2
level of scheme membership	0.6	0.7	0.3	0.3	0.1	0.1
private sector preservation	0.4	0.7	0.4	0.5	0.3	0.5

out years to be 18.9 years for males and 6.9 years for females. Using the bases that correspond most closely to those of Field, we obtain estimates of 18.6 years and 4.2 years respectively. As with effective pensionable service, the estimates agree closely for males. For both sexes, as before, a wide range of results emerge depending on the underlying assumption. The ranges are as follows:

$$\text{Males}\quad 16.0 - 21.7\ \text{yrs}$$
$$\text{Females}\quad 3.7 - 9.9\ \text{yrs}$$

Weekly pensions per head In order to estimate the weekly GMP per head for 2031 the following general formula is used, where YCO denotes the estimate of years contracted out:

$$\text{For males}\quad GMP = YCO \times \frac{105}{196}\ \text{at age 65}$$
$$\text{For females}\quad GMP = YCO \times \frac{66}{176}\ \text{at age 60}$$

To estimate the average GMP in payment at ages 65–69 for males and 60–64 for females (that is, two and a half years after retirement on average), these estimates are to be adjusted by an 'inflation loss factor', f, where $f = (1.08)^{-2.5}$ on the bases being considered.

In order to calculate the weekly pension (P) per head for 2031, the following general formula is used:

$$\text{For males}\quad P = EPS \times \frac{142}{85}\ \text{at age 65}$$
$$\text{For females}\quad P = EPS \times \frac{96}{84}\ \text{at age 60}$$

To estimate the average pension in payment 2.5 years later, the general formula to be used is:

$$(P - GMP)g + GMP.f$$

where g is the inflation loss factor for the pension in excess of GMP allowing for the different features of the private and public sectors and the particular assumptions being made. The factor f is the same for both economic bases, being determined solely by the earnings growth assumption and the fact that the GMPs are not dynamized by occupational pension schemes. Approximate values are $f = 0.824$, and $g = 0.924$ for males and 0.927 for females on the 8/6 basis and 0.960 and 0.966 on the 8/8 basis.

Table 11.18   *Average pensions per head at retirement for males: 2031 (£ per week in terms of 1981 earnings)*

		01			02		
		U1	U2	U3	U1	U2	U3
Basis V1 (8/6)							
M1	W1	28.6	27.6	26.2	29.6	28.4	27.2
M1	W2	30.1	28.9	27.7	31.1	29.7	28.6
M2	W1	31.2	30.1	28.7	32.4	31.1	29.6
M2	W2	32.9	31.6	30.2	34.1	32.7	31.2
Basis V2 (8/8)							
M1	W1	30.4	29.2	27.9	31.4	30.2	29.1
M1	W2	32.6	31.2	30.1	33.7	32.4	31.1
M2	W1	33.1	31.9	30.7	34.4	32.9	31.6
M2	W2	35.6	34.2	32.7	36.8	35.4	33.9

The results of these calculations are given in Tables 11.18 and 11.19. In each cell, the figure shown is the estimate of the weekly pension per head at retirement in 2031. Estimates of the pension per head on average 2.5 years after retirement are not tabulated to save space. Table 11.18 shows that for males the weekly pension varies between £26.20 and £34.10 on the 8/6 basis and between £27.90 and £36.80 on the 8/8 basis. For females, from Table 11.19, the range of variation is, according to the employment assumption:

	8/6	8/8
E1	£7.70–10.10	£9.00–12.00
E2	£5.60–7.30	£6.70–8.90
E3	£3.50–4.70	£4.50–6.10

Table 11.19 *Average pensions per head at retirement for females: 2031*
(£ per week in terms of 1981 earnings)

			01			02		
			U1	U2	U3	U1	U2	U3
Basis VI (8/6)								
M1	W1	E1	8.6	8.1	7.7	8.9	8.3	7.9
M1	W1	E2	6.3	5.9	5.6	6.4	6.1	5.7
M1	W1	E3	4.0	3.8	3.5	4.1	4.0	3.8
M1	W2	E1	9.0	8.6	8.1	9.4	8.8	8.3
M1	W2	E2	6.6	6.3	5.9	6.9	6.5	6.2
M1	W2	E3	4.3	4.1	3.9	4.6	4.2	4.0
M2	W1	E1	9.4	8.8	8.3	9.6	9.0	8.6
M2	W1	E2	6.5	6.2	5.8	6.7	6.4	5.9
M2	W1	E3	4.1	3.9	3.7	4.3	4.0	3.8
M2	W2	E1	9.8	9.3	8.7	10.1	9.6	9.0
M2	W2	E2	7.1	6.6	6.3	7.3	6.9	6.5
M2	W2	E3	4.6	4.3	4.0	4.7	4.5	4.1
Basis V2 (8/8)								
M1	W1	E1	10.1	9.6	9.0	10.4	9.8	9.4
M1	W1	E2	7.7	7.2	6.7	7.9	7.4	7.0
M1	W1	E3	5.1	4.8	4.5	5.3	5.0	4.7
M1	W2	E1	11.0	10.3	9.7	11.2	10.6	9.9
M1	W2	E2	8.2	7.8	7.3	8.5	8.0	7.5
M1	W2	E3	5.7	5.4	5.0	5.9	5.6	5.3
M2	W1	E1	10.6	10.1	9.5	11.2	10.5	9.9
M2	W1	E2	8.0	7.5	7.1	8.1	7.7	7.2
M2	W1	E3	5.3	4.9	4.6	5.5	5.1	4.8
M2	W2	E1	11.8	11.1	10.5	12.0	11.4	10.9
M2	W2	E2	8.6	8.1	7.5	8.9	8.3	7.9
M2	W2	E3	5.9	5.6	5.3	6.1	5.7	5.4

These figures should be compared with the estimate provided by Field that the average pension per head per week at retirement in 1979 of £11.10 for males and £2.40 for females using data from the 1979 General Household Survey. These figures are in terms of 1979 earnings. Earnings inflation between 1979 and 1981 was about 36 per cent, which crudely suggests growth in average pension per head over the coming fifty years of 75–140 per cent for males and 10–270 per cent for females, depending on the assumptions made.

These trends mask changes in the levels of membership in occupational pension schemes. Approximate estimates of the averages per person receiving an occupational pension are shown in Tables 11.20 and 11.21

Table 11.20 *Average weekly pension at retirement*
per recipient for males: 2031
(£ per week in terms of 1981 earnings)

		01			02		
		U1	*U2*	*U3*	*U1*	*U2*	*U3*
V1	W1	47.90	46.20	43.90	47.60	47.60	45.60
V1	W2	50.40	48.40	46.40	52.20	49.70	47.90
V2	W1	50.90	48.90	46.70	52.60	50.60	48.70
V2	W2	54.60	52.30	50.40	56.40	54.30	52.10

for males and females respectively. Table 11.20 shows that for males the
pension per recipient varies between £43.90 and £52.20 on the 8/6 basis
and between £46.70 and £56.40 on the 8/8 basis. For females the range
of variation is:

	8/6	*8/8*
E1	£26.30–32.10	£30.80–38.30
E2	£24.00–29.60	£28.70–36.50
E3	£21.40–28.20	£27.50–36.10

The Occupational Pension Survey of 1979 indicates that, for new
awards in 1979, approximate average pensions for males and females are
£23 and £18 per week respectively. These figures are in terms of 1979
earnings as above. These suggest a crude growth in pensions per recipient
over the coming fifty years of 40–85 per cent for males and up to 55 per
cent for females.

The averages expressed per occupational pensioner are of course higher
because some of the population will not have an occupational pension.
Such averages are tentative because of the doubt attaching to estimates of
the number of small pensions, which are sensitive to the treatment, in the
model, of short periods of membership, although the aggregate amount of
pensions paid is less sensitive to those short periods. Looking at the trends
in average pension described in the previous paragraphs, we note that
there is a less sharp rise in the average expressed per recipient. This is
because the number of pensioners and the size of average pensions are
both estimated to increase. The upward trend in pensions per recipient
is estimated to be less steep for females because, although some pensions
will be larger (for example as a result of improved preservation
allowances), there will be many pensioners ultimately who will obtain a
small pension but who under present circumstances would not receive any
occupational scheme pension at all.

Table 11.21   *Average weekly pension at retirement per recipient for females:*
2031 (years per person)
(£ per week in terms of 1981 earnings)

			01			02		
			U1	*U2*	*U3*	*U1*	*U2*	*U3*
V1	W1	E1	29.4	27.7	26.3	30.4	28.4	27.0
V1	W1	E2	27.0	25.3	24.0	27.5	26.2	24.5
V1	W1	E3	24.5	23.3	21.4	25.1	24.5	23.3
V1	W2	E1	30.8	29.4	27.7	32.1	30.1	28.4
V1	W2	E2	28.3	27.0	25.3	29.6	27.9	26.6
V1	W2	E3	26.3	25.1	23.9	28.2	25.7	24.5
V2	W1	E1	34.5	32.8	30.8	35.6	33.5	32.1
V2	W1	E2	33.0	30.9	28.7	33.9	31.7	30.0
V2	W1	E3	31.2	29.4	27.5	32.4	30.6	28.8
V2	W2	E1	37.6	35.2	33.2	38.3	36.3	33.9
V2	W2	E2	35.2	33.5	31.3	36.5	34.3	32.2
V2	W2	E3	34.9	33.0	30.6	36.1	34.3	32.2

Total benefit expenditure   In order to calculate the total annual pension expenditure in 2031, we need to combine the results of the population projection with the estimates of penions and GMP per head described earlier. As an illustration of the approach, consider a male population projection that gives estimates of the population in 2031 aged 65–69 of M_0. Let M_i be the estimate for age group $65+5i$ to $69+5i$.

Then the annual pension expenditure for 2031 on retirement pensions, X, for males would be given by

$$X = 52.18\, M_0\, [(P - GMP)g + GMPf]$$

$$+ 52.18(P - GMP) \sum {}_i\!M_i g^{2i} + 52.18\, GMP \sum {}_i\!M_i f^{2i}.$$

(In quoting expenditure estimates we use a billion to mean a thousand million and use the shorthand £b.)

Lump-sum retirement benefits are estimated similarly for the annual number of persons reaching retirement age.

Following Field (1983), we assume an arbitrary allowance of £0.5b for returns of contributions, state scheme premiums, and other miscellaneous items. This figure is in line with recent expenditure under this heading.

The estimates of the annual cost of lump-sum death in service benefits for males are as follows (in £b):

	A/C		B/D	
	M1	*M2*	*M1*	*M2*
U1	0.28	0.31	0.14	0.16
U2	0.27	0.30	0.14	0.15
U3	0.26	0.29	0.13	0.15

For females the approximate costs are £0.02b and and £0.01b under demographic assumptions A/C and B/D respectively.

Allowance is made for the level of GMP in estimating the expenditure on pensions to the surviving widows and widowers of members. These annual estimates are as follows:

- Death in service – widowers' pensions: approximate calculations give estimates of up to £0.10b depending on the assumptions used.
- Death after retirement – widowers' pensions: approximate calculations give estimates of £0.04–0.08b depending on the assumptions used.
- Death in service – widows' pensions: approximate calculations give estimates of £0.30–0.80b depending on the assumptions used.
- Death after retirement – widows' pensions: a full set of results is given in Table 11.22.

The total estimated expenditure in 2031 is presented in Table 11.23 under the various bases. Thus, on the 8/6 valuation basis (V1), using the medium mortality assumption (A/C), medium female employment assumption (E2), 6 per cent unemployment assumption (U1), zero private sector preservation (W1), 60 per cent ultimate scheme membership for males in private sector (M1), non-contracted out schemes providing half the aggregate benefit of those contracted out (O1), the total 2031 expenditure is estimated to be £12.0. On the 8/8 valuation basis (V2), the estimate is £15.0b. Interpolating from Field's Table 5, his figures are £12.86b and £15.0b on a set of assumptions corresponding fairly closely to those described above. The similarity between these results is marked, and should be compared with the 1981 expenditure estimate of £7.5b.

From the results in Table 11.23 we note their sensitivity to a change in the assumptions, one at a time. For example, we shall begin with the V1/AC/M1/W1/E2 figure of £12.0b. Changing the assumptions individually gives the following adjustments:

Table 11.22 Estimated annual cost of widows' pension on death after retirement: 2031 (£b in terms of 1981 earnings)

| | | | 01 | | | | | | | 02 | | | | | |
| | | U1 | | U2 | | U3 | | U1 | | U2 | | U3 | | | |
		V1	V2	V1	V2	V1	V2	V1	V2	V1	V2	V1	V2		
A/C	M1	W1	1.81	2.55	1.73	2.47	1.65	2.39	1.90	2.64	1.81	2.55	1.73	2.47
A/C	M1	W2	1.90	2.72	1.81	2.64	1.73	2.55	1.98	2.72	1.90	2.64	1.81	2.55
A/C	M2	W1	1.98	2.80	1.90	2.72	1.81	2.64	2.07	2.88	1.98	2.80	1.90	2.72
A/C	M2	W2	2.07	2.88	1.99	2.80	1.91	2.72	2.22	2.96	2.07	2.88	1.99	2.80
B/D	M1	W1	3.05	4.26	2.91	4.12	2.76	3.97	3.20	4.41	3.05	4.26	2.91	4.12
B/D	M1	W2	3.20	4.41	3.05	4.26	2.91	4.12	3.35	4.56	3.20	4.41	3.05	4.26
B/D	M2	W1	3.35	4.56	3.20	4.41	3.05	4.26	3.43	4.70	3.35	4.56	3.20	4.41
B/D	M2	W2	3.50	4.70	3.43	4.63	3.20	4.41	3.58	4.85	3.50	4.70	3.43	4.63

		% change in expenditure
Optimistic mortality projection (A/C – B/D)	+ £2.4b	+20%
Rate of increase in prices 8 per cent (V1 – V2)	+ £2.2b	+18%
70 per cent male scheme membership in private sector (M1 – M2)	+ £1.0b	+8%
Non-contracted-out schemes providing 75 per cent of benefits in contracted-out schemes (01–02)	+ £0.9b	+7.5%
Increase in female employment rates (E2 – E1)	+ £0.8b	+7%
Private sector schemes providing preservation at half price inflation (W1 – W2)	+£.06b	+5%
9 per cent unemployment rate (U1 – U2)	– £0.5b	–4%
Decrease in female employment rates (E2 – E3)	– £0.7b	–6%

The sensitivity to the demographic and economic parameters is most marked.

It should also be noted that the expenditure estimates are particularly sensitive to the combination of economic assumptions used. These expenditure estimates for occupational pension schemes would be higher if lower rates of increases in earnings occurred because

(a) the state would be bearing a smaller proportion of the total burden of the GMPs plus their indexing;
(b) private sector pensions in excess of GMPs might be increased more nearly in line with prices than has been assumed under either assumptions W1 or W2.

The estimates here may be combined with those from the Quinquennial Review (QR) of the National Insurance Scheme, which covers state retirement pensions. This chapter refers to the United Kingdom and to calendar years whereas the QR refers to Great Britain and to financial years (1 April – 31 March). These two differences act roughly equally and in opposite directions on amounts of expenditure, so the two sets of figures are roughly compatible (and are compatible with the figures given in the annual National Income and Expenditure publication for the United Kingdom – the 'Blue Book'). Interpolating from the figures given in Appendix H of the QR and from Field's estimates, the approximate expenditure per annum on state retirement pensions as at 2031 is estimated to be

Table 11.23   *Estimated total expenditure from UK occupational*
pension schemes 2031:
(£b in terms of 1981 earnings)

				01			02		
				U1	U2	U3	U1	U2	U3
Basis VI (8/6)									
A/C	M1	W1	E1	12.8	12.2	11.6	13.7	13.1	12.6
			E2	12.0	11.5	10.9	12.9	12.4	11.8
			E3	11.3	10.8	10.1	12.1	11.7	11.2
A/C	M1	W2	E1	13.3	12.8	12.3	14.3	13.7	13.1
			E2	12.6	12.1	11.6	13.5	12.9	12.4
			E3	11.8	11.3	10.9	12.6	12.0	11.5
A/C	M2	W1	E1	14.0	13.4	12.7	14.9	14.3	13.6
			E2	13.0	12.6	11.9	14.0	13.5	12.7
			E3	12.0	11.8	11.2	13.2	12.7	12.0
A/C	M2	W2	E1	14.5	13.9	13.2	15.7	14.9	14.3
			E2	13.6	13.0	12.5	14.8	14.0	13.4
			E3	12.8	12.3	11.8	13.9	13.2	12.6
B/D	M1	W1	E1	15.3	14.8	14.1	16.4	15.7	15.0
			E2	14.4	13.9	13.2	15.4	14.8	14.1
			E3	13.5	13.0	12.4	14.5	14.0	13.4
B/D	M1	W2	E1	16.1	15.4	14.7	17.3	16.4	15.7
			E2	15.1	14.5	13.9	16.3	15.5	14.9
			E3	14.2	13.6	13.1	15.4	14.6	14.0
B/D	M1	W1	E1	16.7	16.0	15.3	17.7	17.0	16.3
			E2	15.5	15.0	14.3	16.6	16.0	15.2
			E3	14.6	14.1	13.5	15.7	15.1	14.4
B/D	M2	W2	E1	17.5	16.9	16.0	18.7	18.0	17.2
			E2	16.5	15.9	15.0	17.6	16.9	16.3
			E3	15.5	15.0	14.2	16.6	16.0	15.3

Table 11.23 *continued*

					01			*02*	
				U1	*U2*	*U3*	*U1*	*U2*	*U3*
Basis V2 (8/8)									
A/C	M1	W1	E1	15.9	15.2	14.4	16.9	16.1	15.6
			E2	15.0	14.3	13.6	15.9	15.2	14.7
			E3	14.0	13.4	12.7	14.9	14.3	13.8
A/C	M1	W1	E1	17.0	16.3	15.5	17.9	17.0	16.5
			E2	15.9	15.0	14.6	16.9	16.0	15.6
			E3	15.0	14.4	13.8	15.9	15.1	14.8
A/C	M2	W1	E1	17.2	16.5	15.8	18.4	17.6	16.8
			E2	16.2	15.5	14.9	17.2	16.5	15.8
			E3	15.2	14.5	14.0	16.3	15.6	14.9
A/C	M2	W2	E1	18.4	17.6	16.8	19.4	18.7	18.0
			E2	17.1	16.5	15.6	18.3	17.5	16.9
			E3	16.1	15.6	14.8	17.2	16.6	15.9
B/D	M1	W1	E1	20.8	19.9	19.0	22.0	21.1	20.3
			E2	19.7	18.7	17.9	20.8	20.0	19.2
			E3	18.5	17.6	16.9	19.6	18.8	18.1
B/D	M1	W2	E1	22.2	21.2	20.3	23.4	22.4	21.6
			E2	20.8	20.0	19.1	22.1	12.2	20.4
			E3	19.6	18.9	18.1	20.8	20.1	19.4
B/D	M2	W1	E1	22.3	21.4	20.6	23.8	23.0	22.1
			E2	21.2	20.2	19.5	22.4	21.7	20.9
			E3	19.9	19.0	18.3	21.2	20.5	19.8
B/D	M2	W2	E1	23.9	23.0	22.0	25.2	24.3	23.4
			E2	22.4	21.6	20.6	23.8	22.9	22.0
			E3	21.2	20.5	19.6	22.5	21.7	20.9

£22b on the 8/6 basis (i.e. V1, U1, A/C, E2 approximately)

£25b on the 8/8 basis (i.e. V2, U1, A/C, E2 approximately)

Table 11.24 summarizes the total provision from state and occupational pension arrangements in terms of current and ultimate expenditure. Given the sensitivity of the results to the mortality and economic assumptions, these are the only ones allowed to vary within Table 11.24 (the rest are fixed at M1, W1, E2, U1, O1). The estimates for state retirement expenditure for the optimistic mortality projection (B/D) have been made on a simplistic *pro rata* basis. The 1981 estimates are taken from Field's paper. The top half of the table compares the two levels of expenditure estimated. Such a comparison is not too precise. The lower half of the table attempts to rectify this by concentrating on:

(a) occupational scheme expenditure on pensions to former employees and their dependants aged over state pension age (excluding all lump-sum benefits);
(b) state retirement provision with a deduction of about 6 per cent to allow for benefits arising from periods of self-employment;
(c) a somewhat arbitrary allowance for other state benefits payable to persons aged over state pension age, for example, war pensions, invalidity and disablement benefits, supplementary benefits (based on Appendix H of QR).

The figures shown for total wages and salaries (including those of the armed forces) have been projected simply in proportion to the numbers aged 16–64 (or 59) from the demographic projections. It should be noted that all of these estimates are gross in that no deductions have been made in respect of income tax.

The allowance for supplementary benefits (and other means-tested benefits) has been taken as fixed in Table 11.24 for simplicity, although the increases in scheme membership projected (and illustrated in Tables 11.10–11.13) are likely to mean that fewer persons will be in need of such benefits.

Table 11.24 shows a total expenditure in terms of retirement benefits of £34b using economic assumptions of 6 per cent prices growth and 8 per cent earnings growth and a medium mortality assumption and £40b with an optimistic mortality assumption, relative to current expenditure of about £20b. These implied increases would be more dramatic were prices growth to be 8 per cent and should be seen in the light of the moderate changes anticipated in total UK wages and salaries. This will be discussed further. The figures in Table 11.24 relate to the particular assumptions described earlier. Some idea of the effect of the full range of

Table 11.24 Estimated total expenditure from UK occupational pension schemes and state retirement pensions:
1981 and 2031

(£b in terms of 1981 earnings)

Expenditure	1981	2031 Basis V1 (8/6)		2031 Basis V2 (8/8)	
		A/C	B/D	A/C	B/D
Total occupational pension schemes	7.5	12.0	14.4	15.0	19.7
State retirement pensions	12	22	26	25	33
Total (rounded)	20	34	40	40	53
UK wages and salaries	125	127(A)	128(B)	127(A)	128(B)
		124(C)	125(D)	124(C)	125(D)
Expenditure for persons aged over 65/60, excl. self-employed					
Occupational pension schemes (members' and dependants' pensions only)	4	8.8	11.8	11.5	16.7
State retirement pensions (excl. self-employed)	11.5	21	24	23	31
Other state benefits	2	2	3	2	3
Total (rounded)	17	32	39	37	51

Table 11.25 Range of variation in estimated total expenditure from UK occupational pension schemes and state retirement pensions
(£b in terms of 1981 earnings)

Expenditure	1981	2031 Basis V1 (8/6)				2031 Basis V2 (8/8)			
		A	C	B	D	A	C	B	D
Total occupational pensions	7.5	10.1–15.7	10.1–15.7	12.4–18.7	12.4–18.7	12.7–19.4	12.7–19.4	16.9–25.2	16.9–25.2
State retirement pensions	12	22	22	26	26	25	25	33	33
Total (rounded)	20	32–38	32–38	38–45	38–45	38–44	38–44	50–58	50–58
UK wages and salaries	125	127	124	128	125	127	124	128	125

assumptions for each combination of economic and demographic parameters is given by the results quoted in Table 11.25.

These figures should be viewed relative to the size of the national income of the UK. Since all of the income in the UK should belong to people in some way somewhere (and assuming a closed economy), we shall use the aggregate of UK wages and salaries and pensions expenditure as a substitute for national income. This surrogate definition excludes investment income. Adjustments are made for the state benefits payable for periods of self-employment, for means-linked state benefits and for occupational pension scheme expenditure on lump-sum benefits not payable to pensioners. Table 11.26 then shows the expenditure on pensions (modified as described) relative to the total wages, salaries and pensions (TWSP) for 1981 and 2031 (on the M1/ W1/E1/U1/O1 basis). The figures in parentheses indicate the effect of the full range of underlying assumptions. Also shown are the UK pensioner population (that is, persons aged over 65/60) for 1981 and 2031 relative to the total population and the total adult population (that is, persons aged over 15). Both are presented since it is not clear how much weight should be given to the consumption of (or expenditure on) children (for example, half may be appropriate). Table 11.26 indicates that pension expenditure, expressed as a percentage of TWSP, is projected to increase from 12.0 per cent to 19.3–30.5 per cent by 2031 at the same time as the pensioner population, expressed as a percentage of the total population, is projected to increase from 17.9 per cent to 22.1–29.0 per cent (and from 22.5 per cent to 27.7–35.1 per cent when expressed as a percentage of the adult population). The increase in pension expenditure is, therefore, projected to increase by 7.3–18.5 percentage points (relative to the TWSP) at the same time as the pensioner population is projected to increase by 4.2–11.1 percentage points (relative to total population).

These estimates assume that pensioners will purchase goods and services to the full extent of their pensions and ignore, as mentioned earlier, the incidence of income tax.

Stewart (1983) has estimated the combined cost of the state and occupational pension provision to be 16.7 per cent for 1985/86 rising to 31.7 per cent relative to UK total wages and salaries (that is, a different denominator to that used in the first line of Table 11.26). These estimates are in line with the more detailed figures presented here.

More detailed calculations along the lines of Table 11.26 indicate that most of the increase in pensions expenditure projected is postponed until the first quarter of the next century for reasons of demography (as mentioned in Chapter 10) and the current immaturity of occupational pension schemes. These projections indicate that the pace of change is slow now but that over the next fifty years the income of the retired relative to the economically active should increase substantially.

Table 11.26 *Pensioners' share of the national income (TWSP) and total population: 1981 and 2031*

Expenditure	*1981*	*2031 Basis V1 (8/6)*				*2031 Basis V2 (8/8)*			
		A	*C*	*B*	*D*	*A*	*C*	*B*	*D*
Pension expenditure as a proportion of total wages, salaries and pensions	12.0%	20.0%	20.4%	23.3%	23.7%	22.3%	22.7%	28.4%	28.9%
(Range of variation)		(19.3 – 21.2)	(19.7 – 21.6)	(22.4 – 24.6)	(22.9 – 25.1)	(21.5 – 23.7)	(21.9 – 24.2)	(27.4 – 30.0)	(27.9 – 30.5)
UK pensioner population as a proportion of total population	17.9%	22.1%	22.7%	28.3%	29.0%	22.1%	22.7%	28.3%	29.0%
UK pensioner population as a proportion of adult population	22.5%	27.7%	28.1%	34.7%	35.1%	27.7%	28.1%	34.7%	35.1%

Recent historical analyses and projections published by the DHSS throw more light on the growth in pensioners' incomes (DHSS, 1984). Current statistics show that for 1981/82 pensioners had a 14.5 per cent share in TPDI (total personal disposable income) – which is made up of earnings and income from self-employment, income from savings and investment, pensions, other social security benefits – and that over the previous decade real disposable income per head increased by 31 per cent for pensioners and only 10 per cent for non-pensioners. Disposable income per head for pensioners in 1981 was about 70 per cent of that of non-pensioners, whereas in 1951 it was only 40 per cent. The main source of this improvement was through the growing real value of the state basic pension compared with average take-home pay: basic pension rose from 20 per cent in 1951 to 33 per cent in 1981/82 of the average *net* earnings for a male manual worker. National insurance pensions and other social security benefits rose as a proportion of pensioners' total gross income, from about 40 per cent in 1951 to about 60 per cent in 1981. Occupational pensions also contributed to the rise in pensioners' incomes, with the share up from 15 per cent to 22 per cent of their total gross income. These rises were at the expense of income from employment and investment income.

Using a long-term demographic basis similar to assumption A here and an unemployment assumption of 6 per cent, projections of TPDI up to 2025/26 have been prepared by DHSS. These indicate that pensioners' share of TPDI would increase to 17.5 per cent on the basis of prices uprating of flat-rate and means-tested social security benefits and 20 per cent on the basis of earnings uprating. Pensioners' disposable income per head relative to non-pensioners is projected to stay fairly stable at 70 per cent under prices uprating but to increase to over 80 per cent under earnings uprating.

The earlier discussion indicates that, expressed relative to the national income, the problem created by the projected growth of pension rights does not appear beyond solution. However, unless the total amount available for consumption is increased, the anticipated growth in pensions expenditure will reduce that available for consumption by the non-pensioner section of the population. Taking national income as being made up of two components only – wages and salaries, and pensions expenditure – as we have, implies that the 7.3–18.5 percentage points anticipated increase for the pensioners' share of national income would be accompanied by a corresponding fall in the share of the non-pensioner population (that is, a fall of 8.3–21.0 percentage points of their 1981 share). Such a reduction might well provoke severe social and fiscal strains. Bacon, Benjamin and Elphinstone (1954) noted that one economic factor that critically affected the calculations at that time was the level of defence expenditure. Today, defence expenditure remains a significant part of public spending and, to the extent that the amount might be reduced over the next fifty years, the burden of pensions might be more easily accommodated.

It is clear that the only way in which the growth in pensions expenditure can be provided, without reducing the standard of living of the rest of the population or the amount invested in augmenting the country's national resources, is (a) to increase the productivity per head of the working population and/or (b) to increase the numbers of persons working by postponing the normal ages of retirement and putting back to work the current numbers unemployed. As discussed in Chapter 9, the possibilities of (b) look remote in the near future. However, were pensioners themselves to do more part-time work, this would reduce the level of economic growth needed to facilitate the transfer of resources described earlier. Therefore, let us concentrate on option (a).

We have assumed in the calculations underlying Tables 11.24–11.26 that total wages and salaries in the UK will be proportional to the numbers of persons of working age, that is, 16–65 or 16–60. The level of and growth in pensions expenditure per person aged over state pension age are given in Table 11.27 for the range of assumptions in Table 11.26 (the level of pensions expenditure has been modified as in Table 11.26).

The low figures for the optimistic mortality projections (B/D) under the assumption of a 6 per cent per annum growth in prices arise from the interaction of the loss in value of pension payment and the very old age structure of the population in 2031 arising from this projection. The figures in Table 11.27 indicate that the annual expenditure on pensions benefits per pensioner will increase by 17–76 percentage points over the next fifty years, depending on the set of assumptions used. The percentage growths are projected to occur over fifty years. Converting to an annual basis, we see that these increases correspond to rates of 0.5–1.25 per cent per annum.

Table 11.27   *Projected growth in pensions expenditure: 1981–2031*

| | | 2031 | | | |
| | | *Basis V1 (8/6)* | | *Basis V2 (8/8)* | |
	1981	*A/C*	*B/D*	*A/C*	*B/D*
Pensions					
– annual					
expenditure					
per pensioner					
(£)	1,680	2,260 – 2,550	1,960 – 2,230	2,590 – 2,950	2,570 – 2,920
Growth since					
1981	—	35 – 52%	17 – 33%	54 – 76%	53 – 74%

Hence if the per capita level of real wages and salaries (relative to the non-pensioner adult population or including a reduced weight for children) were to increase over the next fifty years by an average of 0.5–1.25 per cent per annum, we would find that the non-pensioner population would maintain its standard of living relative to the pensioners. These are the required levels of annual increases in productivity per head of the working population. Annual increases in productivity per head of more than 1.25 per cent would make the transfer of resources, indicated by the figures quoted above, possible without detriment to the non-pensioner sections of the community; indeed, at higher rates, an improvement in the standard of living would be possible for *all* sections of the population. However, very low growth or the absence of any growth would mean that these 'promises' to future pensioners (and the expectations of these pensioners who are currently entering the workforce) could be implemented only by a reduction in the share of the national income allocated to the working population and their non-pensioner dependants (including children, the unemployed, the permanently incapacitated). These levels of productivity growth mentioned above are of the same order of magnitude as those suggested by Bacon, Benjamin and Elphinstone (1954) as being required to facilitate the necessary transfer resources as viewed thirty years ago.

We have shown that the relationship between the shares of the national income (as represented by TWSP) allocated to active persons, their non-pensioner dependants and pensioners depends on many factors, including the prevailing tax structure, price and earnings inflation, mortality and fertility, trends in unemployment and employment levels, improvements to pension scheme benefit provision, and trends in membership of occupational schemes. In Chapter 5, more attention has been devoted to the relationships between these contributions to the national income.

Total contribution income Ultimately, if the provision of pensions in the UK were regarded as tending over time towards a stationary fund, annual expenditure would balance the combined annual income from contributions and investments. Trial calculations for this ultimate situation along the lines described in the Appendix to Stewart (1983) indicate that the ratio of annual contribution income to pensions expenditure (considering only the provision of retirement pensions for members) would be approximately as follows:

Real rate of return on investment (relative to earnings)	*Ratio of contributions: expenditure*
0.5%	87%
1.5%	65%

According to the 1979 Survey of Occupational Pension Schemes, contribution income was about 1.78 times benefit expenditure. Further, private and public sector schemes are estimated to have generated about £8.10b as a net growth in funds for 1979. This represents about twice their aggregate investment income (of £4.15b) and, because of the immaturity of so many of the schemes in the private sector, this relationship is unlikely to decrease quickly even with a fall in interest rates. In 1979 this inflow represented about 5.7 per cent of national income, although this level has probably deteriorated recently due to the economic recession. Hence substantial sums of money are likely to be available for the acquisition of assets.

Detailed projections of contribution income have not been prepared here principally for the following reasons. First, the ultimate balance means that, given the real rate of return on investments and the level of expenditure, the flow of contribution income is approximately determined. Secondly, the system currently operating in the UK is one of pension provision for the employed being on a defined benefits basis (as described in detail in Chapters 2 and 4) rather than a defined contributions basis. Further, at any one time, a wide range of funding methods and contribution levels are in use and any improvements in benefits (for example, in terms of deferred pension preservation) similarly lead to a wide range of revised contribution levels.

Conclusions

Estimates of future pension expenditure in relation to the UK national income have been carried out and analysed.

Relative to the aggregate of UK wages, salaries and pensions expenditure (TWSP), the total pensions expenditure for 2031 is projected to lie between 19 per cent and 25 per cent. For 1981, the total equivalent is estimated to be 12 per cent TWSP. These figures should be viewed against the background of a pensioner population that is 18 per cent of the total UK population and that is projected to be between 22 per cent and 29 per cent of the UK population in 2031. The striking point behind these complex comparisons is that total pension expenditure is projected to be a percentage of TWSP that is closer (than at present) to the proportion of the population that pensioners are projected to form.

If pensioners are anticipated to increase their share of 'national income', this will be at the expense of the rest of the population – principally, the economically active.

This growth in pension expenditure could be accommodated, without depleting the standard of living of the rest of the population or decreasing the amount devoted to new investment, by the possible use of two control mechanisms – by increasing the productivity per head of the working population or by postponing the normal pattern of retirement. In the absence of either of these controls, the promises to pay improved pensions (implied by the projections) can be implemented only by non-pensioners having a depleted standard of living.

The increased financial strains caused by the continued ageing of the UK population, the maturing of the State Earnings Related Pension Scheme and the possible increase in coverage of occupational pension schemes can be met if there is moderate growth in the future. These conclusions are similar in tone to those of Bacon et al. (1954). The critical time is likely to be the second or third decade of the twenty-first century when the post-war bulge of births centred on the early 1960s reaches normal retirement age and those born in the current fertility trough are still economically active.

References

Bacon, F. W., Benjamin, B. and Elphinstone, M. D. W. (1954), 'The growth of pension rights and their impact on the national economy', *Journal of the Institute of Actuaries*, vol. 80, pp. 141–202 (with discussion)

Department of Employment (1980), *New Earnings Survey Part E 1979*, London: HMSO

Department of Employment (1982), *New Earnings Survey Part A 1981*, London: HMSO

Department of Health and Social Security (1984), *Population, Pension Costs and Pensioners' Incomes*, Background Paper for the Inquiry into Provision for Retirement, London: HMSO

Field, J. L. (1983) 'Projections of the costs of occupational and state pensions', *Journal of the Institute of Actuaries*, vol. 110, pp. 243–270

Government Actuary (1980), *A Projection of Occupational Pension Schemes to the End of this Century*, Report of the Committee to Review the Functioning of Financial Institutions, Appendix 5, Cmnd 7937, London: HMSO

Government Actuary (1981), *Occupational Pension Schemes 1979*, Sixth Survey by the Government Actuary, London: HMSO

Government Actuary (1982), *National Insurance Fund Long Term Financial Estimates*, Report by the Government Actuary on the First Quinquennial Review under section 137 of the Social Security Act 1975, London: HMSO

Government Actuary (1986), *Occupational Pension Schemes 1983*, Seventh Survey by the Government Actuary, London: HMSO

McKormick, B. and Hughes, G. (1984), 'Influence of pensions on job mobility', *Journal of Public Economics*, vol. 23, pp. 183–206

Main, B. G. M. (1982), 'The length of a job in Great Britain', *Economica*, vol. 49, pp. 325–333

National Association of Pension Funds (1982), *Eighth Annual Survey of Occupational Pension Schemes 1982*, Croydon: NAPF

Occupational Pensions Board (1981), *Improved Protection for the Occupational Pension Rights and Expectations of Early Leavers*, Cmnd 8271, London: HMSO

Occupational Pensions Board (1982), *Greater Security for the Rights and Expectations of Members of Occupational Pension Schemes*, Cmnd 8649, London: HMSO

Parker, S. (1980), *Older Workers and Retirement*, London: HMSO

Stewart, C. M. (1983), 'Pension problems and their solutions', *Journal of the Institute of Actuaries*, vol. 110, pp. 289–332 (with discussion)

Stewart, M. B. and Greenhalgh, C. A. (1984), 'Work history patterns and the occupational attainment of women', *Economic Journal*, vol. 94, pp. 493–519

Index

Index

For Product Safety Concerns and Information please contact our EU representative GPSR@taylorandfrancis.com Taylor & Francis Verlag GmbH, Kaufingerstraße 24, 80331 München, Germany

Printed and bound by CPI Group (UK) Ltd, Croydon, CR0 4YY

08/05/2025

01864396-0001